DARK MATTERS

DARK MATTERS

ON THE SURVEILLANCE OF BLACKNESS

SIMONE BROWNE

———

Duke University Press   Durham and London   2015

Printed in the United States of America on acid-free paper ∞
Designed by Natalie F. Smith
Typeset in Arno Pro by Graphic Composition, Inc., Athens, GA

Library of Congress Cataloging-in-Publication Data
Browne, Simone, [date] author.
Dark matters : on the surveillance of blackness / Simone Browne.
pages cm
Includes bibliographical references and index.
ISBN 978-0-8223-5919-7 (hardcover : alk. paper)
ISBN 978-0-8223-5938-8 (pbk. : alk. paper)
ISBN 978-0-8223-7530-2 (e-book)
1. African Americans—Social conditions. 2. Blacks—Canada—Social
conditions. 3. United States—Race relations. 4. Canada—Race relations.
5. Electronic surveillance—United States. 6. Government information—
United States. I. Title.
E185.86.B76 2015
305.896'073—dc23   2015012563

COVER ART: Robin Rhode (South African, born 1976), *Pan's Opticon*, 2008.
Photographs, fifteen C-prints face-mounted on four-ply museum board.
Photos courtesy of Lehmann Maupin.

Duke University Press gratefully acknowledges the support of the
Office of the President at the University of Texas at Austin, which provided
funds toward the publication of this book.

CONTENTS

ACKNOWLEDGMENTS

This book began as notes that I scribbled in the margins while I was conducting dissertation research at the University of Toronto. Although it is not based on that work, many of the questions and concerns that shape this book emerged from that project. Thank you to my PhD committee members Kari Dehli, Roxana Ng, Alissa Trotz, and David Lyon for their guidance, support, and sharp readings of that work.

My appreciation goes out to colleagues, past and present, at the University of Texas at Austin who have made suggestions, pointed me in new directions, provided feedback, and read parts of the book along the way. I thank João Costa Vargas, Stephen Marshall, Naomi Paik, Nhi Lieu, Meta DuEwa Jones, Shirley Thompson, and Michael Ray Charles. Ben Carrington commented on many chapter drafts, iterations, and the entire manuscript. I am grateful for the insights that his readings have brought to this book. Ted Gordon's support for me and my work has been unwavering. I thank him for showing me the possibilities of maroon spaces. Special thanks to those who provided words of encouragement and support for this project: Jossianna Arroyo, Ann Cvetkovich, Lyndon Gill, Sam Gosling, Frank Guridy, Charlie Hale, Susan Heinzelman, Neville Hoad, Juliet Hooker, Bob Jensen, Omi Jones, Xavier Livermon, Minkah Makalani, Leonard Moore, Lisa Moore, Deborah Paredez, Anna-Lisa Plant, Cherise Smith, Eric Tang, and Craig Watkins. I would also like to thank my colleagues in the Sociology Department, especially Bob Hummer, Keith Robinson, Mary Rose, Marc Musick, Michael Young, and Maya Charrad. I consider myself truly lucky to have met the many students from my graduate seminars and undergraduate classes who have critically engaged with parts and pieces of what would become this book, with a special thanks to Courtney Williams Barron, Josh Bidwell, Jessica Dunning-Lozano, Amanda Gray, Lily Laux, and Elissa Underwood.

I appreciate the many colleagues and friends who have supported me and have made this book better through their questions, conversations, correspondence, enthusiasm, and advice, with many of those mentioned here having generously read parts, or all, of this book. I thank Cathy N. Davidson, David Theo Goldberg, Avery Gordon, Gary T. Marx, Torin Monahan, Lisa Nakamura, Mark Anthony Neal, Howard Winant, Fiona Barnett, Zach Blas, Marc Böhlen, Eduardo Bonilla-Silva, Micha Cárdenas, Danielle Dirks, Joe Feagin, Allen Feldman, Caitlin Fisher, Martin French, Ahmed Ghappour, Ruthie Gilmore, Sarah Ihmoud, Richard Iton, Joy James, David Leonard, Steve Mann, Nicholas Mirzoeff, Alondra Nelson, Tamara K. Nopper, Mark Olson, Jenny Rhee, Mark B. Salter, Christina Sharpe, Maggie Tate, France Winddance Twine, David Murakami Wood, and Clyde Woods. I am especially grateful for Katherine McKittrick's friendship, her brilliance, and her many visits to Austin. Her fierce commentary on so many parts of this book has been invaluable. My sincerest appreciation goes to Rinaldo Walcott for his encouragement, his mentorship, his generous feedback, and for the semester that he sojourned in Austin.

I've had opportunities to present my research at various venues, which have greatly enriched this book. I am thankful for all that I've learned from the rigorous questions and comments, and in particular those from audiences at the Surveillance Studies Center at Queen's University, HASTAC conferences in Durham and Toronto, CUNY Graduate Center, University of California at Berkeley, University of California at Santa Barbara, University of Ottawa, and New York University.

Chapter 2 benefited from financial support from the John L. Warfield Center for African American Studies that allowed me to take research trips to the National Archives in London and to Fraunces Tavern in New York City. A workshop at the John Hope Franklin Humanities Institute at Duke University organized by Cathy Davidson provided me with generous feedback and guidance on this chapter. I am so grateful to Cathy for her incredible kindness and for creating a timely and safe space for me at the Franklin Center.

Duke University Press has been a dream (come true) to publish with. Since our first meeting at Parker and Otis, Courtney Berger has been an amazing editor. I deeply thank her for her commitment to this book and for her insights and advice throughout. Thank you to Erin Hanas for her step-by-step guidance through the editorial process. I also want to thank the production team at Duke, and in particular Christopher Robinson,

Danielle Houtz, and Karen M. Fisher. A big thanks also to Ken Wissoker. I am especially indebted to the two anonymous reviewers for their fierce critique and for investing their time in order to make this book so much better.

I am eternally grateful for the friendship and support of Samia Rizek-Benisty and Samuel Benisty, Danielle Chow-Leong, Aliyah Hamirani, Almira Hamirani, Zahra Hamirani and family, Carrianne Leung, and Stella Meghie.

This book is dedicated with love to my family, especially James Bailey, Ena Bailey, and Elsa Constantine. To my mother, Carmel Browne, thank you for everything and for singing to me (or my answering machine) every day. To my father, Eardley Browne, thank you for all of your insights and encouragement and reading all of it. Again and again. To my brother, Kevin Browne, who has taught me so much about strength, love, survival, kindness, and humour.

AN EARLIER VERSION of chapter 2 appeared as "Everybody's Got a Little Light under the Sun: Black Luminosity and the Visual Culture of Surveillance," *Cultural Studies* 26, no. 4 (2012): 542–564. Parts of chapter 3 have been revised from "Digital Epidermalization: Race, Identity and Biometrics," *Critical Sociology* 36, no. 1 (2010): 131–150.

INTRODUCTION, AND OTHER DARK MATTERS

"The CIA can neither confirm nor deny the existence or nonexistence of records responsive to your request." Sometime in the spring of 2011, I wrote to the Central Intelligence Agency (CIA) and to the Federal Bureau of Investigation (FBI) to request the release of any documents pertaining to Frantz Fanon under the Freedom of Information Act (FOIA). At the time, I was interested in Fanon's travels to the United States of America in 1961, possibly under the nom de guerre Ibrahim Fanon, to receive treatment for myeloid leukemia. He arrived in the United States on October 3, staying at a hotel in Washington, DC, where he was "left to rot," according to Simone de Beauvoir, "alone and without medical attention."[1] Fanon was a patient at the National Institutes of Health Clinical Center in Bethesda, Maryland, from October 10, 1961, until he died of pneumonia on December 6, 1961. He was thirty-six. I didn't get any documents from the CIA except a letter citing Executive Order 13526 with the standard refrain that the agency "can neither confirm nor deny the existence or nonexistence of records," and further stating that "the fact of the existence or nonexistence of requested records is currently and properly classified and is intelligence sources and methods information that is protected from disclosure."

Fanon's FOIA files that were released to me by the FBI consist only of three declassified documents: Document #105-96959-A—a clipping of a 1971 *Washington Post-Times Herald* article on Fanon's "Black Power Message" and its continuing influence on the Caribbean island of Martinique, where he was born; Document #105-96959-1—a once "SECRET" memo on Fanon dated March 9, 1961; and Document #105-96959-2—a book review of David Caute's 1970 biography *Frantz Fanon*, filed under "extremist matters," which says of Caute that "his methodology bears the Marxist stamp" and that "he is no friend of the United States or of a free society." Document #105-96959-A, the news clipping, names *The Wretched of the Earth* (1963) as Fanon's most important book, stating, "its sales have run unusually high lately, especially among young Negroes." Document #105-96959-2, the FBI's own review of Caute's biography, describes Fanon as a "black intellectual," a "radical revolutionary," and "a philosophical disciple of Karl Marx and Jean Paul Sartre, [who] preached global revolt of the blacks against white colonial rule," and says that Fanon's *The Wretched of the Earth* is "often quoted and misquoted by Stokely Carmichael and other black power advocates, both foreign and domestic." This review also claims that "Fanon's importance has been inflated into exaggerated dimensions by the need of black revolutionaries for philosophical justification and leadership." Traces of Fanon's influence appear in other declassified FBI documents where either he or his published books are named, including some documents that detail the bureau's surveillance of the Black Panther Party.

Although much of the information on the once "SECRET" FBI memo on Fanon, Document #105-96959-1 (figure I.1), has been redacted, meaning that some of its information is censored, concealed, or otherwise covered up, this memo names Fanon as "the Algerian representative in Ghana for the Algerian Front for National Liberation (FLN)" and notes that he was, at the time, in Tunisia preparing to travel to Washington, DC, for "extensive medical treatment." This memo is from Sam J. Papich, the bureau's liaison to the CIA. It is interesting to note here that the redaction of Document #105-96959-1 took the form of a whiteout, concealing a good portion of the original text with white blocks, in this way deviating from the method of censoring the redacted data with opaque black blocks, rendering any information in the dark. We can think of the redaction here as the willful absenting of the record and as the state's disavowal of the bureaucratic traces of Fanon, at least those which are made publicly available. Here Frantz Fanon is a nonnameable matter. Now dead, yet still a "currently and properly classified" security risk, apparently, as "the fact of the existence or nonexistence" of Fanon's records itself is "intelligence sources and methods information that is protected from disclosure." With this, the redaction and Executive Order 13526 could be understood as a form of security theater where certain "intelligence sources and methods," if in existence, could still be put into operation, and as such could not be declassified.

Fanon's FOIA files form a part of the long history of the collection of intelligence on the many black radicals, artists, activists, and intellectuals who were targeted for surveillance by the FBI. This list includes Assata Shakur,

James Baldwin, Lorraine Hansberry, Stokely Carmichael, the Student Nonviolent Coordinating Committee, the Freedom Riders, Martin Luther King Jr., Elijah Muhammad and the Nation of Islam, Claudia Jones, Malcolm X, Fred Hampton, William Edward Burghart DuBois, Fannie Lou Hamer, Cyril Lionel Robert James, Mumia Abu-Jamal, Angela Yvonne Davis, Richard Wright, Ralph Ellison, Josephine Baker, Billie Holiday, the Black Panther Party, Kathleen Cleaver, Muhammad Ali, Jimi Hendrix, and Russell Jones aka Ol' Dirty Bastard of the Wu-Tang Clan, among many, many others. The declassified printed matter released to me by the FBI was not particularly revealing regarding any surveillance and monitoring of Frantz Fanon. I was disappointed. My own surveillance of the records of the FBI's surveillance of Fanon had apparently been stalled.

In the foreword to the 2005 edition of *The Wretched of the Earth*, Homi Bhabha describes Fanon's dying days as filled with delirium and with a love for liberation:

> his body was stricken, but his fighting days were not quite over; he resisted his death "minute by minute," a friend reported from his bedside, as his political opinions and beliefs turned into the delirious fantasies of a mind raging against the dying of the light. His hatred of racist Americans now turned into a distrust of the nursing staff, and he awoke on his last morning, having probably had a blood transfusion through the night, obsessed with the idea that "they put me through the washing machine last night." His death was inevitable.[2]

Les damnés de la terre (1961) would be the last of his books that Fanon would live to see published. He was in the hospital in Maryland when he heard some initial reviews of the book and he reportedly stated, "That's not going to get me my marrow back."[3] A letter to a friend penned from his hospital bed captures Fanon's rage "against the dying of the light" as both a battle of the body against disease and an anticolonial praxis:

> During a night and day surveillance, they inject me with the components of blood for which I have a terrible need, and where they give me huge transfusions to keep me in shape—that's to say, alive.... What shocks me here in this bed, as I grow weaker, is not that I'm dying, but that I'm dying in Washington of leukemia considering that I could have died in battle with the enemy three months ago when I

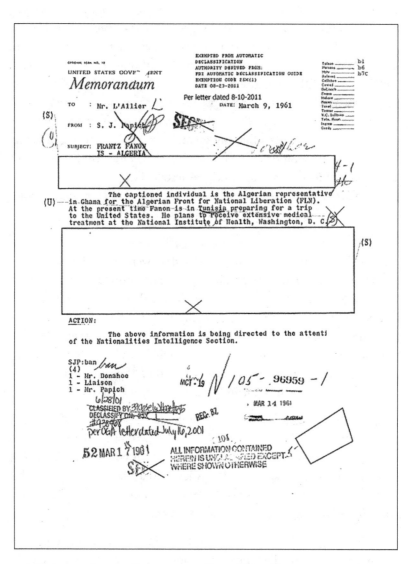

FIGURE I.1. "SECRET" FBI memo on Frantz Fanon, Document #105-96959-1.

knew I had this disease. We are nothing on earth if we are not, first of all, slaves of a cause, the cause of the people, the cause of justice, the cause of liberty.[4]

Fanon wrote much of the anticolonial *Les damnés de la terre* as his time was running out. He knew that his cancer was terminal, which brought writing the book "down to the wire," as he put it.[5] At the time he was in exile in Tunisia after being expelled from Algeria in January 1957 by the French authorities for his work with the Front de Libération Nationale (FLN). During his exile in Tunisia, home to the FLN's headquarters, Fanon took on multiple roles. He worked at the FLN's newspaper *El Moudjahid*, served in refugee camps run by the FLN near the Algerian border, was *chef de service* at the psychiatric hospital of Manouba, and was also the Algerian provisional government's delegate to Mali and other African nations. While in exile, Fanon gave a series of lectures at the University of Tunis on surveillance, the psychic effects of war and colonialism on the colonized, and antiblack racism in the United States.[6] In the notes from these lectures, Fanon speaks of the problem of racial segregation in the United States, or the "color bar" as he names it, where antiblack racism is constant and multi-layered, emotional and affective. He mentions the themes of escape and blackness on the move found in Negro spirituals, the haunting lyrics of blues music and social death, Harlem and the writings of African American novelist Chester Himes, the rigidity of the color line and its nagging presence, African American vernacular and code-switching ("quand un Noir s'adresse à un Blanc") and repressive policing practices ("Quand un Noir tue un Noir, il ne se passe rien; quand un Noir tue un Blanc, toute la police est mobilisée").[7] Fanon's lectures on surveillance at the University of Tunis were eventually canceled, by order of the Tunisian government.[8]

During these lectures Fanon put forth the idea that modernity can be characterized by the "mise en fiches de l'homme." These are the records, files, time sheets, and identity documents that together form a biography, and sometimes an unauthorized one, of the modern subject. In a manner similar to the detailed case histories of colonial war and mental disorders found in the fifth chapter of *The Wretched of the Earth*, in a section of the notes on these lectures titled "Le contrôle et la surveillance" (in English "Surveillance and Control"), Fanon demonstrates his role as both psychiatrist and social theorist, by making observations, or social diagnoses, on the embodied effects and outcomes of surveillance practices on different categories of laborers when attempts are made by way of workforce supervision to reduce their labor to an automation: factory assembly line workers subjected to time management by punch clocks and time sheets, the eavesdropping done by telephone switchboard supervisors as they secretly listened in on calls in order to monitor the conversations of switchboard operators, and the effects of closed-circuit television (CCTV) surveillance on sales clerks in large department stores in the United States. This is control by quantification, as Fanon put it. The embodied psychic effects of surveillance that Fanon described include nervous tensions, insomnia, fatigue, accidents, lightheadedness, and less control over reflexes. Nightmares too: a train that departs and leaves one behind, or a gate closing, or a door that won't open. Although Fanon's remarks on CCTV surveillance are short, they are revealing as he suggests that these cameras are trained not only on the potential thief, but also on the employee working on the shop floor who is put on notice that the video surveillance is perpetual. He also noted that workers displayed microresistances to managerial control in the way of sick leave, expressing boredom on the job, arriving late, and sometimes not arriving at work at all. Rather than being thought of as unproductive, such acts must be understood as disalienating, as they are strategic means of contesting surveillance in the workplace.

Although only the notes from these lectures remain, Fanon's observations on the monitoring of audio communications and CCTV are nevertheless instructive for the social diagnosis of alienation and the effects of modernity, surveillance, and resistance that he offers. If one were to read these lectures "optimistically," as Nicholas Mirzoeff has suggested, "had he lived longer, Fanon might have moved away from his emphasis on masculinity to imagine new modes of postrevolutionary gender identity, as part of this analysis of the racialized disciplinary society, a connection made by many radical black feminists in the United States from Angela Davis to Toni Cade Bambara and bell hooks."[9] I enter *Dark Matters: On the Surveillance of Blackness* with this sense of optimism in mind: that in Fanon's works and in the writings of black feminist scholars, another mode of reading surveillance can be had.

Dark Matters begins with a discussion of my failed attempt to get my hands on any information from the CIA pertaining to Fanon, his FBI FOIA file, the short notes that remain from his lectures on surveillance, and an excerpt from his letter to a friend recounting the "night and day surveillance" that he experienced as he was on the brink of death as a way to cue surveillance in and of black life as a fact of blackness. My gesture to "The Fact of

Blackness," one of the English translations of the title of the fifth chapter of Fanon's *Black Skin, White Masks*, is a deliberate signal to the facticity of surveillance in black life. First published in 1952 as *Peau Noire, Masques Blancs*, the book's fifth chapter in the French original is "L'expérience vécue du Noir." As Sylvia Wynter and others have noted, the translation of that chapter's title into English as "The Lived Experience of the Black" in later editions offers a more accurate understanding. It is this slight difference between the two titles—"The Fact of Blackness" and "The Lived Experience of the Black"—that I want to signal here. The "Blackness" in the former could be taken to mean, as Wynter has put it, "Blackness as an objective fact" while "The Lived Experience of the Black" speaks to a focus on the imposition of race in black life, where one's being is experienced through others.[10] Wynter continues her discussion of Fanon and sociogeny to say that "The Lived Experience of the Black" makes clear that Fanon is dealing "with the 'subjective character' of the experience of the black, of, therefore, what it is *like* to be black, within the terms of the mode of being human specific to our contemporary culture."[11]

Sociogeny, or what Wynter calls "the sociogenic principle," is understood as the organizational framework of our present human condition that names what is and what is not bounded within the category of the human, and that fixes and frames blackness as an object of surveillance. Take, for example, Fanon's often-cited "Look, a Negro!" passage in *Black Skin, White Masks* on the experience of epidermalization, where the white gaze fixes him as an object among objects and, he says, "the white gaze, the only valid one, is already dissecting me."[12] Epidermalization here is the imposition of race on the body. For Fanon, there is no "ontological resistance" in spaces, like that train he rode in France, that are shaped for and by whiteness, where "instead of one seat, they left me two or three," he writes.[13] *Dark Matters* takes up blackness, as metaphor and as lived materiality, and applies it to an understanding of surveillance. I work across multiple spaces (the airport, the plan of the *Brooks* slave ship, the plan for Jeremy Bentham's Panopticon, Internet art) and different segments of time (the period of transatlantic chattel slavery, the British occupation of New York City during the American Revolution, post-9/11) to think through the multiplicities of blackness. This method of analyzing surveillance and the conditions of racial blackness brings historical documents, art, photography, contemporary popular film and television, and various other forms of cultural production into dialogue with critical race scholarship, sociological theory, and feminist theorizing. For this study, I look to Pamela Z's multimedia project on travel and security, *Baggage Allowance*; Adrian Piper's *What It's Like, What It Is #3*; Caryl Phillips's epistolary story "The Cargo Rap" on prisons, politics, and slavery; and Hank Willis Thomas's commentary on branding and the afterlife of slavery in his *B®anded* series. Part of the argument presented here is that with certain acts of cultural production we can find performances of freedom and suggestions of alternatives to ways of living under a routinized surveillance. In this fashion, I am indebted to Stuart Hall's unsettling of understandings of "cultural identity" that does not see the black diaspora and black experiences as static or singular, but instead as "a result of a long and discontinuous series of transformations."[14] Following Rinaldo Walcott here, my use of the term "blackness" is to "signal blackness as a sign, one that carries with it particular histories of resistance and domination" that is "never closed and always under contestation."[15] Blackness is identity and culture, history and present, signifier and signified, but never fixed. As Ralph Ellison names it in *Invisible Man*, "Black is . . . an' black ain't."[16]

Fanon's "Look, a Negro!," his articulations of epidermalization, and his anticolonial thought have influenced the formation of this book. *Dark Matters* suggests that an understanding of the ontological conditions of blackness is integral to developing a general theory of surveillance and, in particular, racializing surveillance—when enactments of surveillance reify boundaries along racial lines, thereby reifying race, and where the outcome of this is often discriminatory and violent treatment. Of course, this is not the entire story of surveillance, but it is a part that often escapes notice. Although "race" might be a term found in the index of many of the recent edited collections and special journal issues dedicated to the study of surveillance, within the field of surveillance studies race remains undertheorized, and serious consideration has yet to be given to the racial subject in general, and to the role of surveillance in the archive of slavery and the transatlantic slave trade in particular. It is through this archive and that of black life after the Middle Passage that I want to further complicate understandings of surveillance by questioning how a realization of the conditions of blackness—the historical, the present, and the historical present—can help social theorists understand our contemporary conditions of surveillance. Put another way, rather than seeing surveillance as something inaugurated by new technologies, such as automated facial recognition or unmanned autonomous vehicles (or drones), to see it as ongoing is to insist that we factor in how racism and antiblackness undergird and sustain the intersecting surveillances of our present order. Patricia Hill Collins uses the term "intersectional paradigms" to signal that "oppression cannot be reduced to one fundamental type, and that oppressions work together in producing injustice."[17] Indebted to black feminist scholarship, by "intersecting surveillances" I am referring to the interdependent and interlocking ways that practices, performances, and policies regarding surveillance operate.

The concept of dark matter might bring to mind opacity, the color black, limitlessness and the limitations imposed on blackness, the dark, antimatter, that which is not optically available, black holes, the Big Bang theory, and other concerns of cosmology where dark matter is that nonluminous component of the universe that is said to exist but cannot be observed, cannot be re-created in laboratory conditions. Its distribution cannot be measured; its properties cannot be determined; and so it remains undetectable. The gravitational pull of this unseen matter is said to move galaxies. Invisible and unknowable, yet somehow still there, dark matter, in this planetary sense, is theoretical. If the term "dark matter" is a way to think about race, where race, as Howard Winant puts it, "remains the *dark matter*, the often invisible substance that in many ways structures the universe of modernity," then one must ask here, invisible to whom?[18] If it is often invisible, then how is it sensed, experienced, and lived? Is it really invisible, or is it rather unseen and unperceived by many? In her essay "Black (W)holes and the Geometry of Black Female Sexuality," Evelyn Hammonds takes up the astrophysics of black holes found in Michele Wallace's discussion of the negation of black creative genius to say that if "we can detect the presence of a black hole by its effects on the region of space where it is located," where, unseen, its energy distorts and disrupts that around it, from that understanding we can then use this theorizing as a way to "develop reading strategies that allow us to make visible the distorting and productive effects" of black female sexualities in particular, and blackness in general.[19] Taking up blackness in surveillance studies in this way, as rather unperceived yet producing a productive disruption of that around it, *Dark Matters* names the surveillance of blackness as often unperceivable within the study of surveillance, all the while blackness being that nonnameable matter that matters the racialized disciplinary society. It is from this insight that I situate *Dark Matters* as a black diasporic, archival, historical, and contemporary study that locates blackness as a key site through which surveillance is practiced, narrated, and enacted.

Surveillance is nothing new to black folks. It is the fact of antiblackness. This book is not intended to be a comprehensive overview of the ways that black people and blackness have come under, or up against, surveillance. Of the scholars that have written about surveillance as it concerns black people, many have taken as their focus the FBI Counterintelligence Program (COINTELPRO) that ran from 1956 until 1971 and that saw individuals and domestic political organizations deemed subversive, or potentially so, come under investigation by the bureau with the aim of disrupting their activities, discrediting their efforts, and neutralizing their effects, often through infiltration, disinformation, and the work of informants. Sociologist Mike Forrest Keen's study of the FBI's surveillance of sociologists such as W. E. B. DuBois and E. Franklin Frazier, David Garrow's *The FBI and Martin Luther King Jr.*, Theodore Kornweibel on the FBI's surveillance of the activities of Marcus Garvey and the United Negro Improvement Association through the use of informants and disinformation, or Carole Boyce Davies's writings on the intense FBI scrutiny of Trinidadian activist, Marxist, and journalist Claudia Jones, for example, form part of this scholarly work. Other research examines policing with a focus on racism, state power, and incarceration, such as the works of Ruth Wilson Gilmore, Angela Davis, Joy James, Dylan Rodriguez, and more. James Baldwin, Toni Cade Bambara, bell hooks, and Ralph Ellison have all, in different ways, written on being looked at and on seeing black life. For instance, in *The Evidence of Things Not Seen*, James Baldwin describes black suffering under the conditions of antiblackness where, as he puts it, "it is a very grave matter to be forced to imitate a people for whom you know—which is the price of your performance and survival—you do not exist. It is hard to imitate a people whose existence appears, mainly, to be made tolerable by their bottomless gratitude that they are not, thank heaven, *you*."[20] Toni Cade Bambara's call for emancipatory texts to "heal our imperialized eyes" as well as bell hooks's naming of the interrogating, "oppositional gaze" as "one that 'looks' to document" form part of this critical take on black looks.[21] Ralph Ellison's critiques and quarrels with what is taken as canonical sociology and the ways in which much of its early racial knowledge production was achieved by distorting blackness has been detailed by Roderick Ferguson. In *Aberrations in Black: Toward a Queer of Color Critique*, Ferguson offers an analysis of an unpublished chapter of Ellison's *Invisible Man* where he examines the ways that canonical sociology made itself out to be a discipline through the "sociologization" of black sexuality by way of surveillance. On sociologization, Ferguson writes, "canonical sociology would help transform observation into an epistemological and 'objective' technique for the good of modern state power. This was a way of defining surveillance as a scientifically acceptable and socially necessary practice. It established the sociological onlooker as safely removed and insulated from the prurient practices of African American men, women and children."[22]

As ethnography, tallying, and "statistics helped to produce surveillance as one mode, alongside confession, for producing the truth of sexuality in Western society," when this mode concerned the measurement of black human life in the post-Emancipation United States, such racial logics often made for sociology as a population management technology of the state.[23] One example of how such sociologization functioned in relation to blackness is "The Conflict and Fusion of Cultures with Special Reference to the Negro," Robert Park's 1918 address to the meeting of the American Sociological Society in which he stated, "The Negro is, by natural disposition, neither an intellectual nor an idealist like the Jew, nor a brooding introspective like the East Indian, nor a pioneer and frontiersman, like the Anglo-Saxon. He is primarily an artist, loving life for its own sake."[24] Park, who in 1925 would become president of the American Sociological Society, continued his address by saying, "The Negro is, so to speak, the lady among the races."[25] Park's address is instructive regarding the tenets of gendered antiblack racism that shaped the discipline of sociology in the early twentieth century. It is accounts of blackness like these that influenced Ellison's quarrels with sociological discourse, or what he called in his introduction to *Invisible Man* "the bland assertions of sociologists," where in observing, tallying, quantifying, indexing, and surveilling, black life was made "unvisible."[26]

Dark Matters stems from a questioning of what would happen if some of the ideas occurring in the emerging field of surveillance studies were put into conversation with the enduring archive of transatlantic slavery and its afterlife, in this way making visible the many ways that race continues to structure surveillance practices. This study's objects of investigation include the plan of the *Brooks* slave ship, the Panopticon, the *Book of Negroes* as a record of black escape from New York in the late 1700s, branding of enslaved people in transatlantic slavery, slave passes and runaway notices, lantern laws in eighteenth-century New York City that mandated enslaved people carry lit candles as they moved about the city after dark, a set of rules from the 1800s specifying the management of slaves on an East Texas plantation, and the life of a young woman named Coobah who was enslaved in eighteenth-century Jamaica. If we are to take transatlantic slavery as antecedent to contemporary surveillance technologies and practices as they concern inventories of ships' cargo and the cheek-by-jowl arrangement laid out in the stowage plan of the *Brooks* slave ship, biometric identification by branding the slave's body with hot irons, slave markets and auction blocks as exercises of synoptic power where the many watched the few, slave passes and patrols, manumission papers and free badges, black codes and fugitive slave notices, it is to the archives, slave narratives, and often to black expressive practices, creative texts, and other efforts that we can look for moments of refusal and critique. Slave narratives, as Avery Gordon demonstrates, offer us "a sociology of slavery and freedom."[27] To paraphrase Gordon here, through their rendering of the autobiographical, the ethnographic, the historical, the literary, and the political, slave narratives are sociological in that they reveal the social life of the slave condition, speak of freedom practices, and detail the workings of power in the making of what is exceptional—the slave life—into the everyday through acts of violence.[28]

Surveillance Studies

In this section, I provide a brief overview of key terms and concepts, some of them overlapping, as they relate to the concerns of this book. This is not meant to be a comprehensive review of the field of surveillance studies, but rather it is done to put this book into conversation with that body of research and writing and to also introduce the two main, interrelated conceptual schemes of this book: racializing surveillance and dark sousveillance. Research and writing that falls under the rubric of surveillance studies has come from a range of disciplines including sociology, geography, cultural studies, organization studies, science and technology studies, criminology, and critical theory. As an interdisciplinary field of study, the questions that shape surveillance studies center on the management of everyday and exceptional life—personal data, privacy, security, and terrorism, for example. In their introduction to *The Surveillance Studies Reader*, Sean Hier and Joshua Greenberg note that although "a qualitative shift in surveillance took place after 9/11," there still remains a certain absence in the literature "on the pre-9/11 forms of surveillance that made post-9/11 surveillance possible."[29] *Dark Matters* seeks to make an intervention in the literature by naming the "absented presence" of blackness as part of that absence in the literature that Hier and Greenberg point to. In the sense that blackness is often absented from what is theorized and who is cited, it is ever present in the subjection of black motorists to a disproportionate number of traffic stops (driving while black), stop-and-frisk policing practices that subject black and Latino pedestrians in New York City and other urban spaces to just that, CCTV and urban renewal projects that displace those living in black city spaces, and mass incarceration in the United States where, for example, black men between the ages of twenty and twenty-four are imprisoned at a rate seven times higher than white men of that age group, and the various exclusions and other matters where blackness meets surveillance and then reveals the ongoing racisms of unfinished emancipation.[30] Unfinished emancipation suggests that slavery matters and the archive of transatlantic slavery must be engaged if we are to create a surveillance studies that grapples with its constitutive genealogies, where the archive of slavery is taken up in a way that does not replicate the racial schema that spawned it and that it reproduced, but at the same time does not erase its violence.

Since its emergence, surveillance studies has been primarily concerned with how and why populations are tracked, profiled, policed, and governed at state borders, in cities, at airports, in public and private spaces, through biometrics, telecommunications technology, CCTV, identification documents, and more recently by way of Internet-based social network sites such as Twitter and Facebook. Also of focus are the ways that those who are often subject to surveillance subvert, adopt, endorse, resist, innovate, limit, comply with, and monitor that very surveillance.[31] Most surveillance, as David Lyon suggests, is "practiced with a view to enhancing efficiency, productivity, participation, welfare, health or safety," leaving social control "seldom a motivation for installing surveillance systems even though that may be an unintended or secondary consequence of their deployment."[32] Lyon has argued that the "surveillance society" as a concept might be misleading, for it suggests "a total, homogeneous situation of being under surveillance" rather than a more nuanced understanding of the sometimes discreet and varying ways that surveillance operates.[33] He suggests that we should look more closely at "sites of surveillance," such as the military, the state, the workplace, policing, and the marketplace in order to come to an understanding of the commonalities that exist at these various sites. For Lyon, looking at contemporary sites of surveillance requires us to examine some "common threads" including rationalization (where reason "rather than tradition, emotion or common-sense knowledge" is the justification given for standardization), technology (the use of high-technology applications), sorting (the social sorting of people into categories as a means of management and ascribing differential treatment), knowledgeability (the notion that how surveillance operates depends on "the different levels of knowledgeability and willing participation on the part of those whose life-details are under scrutiny"), and urgency (where panic prevails in risk and threat assessments, and in the adoption of security measures, especially post-9/11).[34]

In *Private Lives and Public Surveillance* (1973), James Rule set out to explore commonalities within sites of surveillance as well by asking whether the "sociological qualities" of the totalizing system of surveillance as depicted in George Orwell's *1984* could be seen in computer-mediated modern systems of mass surveillance in the United States and Britain, such as policing, banking, and national health care schemes.[35] Rule found that although the bureaucratic systems he studied did not function as malevolently as in *1984*, Orwell's novel served as a "theoretical extreme" from which to analyze a given system's capacity for surveillance, in other words, how near it comes to replicating an Orwellian system of total control.[36] Using this rubric, Rule concludes that a large-scale and long-enduring surveillance system could be limited in its surveillance capacity in four ways: due to size, the centralization of its files, the speed of information flow, and restrictions to its points of contact with its clientele. Although much has changed with regard to innovations in information technologies, machine intelligence, telecommunications, and networked cloud computing since the time of Rule's study in the late 1960s and early 1970s, *Private Lives* is instructive in its understanding of the workings of centralized and diffused power by state and private actors and institutions, and for identifying earlier developments in what Gary T. Marx has called "the new surveillance."[37]

What makes "the new surveillance" quite different from older and more traditional forms of social control is laid out by Marx in a set of ten characteristics that these new technologies, practices, and forms of surveillance share to varying degrees: (1) it is no longer impeded by distance or physical barriers; (2) data can be shared, permanently stored, compressed, and aggregated more easily due to advances in computing and telecommunications; (3) it is often undetected, meaning that "surveillance devices can either be made to appear as something else (one-way mirrors, cameras hidden in a fire extinguisher, undercover agents) or can be virtually invisible (electronic snooping into microwave transmission or computer files)"; (4) data collection is often done without the consent of the target, for example with noncooperative biometric tagging and matching at a casino or a sporting event, or Facebook's prompt to "tag your friends" using the photo tag suggest feature; (5) surveillance is about the prevention and management of risk through predictive or anticipatory means; (6) it is less labor intensive than before, opening up the possibility for monitoring that which was previously left unobserved, like the detection of illegal marijuana grow-ops by thermal cameras set to sense unusually high temperatures or the detection of illicit bomb making by collecting and testing chemical air samples; (7) it involves more self-surveillance by way of wearable computing or "electronic leashes" such as fitness trackers or other means by which people come to monitor themselves; (8) the presumption of guilt is assigned to some based on their membership within a particular category or grouping; (9) technological innovations have made for a more intensive and interiorizing surveillance where the body is concerned, for example, with voice analysis that is said to measure stress as a way to differentiate between lies and truths; and (10) it is now so intense and with reduced opportunities to evade it that "the uncertainty over whether or not surveillance is present is an important strategic element."[38] With these developments regarding the scope and scale of surveillance, Marx has suggested that perhaps we have become a "maximum-security society."

For Marx, the maximum-security society is a way to conceptualize how the surveillance that was once figured as contained inside the military base or the maximum-security prison ("perimeter security, thick walls with guard towers, spotlights, and a high degree of electronic surveillance") now extends out to the whole society.[39] According to Marx, the maximum-security society is predictive, porous, monitored and self-monitored, and made up of computerized records and dossiers, where increasingly choices are engineered and limited by social location. In it, everyone is rendered suspicious at some time or another, while some individuals might be more often subject to what Marx terms "categorical suspicion" given their ascribed membership in certain groups. Notably, for Marx, the maximum security society is also "a *transparent* society, in which the boundaries of time, distance, darkness, and physical barriers that traditionally protected information are weakened."[40] Marx's concept of "electronic leashes" and also what William Staples calls "participatory monitoring" are ways of understanding how people, objects, and things come to be monitored in remote, routinized, and continuous ways—think of electronic ankle bracelets as a requirement of house arrest or car ignitions fitted with breathalyzers that measure a driver's breath alcohol content before the engine can be started.[41] People who are subject to such monitoring are also tasked with actively participating in their own confinement by partnering, in a way, with the overseeing body or agency in the check for violations and infractions.

Oscar Gandy's "panoptic sort" names the processes by which the collection of data on and about individuals and groups as "citizens, employees and consumers" is used to identify, classify, assess, sort, or otherwise "control their access to the goods and services that define life in the modern capitalist society," for example, with the application of credit scores by lenders to rate the creditworthiness of consumers or put to use for targeted marketing of predatory lending with high-interest loans.[42] The panoptic sort privileges some, while disadvantaging others. These concepts—categorical suspicion, social sorting, maximum-security society, electronic leashes, participatory monitoring, panoptic sorting—along with Kevin Haggerty and Richard Ericson's concept of the "surveillant assemblage," are some of the ways that the field has come to conceptualize surveillance. As a model for understanding surveillance, the surveillant assemblage sees the observed human body "broken down by being abstracted from its territorial setting" and then reassembled elsewhere (a credit reporting database, for example) to then serve as virtual "data doubles," and also as sites of comparison by way of, for example, credit scores or urinalysis drug testing, where one's biological sample is collected and tested for drug use, or when "lie detectors align and compare assorted flows of respiration, pulse and electricity."[43]

I want to add to these understandings of surveillance the concept of racializing surveillance. Racializing surveillance is a technology of social control where surveillance practices, policies, and performances concern the production of norms pertaining to race and exercise a "power to define what is in or out of place."[44] Being mindful here of David Theo Goldberg's caution that the term "racialization," if applied, should be done with a certain precision and not merely called upon to uncritically signal "race-inflected social situations," my use of the term "racializing surveillance" signals those moments when enactments of surveillance reify boundaries, borders, and bodies along racial lines, and where the outcome is often discriminatory treatment of those who are negatively racialized by such surveillance.[45] To say that racializing surveillance is a technology of social control is not to take this form of surveillance as involving a fixed set of practices that maintain a racial order of things. Instead, it suggests that how things get ordered racially by way of surveillance depends on space and time and is subject to change, but most often upholds negating strategies that first accompanied European colonial expansion and transatlantic slavery that sought to structure social relations and institutions in ways that privilege whiteness. Racializing surveillance is not static or only applied to particular human groupings, but it does rely on certain techniques in order to reify boundaries along racial lines, and, in so doing, it reifies race. Race here is understood as operating in an interlocking manner with class, gender, sexuality, and other markers of identity and their various intersections.

John Fiske shows the operation of racializing surveillance in his discussion of video surveillance and the hypermediation of blackness where he argues that "although surveillance is penetrating deeply throughout our society, its penetration is differential."[46] Fiske argues that although Michel Foucault and George Orwell both conceptualized surveillance as integral to modernity, surveillance "has been racialized in a manner that they did not foresee: today's seeing eye is white."[47] Fiske gives the example that "street behaviors of white men (standing still and talking, using a cellular phone, passing an unseen object from one to another) may be coded as normal and thus granted no attention, whereas the same activity performed by Black men will be coded as lying on or beyond the boundary of the normal, and thus subject to disciplinary action."[48] Where public spaces are shaped for and by whiteness, some acts in public are abnormalized by way of racializing surveillance and then coded for disciplinary measures that are punitive in their effects. Racializing surveillance is also a part of the digital sphere with material consequences within and outside of it. For example, what Lyon calls "digital discrimination" signals this differential application of surveillance technologies, where "flows of personal data—abstracted information—are sifted and channeled in the process of risk assessment, to privilege some and disadvantage others, to accept some as legitimately present and to reject others."[49] In this way, data that is abstracted from, or produced about, individuals and groups is then profiled, circulated, and traded within and between databases. Such data is often marked by gender, nation, region, race, socioeconomic status, and other categories where the life chances of many, as Lyon notes, are "more circumscribed by the categories into which they fall. For some, those categories are particularly prejudicial. They already restrict them from consumer choices because of credit ratings, or, more insidiously, relegate them to second-class status because of their color or ethnic background. Now, there is an added category to fear: the terrorist. It's an old story in high-tech guise."[50]

To conceptualize racializing surveillance requires that I also unpack the term "surveillance." Surveillance is understood here as meaning "oversight," with the French prefix *sur-* meaning "from above" and the root word *-veillance* deriving from the French verb *veiller* and taken to mean observing or watching. The root word *-veillance* is differently applied and invoked, for example, with the terms "überveillance" (often defined as electronic surveillance by way of radio-frequency identification or other devices embedded in the living body), "redditveillance" (the crowdsourcing of surveillance through publicly accessible CCTV feeds, photographs uploaded to online image sharing platforms such as Flickr, and online discussion forums, such as Reddit and 4chan), and "dataveillance," to name a few.[51] Lyon has outlined the "potency of dataveillance" in a surveillance society, which, he writes, is marked by "a range of personal data systems, connected by telecommunications networks, with a consistent identification scheme."[52] The prefix *data-* signals that such observing is done through data collection as a way of managing or governing a certain population, for example, through the use of bar-coded customer loyalty cards at point of sale for discounted purchases while also collecting aggregate data on loyalty cardholders, or vehicles equipped with transponders that signal their entry and exit on pay-per-use highways and roads, often replacing toll booths.

The *Guardian* newspaper named "surveillance" and "sousveillance" as the words that mattered in 2013 alongside "Bitcoin," "Obamacare," and "binge-watching."[53] For Steve Mann, who coined the term "sousveillance," both terms—sousveillance and surveillance—fall under the broad concept of veillance, a form of watching that is neutral. Mann situates surveillance as the "more studied, applied and well-known veillance" of the two, defining surveillance as "organizations observing people" where this observing and recording is done by an entity in a position of power relative to the person or persons being observed and recorded.[54] Such oversight could take the form of red-light cameras that photograph vehicles when drivers violate traffic laws, or the monitoring of sales clerks on shop floors with CCTV, as well as, for example, punch clocks that track factory workers' time on the floor to more ubiquitous forms of observation, productivity monitoring, and data collection, such as remote desktop viewing or electronic monitoring software that tracks employees' non-work-related Internet use. Mann

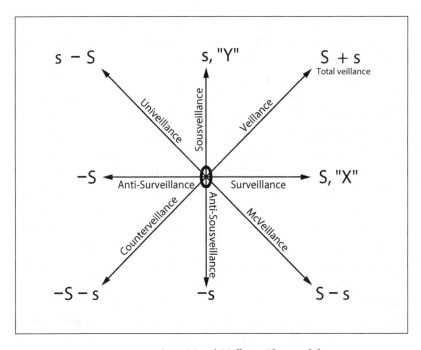

FIGURE I.2. Steve Mann's Veillance Plane and the "8-point compass" model of its directionalities. From Steve Mann, "Veillance and Reciprocal Transparency." Reproduced with permission.

developed the term "sousveillance" as a way of naming an active inversion of the power relations that surveillance entails. Sousveillance, for Mann, is acts of "observing and recording by an entity not in a position of power or authority over the subject of the veillance," often done through the use of handheld or wearable cameras." George Holliday's video recording of the beating of Rodney King by police officers of the Los Angeles Police Department on March 3, 1991, is an example of sousveillance, where Holliday's watching and recording of the police that night functioned as a form of citizen undersight.

Mann's Veillance Plane (figure I.2) places surveillance on the x-axis (uppercase S) and sousveillance on the y-axis (lowercase s). An "8-point compass" model, the Veillance Plane sees sousveillance and surveillance as "orthogonal vectors" or perpendicular, where "the amount of sousveillance can be increased without necessarily decreasing the amount of surveillance."[56] Other directionalities on this plane include univeillance (e.g., when one party to a telephone conversation records said conversation, making this action more aligned with sousveillance, rather than an approach closer to surveillance where a "nonparticipant party" to a conversation does the recording) and McVeillance. McVeillance would include an establishment that sets up a policy that forbids patrons from using cameras and recording devices on its premises, while at the same time recording those very patrons through CCTV surveillance, for example. McVeillance is surveillance minus sousveillance (S – s). Mann describes the "sousveillance era" as occurring prior to the increase and normalization of surveillance cameras recording in public and private spaces. He argues that although "the king or emperor or sheriff had more power" in the sousveillance era, during this era "the observational component of that power was more approximately equal than it is today," where people are often prevented from recording entities in positions of power, for example, when signs are posted in government offices and business establishments warning visitors and patrons that the use of recording devices on the premises is prohibited.[57] On the sousveillance era, Mann further explains, "Before approximately 50 years ago—and going back millions of years—we have what we call the 'sousveillance era' because the only veillance was sousveillance which was given by the body-borne camera formed by the eye, and the body-borne recording device comprised of the mind and brain."[58]

I want to make a link here between Mann's naming of the human eye as a "body-borne camera" and what Judith Butler terms the "racially saturated field of visibility" and what Maurice O. Wallace has called the "picture-taking racial gaze" that fixes and frames the black subject within a "rigid and limited grid of representational possibilities."[59] In other words, these are ways of seeing and conceptualizing blackness through stereotypes, abnormalization, and other means that impose limitations, particularly so in spaces that are shaped for whiteness, as discussed above with reference to Fanon's epidermalization and to Fiske on how some acts and even the mere presence of blackness gets coded as criminal. We can read a rigid framing in how Rodney King's acts of self-defense during a traffic stop in Los Angeles as recorded by Holliday on March 3, 1991, were coded as aggressive and violent. When King raised his hand to protect himself from police baton blows, his actions were met with more police force. Within what Butler has called a "racially saturated field of visibility," such police violence is not read as violence; rather, the racially saturated field of visibility fixed and framed

Rodney King and read his actions, as recorded by Holliday, as that danger from which whiteness must be protected.[60]

Although the observational component of the power of the sheriff might have been equal to that of the citizen in the sousveillance era, in the time of slavery that citizenry (the watchers) was deputized through white supremacy to apprehend any fugitive who escaped from bondage (the watched), making for a cumulative white gaze that functioned as a totalizing surveillance. Under these conditions of terror and the violent regulation of blackness by way of surveillance, the inequities between those who were watched over and those who did the watching are revealed. The violence of this cumulative gaze continues in the postslavery era.

Extending Steve Mann's concept of sousveillance, which he describes as a way of "enhancing the ability of people to access and collect data about their surveillance and to neutralize surveillance,"[61] I use the term "dark sousveillance" as a way to situate the tactics employed to render one's self out of sight, and strategies used in the flight to freedom from slavery as necessarily ones of undersight. Using this model, but imagining Mann's Veillance Plane as operating in three dimensions, I plot dark sousveillance as an imaginative place from which to mobilize a critique of racializing surveillance, a critique that takes form in antisurveillance, countersurveillance, and other freedom practices. Dark sousveillance, then, plots imaginaries that are oppositional and that are hopeful for another way of being. Dark sousveillance is a site of critique, as it speaks to black epistemologies of contending with antiblack surveillance, where the tools of social control in plantation surveillance or lantern laws in city spaces and beyond were appropriated, co-opted, repurposed, and challenged in order to facilitate survival and escape. This might sound like Negro spirituals that would sing of freedom and escape routes, or look like an 1851 handbill distributed by Theodore Parker, a white abolitionist from Massachusetts, that advised "colored people of Boston" to "keep a sharp lookout for kidnappers" who would act as slave catchers under fugitive slave laws that federalized antiblack surveillance (figure 1.3). In this way, acts that might fall under the rubric of dark sousveillance are not strictly enacted by those who fall under the category of blackness.

Dark sousveillance charts possibilities and coordinates modes of responding to, challenging, and confronting a surveillance that was almost all-encompassing. In the *Narrative of the Life of Frederick Douglass*, Frederick Douglass carefully describes how surveillance functioned as a comprehensive and regulating practice on slave life: "at every gate through which we were to pass, we saw a watchman—at every ferry a guard—on every bridge a sentinel—and in every wood a patrol. We were hemmed in upon every side."[62] This sweeping ordering did not, of course, preclude escapes and other forms of resistance, such as antisurveillance "pranks" at the expense of slave patrollers by stretching vines across roads and bridges to trip the patrollers riding on their horses, or counterveillance songs, for example, the folk tune "Run, Nigger, Run," which warned of approaching slave patrols.[63] Recalling acts of antisurveillance and counterveillance, ex-slave Berry Smith of Forest, Mississippi, tells of "the pranks we used to play on them paterollers! Sometimes we tied ropes across the bridge and the paterollers'd hit it and go in the creek. Maybe we'd be fiddling and dancing on the bridge and they'd say, 'Here come the paterollers!' Then we'd put out."[64] Such playful tricks were a means of self-defense. These oral histories of ex-slaves, slave narratives, and runaway notices, in revealing a sociology of slavery, escape, and freedom, recall the brutalities of slavery (instruments of punishment, plantation regulation, slave patrols) and detail how black performative practices and creative acts (fiddling, songs, and dancing) also functioned as sousveillance acts and were employed by people as a way to escape and resist enslavement, and in so being were freedom acts.

As a way of knowing, dark sousveillance speaks not only to observing those in authority (the slave patroller or the plantation overseer, for instance) but also to the use of a keen and experiential insight of plantation surveillance in order to resist it. Forging slave passes and freedom papers or passing as free are examples of this. Others include fugitive slave Ellen Craft escaping to Philadelphia in 1848 with her husband, William, by posing as a white man and as William's owner; Henry "Box" Brown's escape from slavery in 1849 by mailing himself to freedom in a crate "3 feet long and 2 wide"; Harriet Jacobs's escape from slavery to a cramped garret above her grandmother's home that she named as both her prison and her emancipatory "loophole of retreat"; slave spirituals as coded messages to coordinate escape along the Underground Railroad; Harriet "Moses" Tubman and her role in the 1863 Combahee River Raid that saw over seven hundred people escape enslavement in South Carolina; Soujourner Truth's escape to freedom in 1826 when she "walked off, believing that to be alright."[65] Dark sousveillance is also a reading praxis for examining surveillance that allows for a questioning of how certain surveillance technologies installed

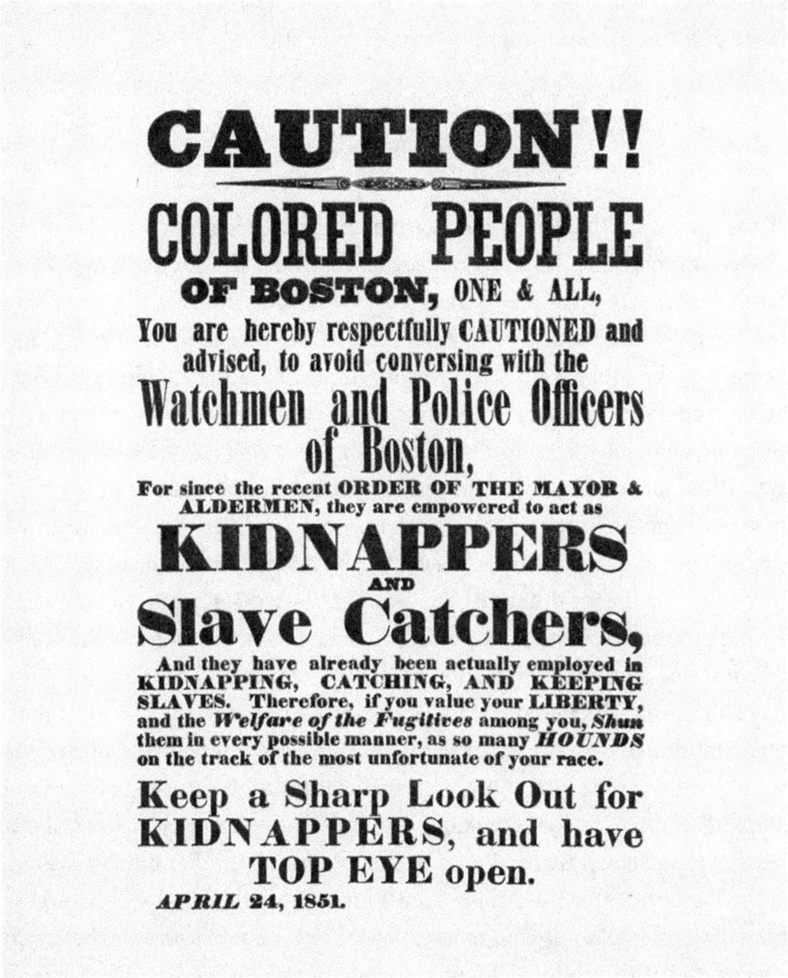

CAUTION!!

COLORED PEOPLE

OF BOSTON, ONE & ALL,

You are hereby respectfully CAUTIONED and advised, to avoid conversing with the

Watchmen and Police Officers of Boston,

For since the recent ORDER OF THE MAYOR & ALDERMEN, they are empowered to act as

KIDNAPPERS

AND

Slave Catchers,

And they have already been actually employed in KIDNAPPING, CATCHING, AND KEEPING SLAVES. Therefore, if you value your LIBERTY, and the *Welfare of the Fugitives* among you, *Shun* them in every possible manner, as so many *HOUNDS* on the track of the most unfortunate of your race.

Keep a Sharp Look Out for KIDNAPPERS, and have TOP EYE open.

APRIL 24, 1851.

FIGURE 1.3. "Caution! Colored People of Boston," handbill (1851). Library of Congress, Printed Ephemera Collection; Portfolio 60, Folder 22. 30.5 x 25 cm.

during slavery to monitor and track blackness as property (for example, branding, the one-drop rule, quantitative plantation records that listed enslaved people alongside livestock and crops, slave passes, slave patrols, and runaway notices) anticipate the contemporary surveillance of racialized subjects, and it also provides a way to frame how the contemporary surveillance of the racial body might be contended with.

The Chapters

If, for Foucault, "the disciplinary gaze of the Panopticon is the archetypical power of modernity," as Lyon has suggested in the introduction to *Surveillance Studies: An Overview*,[66] then it is my contention that the slave ship too must be understood as an operation of the power of modernity, and as part of the violent regulation of blackness. Chapter 1, "Notes on Surveillance Studies: Through the Door of No Return," considers the Panopticon (1786) and the plan of the slave ship *Brooks* (1789) for what these two schematic plans disclose about surveillance, race, and the production of knowledge. My intent in this chapter is not to reify the Panopticon as the definitive model of modern surveillance, but rather I want to complicate it through a reading of the slave ship. Both of these diagrams were published in and around the same time period, and they continue to provoke, in different ways, questions for both surveillance studies and for theorizing the black diaspora. Taking up David Murakami Wood's call for a "critical reinterpretation" of panopticism, what I am suggesting here is that one of the ways that this reinterpretation can be done is through a reading of the slave ship.[67] Panopticism, for Murakami Wood, is understood as "the social trajectory represented by the figure of the Panopticon."[68] Panopticism, then, is the Panopticon as a social practice. I interrogate the Panopticon and the plan of the slave ship *Brooks* to ask: What kinds of subjects were these two spaces meant to produce? How is social control exercised? What acts of subversion and resistance do these structures allow for? Also in this chapter, I explore the operation of disciplinary and sovereign forms of power over black life under slavery by looking at plantation management and running away.

In Jeremy Bentham's plan for the Panopticon, small lamps worked to "extend to the night the security of the day."[69] I examine this idea of the security of the day and surveillance by lamps at night in Chapter 2, "Everybody's Got a Little Light under the Sun: The Making of the *Book of Negroes*." In this chapter I discuss what I call "lantern laws," which were ordinances "For Regulating Negroes and Slaves in the Night Time" in New York City that compelled black, mixed-race, and indigenous slaves to carry small lamps, if in the streets after dark and unescorted by a white person. With this citywide mandate, "No Negro, Mulatto or Indian slave could" be in the streets unaccompanied "an hour after sunset" without "a lanthorn and lighted candle in it, so as the light thereof may be plainly seen" without penalty.[70] Here technologies of seeing that are racializing in their application and effects, from a candle flame to the white gaze, were employed in an attempt to identify who was in place with permission and who was out of place with censure. The title of this chapter is taken, or sampled, from the lyrics of funk band Parliament's song "Flash Light" (1977). I do this to hint at and imagine what it might mean in our present moment to be mandated to carry a handheld flashlight in the streets after dark, illuminating blackness. This chapter also looks to prior histories of surveillance, identification documents, and black mobilities through a reading of the archive of the *Book of Negroes*. Working with treaties, letters and other government documents, maps, memoirs, and fugitive slave advertisements as primary source data, I use this archive to examine the arbitration that took place at Fraunces Tavern in New York City between fugitive slaves who sought to be included in the *Book of Negroes* and those who claimed them as escaped property. The *Book of Negroes* is an eighteenth-century ledger that lists three thousand self-emancipating former slaves who embarked mainly on British ships, like *Danger* and *Generous Friends*, during the British evacuation of New York in 1783 after the American Revolution. The *Book of Negroes*, I argue, is the first government-issued document for state-regulated migration between the United States and Canada that explicitly linked corporeal markers to the right to travel. This linking of gender (often recorded in the ledger as "fine wench," "ordinary fellow," "snug little wench"), race ("healthy Negress," "worn out, half Indian," "fine girl, ¾ white"), labor ("brickmaker," "carpenter by trade," "formerly slave to"), disabilities ("lame of the left arm," "stone blind," "blind & lame"), and other identifying marks, adjectives, and characterizations ("3 scars in her face," "cut in his right eye, Guinea born," "remarkably stout and lusty," "an idiot") points to the ways that biometric information, understood simply as "bio" (of the body) and "metric" (pertaining to measurement), has long been deployed as a technology in the surveillance of black mobilities and of black stabilities and containment. This chapter argues that biometric information technology—as a measure of the black body—has a long history in the technologies of slavery that sought to govern black people on the move, notably those technologies concerned with escape.

Chapter 3, "B®anding Blackness: Biometric Technology and the Surveillance of Blackness," asks broader questions about early applications of biometric surveillance and its role in African American racial formation in particular, and in the black diaspora in general. I begin with a discussion of an 1863 *carte de visite* featuring "Wilson Chinn, a Branded Slave from Louisiana" as a way to locate my analysis of branding within plantation surveillance and punishment practices. To more clearly draw the links between contemporary biometric information technology and transatlantic slavery, I trace its archive, namely the diary of Thomas Thistlewood (an English planter and slave owner) that tells of plantation conditions in eighteenth-century Jamaica and the life of an enslaved woman named Coobah, other written accounts, runaway notices, and cartes de visite. I begin with a discussion of branding during transatlantic slavery as a marking, making, and marketing of blackness as commodity. Branding was a measure of slavery, an act of making the body legible as property that was put to work in the production of the slave as object that could be bought, sold, and traded. I argue here that the history of branding in transatlantic slavery anticipates the "social sorting" outcomes that Lyon's work alerts us to regarding some contemporary surveillance practices, including passports, identification documents, or credit bureau databases.[71] Through Frantz Fanon's concept of epidermalization—that being the imposition of race on the body—I trace and provide a genealogy of modern, digital epidermalization by focusing on branding and the role of prototypical whiteness in the development of contemporary biometric information technology. I consider the way that what Paul Gilroy terms "epidermal thinking" operates in the discourses surrounding research and development (R&D) of contemporary biometric information technologies and their applications: the fingerprint data template technology and retina scans where the human body, or parts and pieces of it, are digitized for automation, identification, and verification purposes or, in keeping with what Haggerty and Ericson argue as the markings of the surveillant assemblages, "reduce flesh to pure information."[72] Epidermal thinking marks the epistemologies concerning sight at the site of the racial body.[73] I look at some R&D reports concerning race and gender within the biometrics industry, including one particular report that uses images of actor Will Smith as the prototypical black male and actor Tom Cruise as the prototypical white male. This chapter also examines the branding of blackness in contemporary capitalism by looking at National Football League quarterback Michael Vick's postincarceration rebranding, artist Hank Willis Thomas's B®anded series, and blockbuster films starring actor Will Smith that feature biometric information technology. I argue in this chapter that the filmic representation of biometrics is one of the ways that the viewing public gains a popular biometric consciousness and comes to understand these surveillance technologies. I also explore the contemporary circulation of branding artifacts for sale online and take up visual artists Mendi + Keith Obadike's Blackness for Sale, where Keith Obadike put his blackness up for sale on eBay.com as a way to question the current trade in slave memorabilia and branding blackness.

Chapter 4, "'What Did TSA Find in Solange's Fro'?: Security Theater at the Airport," asks, broadly, what the experiences of black women in airports can tell us about the airport as a social formation. This chapter also examines art and artworks at and about the airport and popular culture representations of post-9/11 security practices at the airport to form a general theory of security theater. This is far from saying that security measures and security theater at the airport are a strictly post-9/11 formation. Between 1970 and 2000 there were 184 hijackings of U.S. commercial airline flights, while for foreign carriers during that period hijackings totaled 586.[74] Garrett Brock Trapnell hijacked one of those planes, Trans World Airlines Flight 2 from Los Angeles to New York on January 28, 1972, and during this hijacking he reportedly said: "I'm going to tell you exactly what I want. I want $306,800 in cash waiting at Kennedy. I want the San Jose jail notified I want Angela Davis released."[75] Trapnell later claimed that his demand that Angela Davis be released was actually a ploy to garner the attention and support of the black nationalist movement. Trapnell's was one of twenty-six hijackings of U.S. air carriers in 1972, a peak in domestic aerial piracy that led to the introduction of new security measures by way of a Federal Aviation Administration Emergency Order on December 5, 1972.[76] This Emergency Order included preflight screenings of passengers and their carry-on baggage by way of magnetometers, or walk through metal detectors, and the use of handheld metal detectors at many U.S. airports. This was not the first federal intervention into antihijacking efforts. On September 11, 1970, President Richard Nixon announced countermeasures to combat what he called "the menace of air piracy," including dispatching plainclothes armed personnel, or sky marshals, onboard U.S. commercial flights and the expansion of the use of magnetometers at airports.[77] The rash of airplane hijackings in the early 1970s eventually led to the Anti-hijacking or Air Transportation Security Act of 1974, signed into law by Nixon on August 5, 1974, four days before his resignation from the office of the president. On February 22 of that same year, Samuel J. Byck attempted to hijack Delta Airlines Flight 523 out of Baltimore-Washington International Airport with the expressed intent to assassinate President Nixon by weaponizing the plane and crashing it into the White House. Byck killed two people during his failed attempt, including the plane's copilot. Byck died of a self-inflicted gunshot wound during a standoff with police. Delta Flight 523 never left the runway that day.

I recount this short history of hijackings and various countermeasures as a way to situate contemporary security measures in U.S. air travel as having a much earlier history than those measures taken and performances undergone after the tragic attacks by weaponized aircraft in New York City and Washington, DC, on September 11, 2001. This history offers a counterframing to then National Security Advisor Condoleezza Rice's comment during a press briefing in 2002 when, in reference to the 9/11 hijackings, she stated, "I don't think anybody could have predicted . . . that they would try to use an airplane as a missile, a hijacked airplane as a missile."[78] At post-9/11 U.S. airports, passenger screening by the U.S. Transportation Security Administration (TSA) fulfills the usual scripts of confession ("What is the purpose of your travel?" or "What do you do for a living?" and "Are you bringing any goods in with you?"). With increasing procedural delays due to antiliquid policies, pat downs, chat downs, opt outs, the application of trace detection technologies to check for residue of explosive making materials, and with Secondary Security Screening Selection for some, many travelers undergo a certain amount of ontological insecurity at the border, particularly at airports. While the airport is an institutional site where almost everybody is treated with suspicion at one time or another—by TSA agents, by airline workers, and by other travelers—some travelers may be marked as more suspicious than others. In Chapter 4, I introduce the concept of racial baggage in order to name the ways that race and racism weigh some people down at the airport. I also examine the discretionary power wielded by TSA agents and by airline workers by looking at cases of, mainly, black women who were subjected to invasive pat downs, hair searches, and other security theater measures. I do this as a way to question how black women are de-

ployed in narratives about airport security, for example, through representations in popular culture as uninterested, sassy, and ineffective TSA agents.
This chapter suggests that we pay attention to the ways that black women's
bodies come to represent, and also resist, security theater at the airport.

The epilogue brings together this book's key concerns around the question of what happens when blackness enters the frame, whether that be
cameras that "can't see black people" or centering blackness when it comes
to questioning the logics of surveillance.

1

NOTES ON SURVEILLANCE STUDIES

THROUGH THE DOOR OF NO RETURN

The door is a place, real, imaginary and imagined. As islands and dark continents are. It is a place which exists or existed. The door out of which Africans were captured, loaded onto ships heading for the New World. It was the door of a million exits multiplied. It is a door many of us wish never existed.
—DIONNE BRAND, *A Map to the Door of No Return: Notes to Belonging*

In early August 1785, English social reformer Jeremy Bentham set out from Brighton, England, destined for Krichëv, Russia. It was in Russia where Bentham would first conceive of the Panopticon in a series of letters "from Crecheff in White Russia, to a friend in England." At one point during his journey, in an attempt to reach Constantinople, he embarked from Smyrna on a cramped Turkish caïque with "24 passengers on the deck, all Turks; besides 18 young Negresses (slaves) under the hatches."[1] Much of Bentham's writings that addressed slavery were written before this voyage. In those texts he touches on such topics as sugar production, punishment, and abolition. Writing during the 1770s on "afflictive capital punishment," that being when the degree of pain imposed upon the body surpasses that necessary to produce death, Bentham details the severe methods of torture and punishment reserved for "negro slaves" of the European colonies in the West Indies for the crime of rebellion, a crime so named, he writes, "because they are the weakest, but which, if they were the strongest would be called an act of self-defense."[2] While acknowledging Europe's desire for "sugar and coffee" and other crops produced through enslaved labor in the colonies, he suggests that when these goods are obtained by keeping people enslaved "in a state in which they cannot be kept but by the terror of such execution: are there any considerations of luxury or enjoyment that can counterbalance such evils?"[3] On the terror of the codes that governed slave life in the West Indies, Bentham has this to say: "let the colonist reflect upon this: if such a code be necessary the colonies are a disgrace and an outrage on humanity; if not necessary, these laws are a disgrace to the colonists themselves."[4] Bentham arrived in Krichëv in February 1786. One can only wonder if he thought of the terror of "capital punishment" and of the slave's "self-defense" when he came across those eighteen "young Negresses" held captive in the hatches of that cramped Turkish caïque.

That somewhere along a journey that ends in *The Panopticon; or, The Inspection House* Jeremy Bentham traveled with "18 young Negresses (slaves)" guides me to question the ways that the captive black female body asks us to conceptualize the links between race, gender, slavery, and surveillance. In other words, how must we grapple with the Panopticon, with the knowledge that somewhere within the history of its formation are eighteen "young Negresses" held "under the hatches"? If Bentham's Panopticon depended on an exercise of power where the inspector sees everything while remaining unseen, how might the view from "under the hatches" be another site from which to conceptualize the operation of power? This chapter asks that we rethink the Panopticon (1786) through the plan of the slave ship *Brooks* (1789), as a way to link surveillance studies to black feminist scholarship.

The first section of this chapter offers an overview of the Panopticon, disciplinary power, and sovereign power. In the second section I discuss some of the ways that the Panopticon and panopticism have been put to use in theorizing surveillance, and in particular three analytical concepts derived from this model of social control: synopticon, banopticon, and postpanopticism. In the third section I discuss the plan of the slave ship. Following this, I examine surveillance technologies of slavery, such as advertisements for runaway slaves and the census, as well as a set of rules from the 1800s for the management of slaves on an East Texas plantation. I do this in order to understand how racializing surveillance functioned through these technologies. I end this chapter by looking to black feminist theorizing of surveillance, including bell hooks on "talking back" (1989) and "black looks" (1992) and Patricia Hill Collins's concept of "controlling images" (2000) as a way to situate surveillance as both a discursive and a material practice. I also look to artist Robin Rhode's *Pan's Opticon* (2008) and artist Adrian Piper's video installation *What It's Like, What It Is #3* (1991), as these creative texts offer ways to understand black looks and talking back as oppositional practices that challenge the stereotyped representations of controlling images and their material effects. My use of Rhode's *Pan's Opticon* and Piper's *What It's Like, What It Is #3* is a way of drawing on black creative practices in order to articulate a critique of the surveillance of blackness. In this fashion, these works open up a way to think creatively about what happens if we center the conditions of blackness when we theorize surveillance.

Seeing without Being Seen: The Plan of the Panopticon

The Panopticon was conceived by Jeremy Bentham in 1786 and then amended and produced diagrammatically in 1791 with the assistance of English architect Willey Reveley. Bentham first came upon the idea through his brother Samuel, an engineer and naval architect who had envisioned the Panopticon as a model for workforce supervision. Pan, in Greek mythology, is the god of shepherds and flocks, the name derived from *paien*, meaning "pasture" and hinting at the root word of "pastoral," and in this way the prefix *pan-* gestures to pastoral power. Pastoral power is a power that is individualizing, beneficent, and "essentially exercised over a multiplicity in movement."[5] Bentham imagined the Panopticon to be, as the name suggests, all-seeing and also polyvalent, meaning it could be put to use in any establishment where persons were to be kept under watch: prisons, schools, poorhouses, factories, hospitals, lazarettos, or quarantine stations. Or, as he wrote, "No matter how different, or even opposite the purpose: whether it be that of *punishing the incorrigible, guarding the insane, reforming the vicious, confining the suspected, employing the idle, maintaining the helpless, curing the sick, instructing the willing* in any branch of industry, or *training the rising race* in the path of *education*."[6] Of course, "the willing," "the idle," and the so-called rising race might be more able to leave this enclosure at will or by choice than "the suspected" or "the incorrigible." With this "seeing machine," the unverified few could watch the many and "the more constantly the persons to be inspected are under the eyes of the persons who should inspect them, the more perfectly will the purpose of the establishment have been attained."[7] This is control by design, where population management and the transmission of knowledge about the subject could, as Bentham explains, be achieved, "all by a simple idea of Architecture!"[8]

The Panopticon's floor plan is this: a circular building where the prisoners would occupy cells situated along its circumference (figure 1.1). With the inspector's lodge, or tower, at the center, his field of view is unobstructed: at the back of each cell, a window, and in its front a type of iron grating thin enough that it would enable the inspector to observe the goings-on in the prisoner cells. The cells in the Panopticon make use of "protracted partitions"—where the partitions extend beyond the iron grating that covers the front of the cell—so that communication between inmates is minimized, and making for "lateral invisibility."[9] In this enclosed institution the watched are separated from the watchers; the inspector's presence is unverifiable; and there is said to be no privacy for those that are subject to this architecture of control. Security in the Panopticon, as Bentham asserts, is achieved by way of small lamps, lit after dark and located outside each window of the inspection tower, that worked to "extend to the night the security of the day" through the use of reflectors.[10] By employing mirrors in this fashion, a blinding light was used as a means of preventing the prisoner from knowing whether or not the inspection tower was occupied. Power, in the Panopticon, is exercised by a "play of light," as Michel Foucault put it, and by "glance from center to periphery."[11] The inspection tower is

> divided into quarters, by partitions formed by two diameters to the circle, crossing each other at right angles. For these partitions the thinnest materials might serve; and they might be made removeable at pleasure; the height, sufficient to prevent the prisoners seeing over them from cells. Doors to these partitions, if left open at any time, might produce the thorough light, to prevent this, divide each partition into two, at any part required, setting down the one-half at such distance from the other as shall be equal to the aperture of a door.[12]

With Bentham's plan for prison architecture, we can see how light, shadows, mirrors, and walls are all employed in ways that are meant to engender in many a prisoner a certain self-discipline under the threat of external observation, as was its intended function. The Panopticon would allow for a disciplinary exercise of power. Such exercises of power are not ones of pomp and pageantry, like a queen's coronation, a state funeral, or a royal

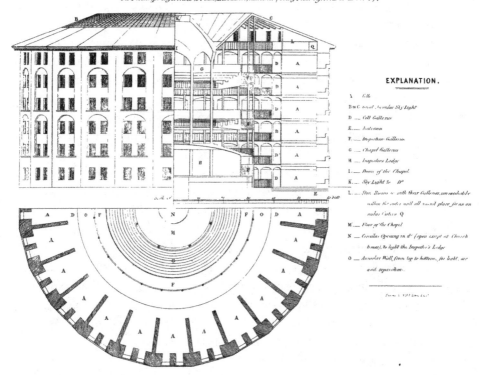

A General Idea of a PENITENTIARY PANOPTICON in an Improved, but as yet (Jan.º 23.ª 1791). Unfinished State.
See Postscript References to Plan, Elevation, & Section (being Plate referred to as N.º 2).

FIGURE 1.1. The plan of the Panopticon (1791). Published in 1843 (originally 1791) in *The Works of Jeremy Bentham*, vol. IV, pp. 172–173.

wedding, or of the overt kind of spectacular violence that often accompanies sovereign power. Instead, in this instance, power is covert and achieved by a play of light.

If an act that is deemed criminal is an assault on the sovereign's power, an exercise of sovereign power is that which seeks to make the sovereign's surplus power plainly understood by all. It is spectacular and episodic, and functions "to make everyone aware," often through ceremonial terror, "of the unrestrained presence of the sovereign."[13] This is a power exercised through excessive means and force, like the public execution of Damiens the regicide, the gruesome scene that opens Foucault's *Discipline and Punish: The Birth of the Prison* (1975). In 1757, Robert-Françoise Damiens was made to make the *amende honorable*, a symbolic apology for his crime against the sovereign. He was carted through the streets of Paris, France, holding a burning torch in one hand and his weapon of choice, a knife, in the other. Boiling resin, sulfur, wax, and oil were combined and poured into his open wounds, and he was drawn by horses, quartered, and eventually hacked apart for his attempt on the life of Louis xv, king of France. With onlookers surrounding, Damiens's body was burned and his ashes were "thrown to the winds."[14]

Another, but less well-known, public execution took place twenty-three years before that of Damiens the regicide in Paris. This time it was in the French colony of Nouvelle-France, and it was a black woman who was subjected to this gruesome exercise of sovereign power. Marie-Joseph Angélique, a Portuguese-born enslaved black woman, was tried and convicted of setting a fire that left much of the town of Montréal in ruins in 1734, the arson itself ruled to be an affront to that same sovereign that Damiens the regicide attempted to assassinate, King Louis xv.[15] Angélique arrived in Montréal from New England after being sold to François Poulin de Francheville in 1725. After Francheville's death in 1733, his wife, Thérèse de Couagne, became Angélique's sole mistress, but through escape, insolence, unruliness, and talking back, Angélique was never quite fully under Madame Francheville's complete control. Madame Francheville would later make arrangements to sell Angélique for six hundred pounds of gunpowder. That sale was never fulfilled as, on the evening of April 10, 1734, a fire broke out on the roof of the Francheville home and Angélique was named the arsonist and arrested the morning after. Claude Thibault, a white indentured servant from France who was under contract to Madame Francheville, was named as Angélique's accomplice. Thibault was Angélique's lover. Angélique and Thibault had escaped from Montréal that previous winter, but were captured and returned. Days after the fire, Thibault disappeared and was never arrested. Angélique's trial lasted two months. Under interrogation she reportedly stated, "No one told me to set the fire. No one helped me, because I did not do it."[16] Later, under repeated torture, she recanted that assertion of her innocence—"*C'est moi*. It's me and no one else. I want to die. *C'est moi*."[17] Condemned to death, she was carted through the streets of Montréal, made to make the amende honorable with a burning torch held in her hand at the door of the town's parish, and hanged. Angélique's body hung in the street for all to observe for hours after her execution, was later burned and her ashes thrown to the winds, as was the ceremony prescribed for the capital punishment of an arsonist according to French law.[18]

The ceremony of Angélique's execution, according to Katherine Mc-Kittrick, achieved at least two things: "spectacular punishment of someone and something that is said not to exist," that something being blackness in and of Canada as absented presence; and "the destroying of bodily evidence."[19] The trial and hanging of Angélique points to the criminalization of black women's resistance to captivity. The will of the sovereign was violently inscribed in Angélique's excruciating and spectacular death (both a public spectacle and spectacularly elaborate in its excessive violence) and made known for all who observed it—both free and enslaved—the expendability of slave life.

Foucault chose to begin "The Body of the Condemned," the first chapter of *Discipline and Punish*, with the brutal public execution of Robert-Françoise Damiens in order to set up, in stark contrast, his discussion of the discrete and also distributed way that exercises of disciplinary power operate in the form of rules "for the House of young prisoners in Paris," where regulation of the subject happened through observation and also through routines, repetition, self-discipline, and by following instructions and timetables. For example, the delinquent's day would be structured like this: "Art. 18 *Rising*. At the first drum roll, the prisoners must rise and dress in silence, as the supervisor opens the cell doors"; "Art. 20. *Work*. . . . They form into work teams and go off to work, which must begin at six in the summer and seven in the winter"; and "Art. 22. *School*. At twenty minutes to eleven, at the drum-roll, the prisoners form into ranks, and proceed in divisions to the school. The class lasts two hours and consists alternately of reading, writing, drawing and arithmetic."[20] The rules for the management of delinquents came eighty years after the execution of Damiens. Foucault cites both the execution and the rules to say that "they each define a certain penal style" and mark the decline of punishment as a public spectacle.[21] Disciplinary power did not do away with or supplant the majestic and often gruesome instantiations of sovereign power, however. Instead, at times, both formulations of power—sovereign and disciplinary—worked together. In reading punishment as public spectacle in the Old France and the New, I chose to recount the hanging of Marie-Joseph Angélique here because her torture and killing evidences blackness and slavery in Canada pre–*Book of Negroes* (1783), pre–Underground Railroad escape of black people from the United States to Canada (early nineteenth century), and pre-Confederation (1867). Putting the life of Marie-Joseph Angélique in conversation with the death of the regicide Robert-Françoise Damiens is my way of interrupting Foucault's reading of discipline and the birth of the prison, as doing so points to an alternative archive from which to understand the hold of both disciplinary and sovereign power on black life under slavery. While Foucault argued that the decline of the spectacle of public torture as punishment might have marked "a slackening of the hold on the body," this chapter contends that when that body is black, the grip hardly loosened during slavery and continued post-Emancipation with, for example, the mob violence of lynching and other acts of racial terrorism.[22]

Panopticon, Panoptical, Panopticism:
A Critical Reinterpretation

Various surveillance studies theorists have employed the Panopticon as an analytical tool in order to question how social control operates on certain bodies and in certain spaces, as well as a way to conceptualize disciplinary power and the ways that it comes to be internalized by some. Some theorists of surveillance have used the metaphor of the Panopticon to generate other ways of conceptualizing surveillance. For example, Thomas Mathiesen's synopticon (1997) is a reversal of the panoptic schema where the many watch the few in a mass-mediated fashion (think here of the reality television show *Big Brother*, where a television audience, as well as an Internet-based one, observe "houseguests" as they compete for prizes by way of twenty-four-hour continuous camera feeds), or Didier Bigo's banopticon, where those whom the state abandons are often banned based on a racialization of risk. Bigo takes the view that the practice of profiling and categorizing some into risk categories and then "projecting them by generalization upon the potential behaviour of each individual pertaining to the risk category" is the disposition of U.S.-led security measures and practices, and increasingly so post-9/11.[23] With the banopticon, certain groups and individuals are labeled as potentially dangerous. This labeling as dangerous is then massively applied to certain nations and their citizens and to those outside the bounds of citizenship, where anxieties and the anticipation of risk stemming from those deemed "dangerous minorities" then shape security measures at borders, on city streets, and other spaces that come to be associated with risk, or with being at risk of becoming risky. According to Bigo, the banopticon is "characterized by the exceptionalism of power (rules of emergency and their tendency to become permanent), by the way it excludes certain groups in the name of their future potential behaviour (profiling) and by the way it normalizes the non-excluded through its production of normative imperatives, the most important of which is free movement."[24] The banopticon might look like trusted traveler programs that speed up border crossings for preapproved travelers who provide some form of biometric-based verification, or free trade zones where goods can be manufactured, transported, imported, and exported without duties or other barriers to trade. The banopticon could also take the form of stop-and-frisk policing practices where categories of suspicion could include "furtive movements," or "fits a relative description," or "change direction at the sight of an officer," or "inappropriate attire for season."[25]

Some scholars have pointed to what they see as an apparent overreliance on the Panopticon in the field of surveillance studies that leaves the role of visibility overstated. Others have suggested that the Panopticon is no longer useful, or that at least as a way of theorizing disciplinary power in the contemporary moment it cannot offer a complete account of, for example, surveillance and exercises of power within social media and cell phone usage, or by way of digital information databases and data aggregators. On this point, Roy Boyne offers a critique of panopticism in which he contends that "post-Panoptical subjects reliably watch over themselves" without need of the physical structure of the Panopticon.[26] He suggests that panopticism has been "transcended by the emergent practice of previsualization" where simulation, profiling, and prevention occur, rather than merely observation.[27] Also, Boyne names the "reversal of the Panoptical polarity," where the many watch the few, as operating in conjunction with the Panopticon, where the few watch the activities of the many, in this way echoing Thomas Mathiesen on the synopticon.[28] John Gilliom and Torin Monahan, in their analysis of social media sites such as Facebook, argue that "rather than being a prisonlike panopticon where trapped people follow the rules because they're afraid someone is watching, with Facebook and similar sites people are probably more afraid that no one is watching, that no one cares what they're up to."[29] With this apparent fear of not being noticed, Gilliom and Monahan say that social media users "discipline themselves in a different way by divulging as much as possible about their lives and thoughts."[30] Other theories, like the "social sorting" of people and populations into categories of risk, are offered as a means of qualifying and understanding forms of surveillance that are sometimes overlooked. On the overrepresentation of the panopticon and accounts that take power as unilaterally exercised, Lyon writes that "not only does this kind of account distract attention from the subtle interplay between surveillance power and the attitudes and activities of those subject to surveillance, it also places all the emphasis on forms of rational control."[31] Likewise, Kevin Haggerty names the Panopticon as "oppressive," not only because of an overreliance placed upon it as an explanatory metaphor in works that analyze surveillance, but also for the way "the panoptic model has become reified, directing scholarly attention to a select subset of attributes of surveillance," which has resulted in the panoptic schema being applied in areas where it is, as he argues, "ill-suited, and important attributes of surveillance that cannot be neatly subsumed under the 'panoptic' rubric have been neglected."[32] One area of contention that Haggerty points to is the claim that in the panoptic schema, who, or what, does the watching is irrespective, or, as Foucault wrote, "Stones can make people docile and knowable."[33] For Haggerty, it is a mistake not to take into account the "attitudes, predispositions, biases, prejudices and personal idiosyncrasies" of those who do the surveillance for how these factors inform the "form, intensity and regularity" of their responses.[34]

The very failure of panopticism to produce docile subjects is an important point of criticism, where, as Boyne puts it, "that failure is announced in many places: prison riots, asylum sub-cultures, ego survival in Gulag or concentration camp."[35] In her observation and interviews at intensive management units housed within prisons run by the Washington State Department of Corrections, Lorna Rhodes names aggressive behavior (throwing feces, urine, and other bodily fluids), passive behavior (such as refusals to eat), and self-harm as instances in which the body is used as a means of resistance, and she argues that these acts are expressions of inmates' struggles with the panopticon.[36] Intensive management units, or special housing units, are solitary confinement units where certain inmates are segregated from the general prison population, spending up to twenty-three hours a day in their individual cells. Prolonged isolation in solitary confinement for many leads to depression, hallucinations, and acts of self-mutilation.

While the prisoner's body is "the very ground of the panoptical relation," under such conditions, as Rhodes contends, "it is also its potential undoing; he has within himself the makings of a perverse opacity."[37] Rhodes cites Lyon here in her naming of this "perverse opacity," a term that, as Lyon explains, points to the idea that such "resistance may not be liberatory—

indeed, it invites further control—but it calls in question both the panopticon and our representations of it."[38] Like Rhodes and Lyon, Boyne also calls the Panopticon into question, but he advises us not to do away with it completely as a way to understand our contemporary condition. Instead, he suggests that we "draw a line through the terms Panopticon, Panoptical, Panopticism. To place these terms under erasure, drawing a black line through them, allowing the idea to be seen at the same time as denying its validity as description, could be the most honest resolution."[39]

Unarguably the most cited work in surveillance studies on the Panopticon as a metaphor for disciplinary exercises of power is Foucault's *Discipline and Punish: The Birth of the Prison*, first published in 1974 as *Surveiller et punir: Naissance de la Prison*, with the book's French title alluding more closely to its focus on surveillance. In *Discipline and Punish*, Foucault argues that "discipline makes individuals" and achieves its success by employing "simple instruments": hierarchical observation (the greater over lesser authority, whether through physical structures or choreographed gazes), normalizing judgment (quantitative measurements, comparisons, establishment and adherence to set rules and norms, exclusions), and the examination.[40] Broadly, Foucault explains that hierarchical observation and normalizing judgment combine in the examination. Hierarchical observation works "as a piece of machinery" designed for "the uninterrupted play of calculated gazes."[41] With this play of gazes in the disciplinary institution, such as the penitentiary or the school campus, surveillance "functioned like a microscope of conduct" and sought to objectify, transform, and improve individuals through architectural arrangements, registration, examination, and documentation.[42] Foucault describes normalizing judgment as that which normalizes by singling out and correcting "that which does not measure up to the rule, that departs from it" with a glance, a gaze that classifies, ranks, and measures.[43] So although disciplinary power is individualizing, by way of normalizing judgment, individual actions are referred "to a whole that is at once a field of comparison, a space of differentiation and the principle of a rule to be followed."[44] The examination places the individual in a "network of writing" as it is "accompanied at the same time by a system of intense registration and of documentary accumulation."[45] The examination in the disciplinary institution seeks to objectify and transform individuals through architectural arrangements, registration, and documentation.

Prefiguring Bentham's design of the Panopticon and the seventeenth- and eighteenth-century disciplinary institutions that Foucault lays out in *Discipline and Punish*, the architectural design, registration, documentation, and examination at slave trafficking forts and ports, through the Door of No Return, and on slave ships during the Middle Passage voyage from Africa to the auction blocks and plantations of the New World were subject defining, but always violent. The violent regulation of blackness as spectacle and as disciplinary combined in the racializing surveillance of the slave system. On this point, Robyn Wiegman states that "the disciplinary power of race, in short, must be read as implicated in both specular and panoptic regimes."[46] Here, black children, women, and men were subject to these "simple" but violent instruments—branding irons fashioned out of silver wire, ships' registers in which African lives were recorded as units of cargo, or listed alongside livestock on slave auction notices, and census categories, estate records, and plantation inventories that catalogued enslaved people as merchandise. The branding of enslaved people as a means of accounting for a particular ship's cargo, for example, was not only individualizing but also a "massifying" practice that constituted a new category of subject, blackness as saleable commodity in the Western Hemisphere. Plantation rules laid out for overseers the prescribed measures for regulating plantation life and "social death."[47] In using Foucault's schemas of sovereign power, discipline, and normalization, as well as the concept of panopticism, I am mindful of their limitations for theorizing the role of trauma, vulnerability, and violence in the making and marking of blackness as property. However, for the concept of racializing surveillance, Foucault's contributions to understanding sovereign power and its "policy of terror" and to conceptualizing discipline and the imposition of norms, for example, offer us a way to understand how acts of making the black body legible as property were put to work in the production of the slave as vendable object to be bought, sold, and traded.[48]

Complicating Foucault's panopticism through the archive of slavery and black feminist scholarship on surveillance is a way of offering a critical reinterpretation of the concept—by "drawing a black line" through it. To do this I now turn to the plan of the slave ship. Drawing a line through panopticism by way of the slave ship is another means of interrupting Foucault's reading of discipline, punishment, and the birth of the prison, because, as Marcus Rediker put it, the slave ship was "a mobile, seagoing prison at a time when the modern prison had not yet been established on land."[49]

OOPS !

"2 feet 7 inches": The Plan of the Slave Ship

The prison didn't come to exist where it does just by happenstance. Those who
inhabit it and feed off its existence are historical products.
—GEORGE L. JACKSON, *Soledad Brother*

Through its creative remembering of the brutalities of slavery and its afterlife, Caryl Phillips's short story "The Cargo Rap" (1989) makes links
between the Panopticon, captivity, the slave ship, plantation slavery, racism, and the contemporary carceral practices of the U.S. prison system.
Racism is, as Ruth Wilson Gilmore explains, "the state-sanctioned or ex-
tralegal production and exploitation of group-differentiated vulnerability
to premature death."[50] Rudi (or sometimes "Rudy") Leroy Williams, the
protagonist of "The Cargo Rap," was sentenced to prison at nineteen years
of age for the attempted theft of forty dollars. Rudi narrates this slow, state-
sanctioned death that is the "negative inheritance" of the slave's progeny
that Stephen Best and Saidiya Hartman alert us to: "the ongoing production of lives lived in intimate relation to premature death (whether civil,
social or literal)."[51]

Phillips writes "The Cargo Rap" in epistolary form—as a series of letters penned by Rudi, namely to family members and to his defense committee, over the course of eighteen months. In this way, "The Cargo Rap"
follows George L. Jackson's *Blood in My Eye* letters, written right before his
death on August 21, 1971, in San Quentin State Prison in California. Like
Rudi, Jackson was convicted and incarcerated for armed robbery, accused
of stealing seventy dollars from a gas station while still a teenager in 1961.
On Jackson's sentence, Foucault had this to say: "ten years in prison for
70 dollars is a political experience—an experience of hostage, of a concentration camp, of class warfare, an experience of the colonized."[52] In one of
his letters written in Soledad Prison on June 10, 1970, Jackson states that
for the black man "being born a slave in a captive society and never experiencing any objective basis for expectation had the effect of preparing me
for the progressively traumatic misfortunes that led so many black men to
the prison gate. I was prepared for prison. It required only minor psychic
adjustments."[53] Both Foucault and Jackson speak of incarceration as a condition of colonization and of captivity.

In "The Cargo Rap" letters, we witness Rudi make sense of the traumatic
misfortunes of the world outside of his solitary confinement, where such
prolonged isolation makes his life one of constant exposure to fluorescent

light and permanent illumination, living in "neither daytime nor night-time. It is no time," as he put it.[54] To understand this constant and tortuous play of light on the body, Rudi asks his reader to "take a desk lamp and shine it into your face. Try to relax, think, act, concentrate, do everything in this position for twenty-four hours."[55] In an attempt to cope with the deliberate disorientation of "no time," Rudi cultivates an ability to tell time by way of certain noises and silences, as some silences are "closer to dawn than others."[56] Rudi tells of isolation, routinization, inspections, prema-ture death, and the harmful toll of prison life: deteriorating eyesight, *The Wretched of the Earth*, a ten-by-four-foot cell, a body atrophied, and the suf-fering of brutalities at the hands of the prison guards. This is a type of cor-poreal violence that was reported to Loïc Wacquant in his study of the Los Angeles County Jail system as "getting the flashlight treatment," where after violent beatings at the hands of prison guards one would be able to "read the brand of their flashlight" on the prisoner's body.[57] During Rudi's brief sojourn in the general prison population, he writes: "I can have darkness. My eyes can rest easy at night."[58] He writes of his desperation to escape the "high-security barracoon" that holds him and of the travels and works of the black activists, writers, athletes, and artists that sustain him while living a slow-motion death in prison: Muhammad Ali, W. E. B. DuBois, Frantz Fanon, Marcus Garvey, Toussaint L'Ouverture, Paul Robeson, Harriet Tubman, Phillis Wheatley.

Readers of Phillips's "The Cargo Rap" are not privy to the responses, if any, to Rudi's letters by his family members or his other correspondents. Instead, we are left only with Rudi's thoughts. His letters are, he writes, "a little cargo rap about the children of Africa who arrived in this country by crossing the water."[59] Rudi's first letter is to his mother, Alice, a domes-tic worker. In it he writes on Darwinism and self-preservation and he re-lates how unthinkable it is for her to even imagine trading places with the wealthy white women who employ her to work in their homes. With each of his letters, the plantation metaphor becomes even more direct as Rudi's physical and mental conditions deteriorate further. Incarceration is a slow-motion death. Rudi's last letter is dated August 1968, in a year that saw the assassinations of both Martin Luther King Jr. and Robert F. Kennedy, the passing of the Fair Housing Act meant to end discrimination in housing in the United States, riots in over one hundred U.S. cities, student coali-tions occupying buildings on university and college campuses demand-ing education reform, and the black-gloved fists raised in protest by African American track and field medalists John Carlos and Tommie Smith during their medal ceremony at the Summer Olympic Games in Mexico City. Rudi's last letter is addressed to his by-then-deceased mother. In it he writes, "the plantation is wide and stretches beyond the horizon. . . . We toil from 'can't see' in the morning to 'can't see' at night. The master is cruel, but nobody 'knows' him better than his slaves. There is strength in this."[60] By now disoriented from doing time under the deliberately disorienting conditions of "no time," in this letter Rudi inquires about the crops and tells of his capture by slavers and his hopes for return to Africa. In this plantation cum prison, he says, "Thirty feet above me a man sits on a watchtower with a rifle."[61] This final letter speaks of loss, prison time management, plantation rules, the Panopticon's inspection tower, and survival of the Middle Passage's cargo hold.

I chose an excerpt from Dionne Brand's *A Map to the Door of No Return* as this chapter's epigraph to point to a symbolic moment and space of diaspora and belonging. This door, while located at La Maison des Esclaves (House of Slaves) museum on Gorée Island, off the coast of Senegal, stands as a symbolic memorial of forced migrations that led to the mass vending of black people across the Atlantic Ocean. On it, Brand writes, "I think that Blacks in the Diaspora feel captive despite the patent freedom we experience, despite the fact that we are several hundred years away from the Door of No Return, despite the fact that the door does not exist."[62] This captive feeling that Brand describes is one of the vestiges of unfinished emancipations. A key aim of this chapter is to question how what Bob Marley names "the Babylon system," and what Howard Winant situates as "the legacy and lessons of the Atlantic slave system,"[63] can help us to think about how blackness is often absented from surveillance studies. "Babylon System" is the fourth track from the album *Survival* by Bob Marley and the Wailers, which was released in 1979. In it, Marley sings of refusal, freedom, and rebellion, with lyrics like, "from the very day we left the shores" and "we've been taken for granted much too long." On the cover of the album is a schematic diagram of a slave ship with tiny figures meant to represent its human cargo. Superimposed on this diagram is the album's title, *Survival*. In 1789, the London Committee of the Society for Effecting the Abolition of the Slave Trade produced and distributed *Description of a Slave Ship* (figure 1.2). Unlike Bentham's blueprint of the Panopticon, this schematic diagram of a maritime prison is populated with tiny figures dressed in loincloths to represent the legally allotted amount of enslaved human cargo that the slave

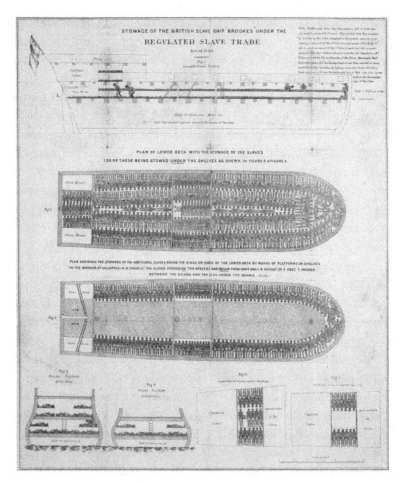

FIGURE 1.2. The plan of the slave ship *Brooks* (1789). Library of Congress, Rare Book and Special Collections Division, Washington, DC.

vessel *Brooks* (often referred to as *Brookes*) could transport under the Dolben Act of 1788, an act that regulated slave carrying and overcrowding.

Some background regarding this plan is necessary here.[64] The ship *Brooks* was built in 1781, commissioned by Liverpool-based slave merchant Joseph Brooks Jr. It was large as slave vessels go, weighing in at around 320 tons and at one point carrying 609 enslaved captives during a 1787 voyage from the Gold Coast of Africa to Kingston, Jamaica.[65] It took its final voyage in 1804 to Montevideo, Uruguay, under Captain William Murdock, where over three hundred people disembarked as slaves after a sixty-two-day voyage from West Africa. *Description of a Slave Ship* was fashioned by the London Committee in the hope of making "an instantaneous impression of horror upon all who saw it."[66] A similar rendering of a slave ship was produced in December 1788 by the Plymouth Committee of the Society for Effecting the Abolition of the Slave Trade. Named the *Plan of an African Ship's lower Deck with Negroes stowed in the Proportion of only One to a Ton*, this earlier version featured an overview of an African ship's cargo hold along with text that laid out the Plymouth Committee's agenda, including the demand that the "cruelty and inhumanity of this trade must be universally admitted and lamented," and advocated for "an end to a practice, which may, without exaggeration be stiled one of the greatest evils at this day existing upon the earth."[67] Copies were circulated in and around Plymouth, with some copies sent to the London Committee. By April 1789 the London Committee had produced their version, which featured seven different views of the *Brooks*: a cutaway longitudinal view of the ship, cross sections of the stern deck and midship, and an overview of the plan of the lower deck with figures of the enslaved lying in a plank position, crammed into all available space. In a later version, *Stowage of the British Slave Ship "Brookes" under the Regulated Slave Trade Act of 1788*, the note for "Figure 3" detailed this cramped configuration: "the stowage of 130 additional slaves round the wings or sides of the lower deck by means of platforms or shelves (in the manner of galleries in a church) the slaves stowed on the shelves or below them have only a height of 2 feet 7 inches between the beams and far less under the beams."[68] Two feet and seven inches. The violence of slavery crudely reduced to geometric units, with room allotted for forty women, twenty-four boys, and sixty men, arranged in a "perfect barbarism," as abolitionist Thomas Clarkson described this formation.[69] This arrangement was, as W. E. B. DuBois put it, "a foretaste of hell."[70] Slave trader Theodore Canot outlined the stowing process:

> The second mate and boatswain descend into the hold, whip in hand, and range the slaves in their regular places: those on the right side of the vessel facing forward, and lying in each other's lap, while those on the left are similarly stowed with their faces towards the stern. In this way each negro lies on his right side, which is considered preferable for the action of the heart.[71]

Without such "*strict* discipline," Canot wrote, "every negro would accommodate himself as if he were a passenger."[72] This spatial arrangement made for a crushing asphyxia: "The men therefore, instead of lying on their backs, were placed, as is usual, in full ships, on their sides, or on each other. In which last situation they are not unfrequently found dead in the morning."[73] The cargo hold is a slow-motion death.[74] Some cheek-by-jowl, this crude arrangement made known that those crossing the Atlantic Ocean in this manner were not "passengers," as they were allotted "half the room afforded soldiers, emigrants or convicts on ships of the same period," but were instead to disembark, if alive, as slaves and as unfree.[75] Rediker names the slave ship as "containing a war within," in which sailors and other crew would function as prison guards who "battled slaves (prisoners)" when attempts at insurrection and other types of resistance were made.[76] Other forms of resistance to this shipping arrangement came by way of refusals to eat, suicides, with some accounts telling of captives rushing all at once to the leeward end of the vessel "in a gale of wind, on purpose to upset the ship, choosing rather to drown themselves" than be subject to a life in slavery.[77] They died from "grief, rage and despair," C. L. R. James remarks in *The Black Jacobins* as he describes how some jumped overboard "uttering cries of triumph as they cleared the vessel and disappeared below the surface."[78]

Noted on one popular version of the *Brooks* diagram is this text:

> The "Brookes" after the Regulation Act of 1788, was allowed to carry 454 Slaves, She could stow this number by following the rule adopted in this plate. Namely of allowing a space of 6 ft. by 1 ft. 4 in. to each man; 5 ft. 10 in. by 1 ft. 4 in. to each woman, & 5 ft. by 1 ft. 2 in. to each boy, but so much space as this was seldom allowed even after the Regulation Act. It was proved by the confession of the Slave Merchant that before the above Act the Brookes had at one time carried as many as 609 Slaves. This was done by taking some out of Irons & locking them spoonwise (to use the technical term) that is by stowing one within the distended legs of the other.[79]

With women, men, girls, and boys locked spoonwise and segregated by age and sex, the production and containment of gendered difference is apparent. This stowage plan is what Hortense Spillers calls the making of "scaled inequalities."[80] Such accounting and architectural practices highlight the scale of the violence and trauma of the Middle Passage, a passage so named as it formed the middle leg of a triangular journey (the Middle Passage was bracketed between the journey from Europe to Africa and that from the New World to Europe). The London Committee version, *Description of a*

Slave Ship, states that the male cargo would be shackled at the ankles, "two by two; the right leg of one to the left leg of the other, and their hands are secured in the same manor,"[81] while the figures representing women and children were, in that rendering, unshackled, but in closer proximity to the captain's cabin. The London Committee noted, "The principal difference is in the men. It must be observed, that the men, from whom only insurrections are to be feared, are kept continually in irons, and must be stowed in the room allotted for them, which is of a more secure construction of the rest."[82] The plan then, in its various versions, highlights the gendering of sexual violence, while diagrammatically and textually absenting the possibilities of women's leadership and resistance in insurrections, as "only insurrections are to be feared" from men.[83]

The *Brooks* diagram, "in serving the cause of the injured African,"[84] offers an overview of the stowage plan of the slave merchant's ship and forces me to reflect on my own surveillance practices in reading the archive of transatlantic slavery. The slave ship schematic is clinical in its architectural logic and provides an almost aerial viewpoint, overlooking the tiny black figures set to represent the enslaved drawn "like so many cartoon figures," as Spillers describes.[85] What does it mean that I now look to this plan, but not from the elevated and seemingly detached manner as it was first intended to be looked upon? When the plan was first fashioned, this vantage point was meant to be that of the predominantly white and male abolitionists and lawmakers. I am reminded here of what Donna Haraway calls the "conquering gaze from nowhere," a gaze that is always unmarked, and therefore already markedly white and male, and one that claims a power to "represent while escaping representation."[86] I am also reminded here of Frantz Fanon's moment of awareness of a "racial epidermal schema" on that train in France and "battered by tom-toms" and "slave-ships" and "dissected under white eyes, the only real eyes," when he says, "I took myself far off from my own presence, far indeed and made myself an object."[87] What this visual representation of the slave ship points to is the primacy given in these abolitionist texts to white gazes and vantage points to the trauma of slavery, where the tiny black figures are made to seem androgynous, interchangeable, and replicable. This is the "god-trick of seeing everything from nowhere," and, as Haraway warns, "this eye fucks the world."[88] So it gets a little tricky when I do this looking, seemingly an aerial reconnaissance mission of the archive of surveillance and of slavery. In the versions of the *Brooks* diagram that were produced in the United States, the slave ship plan as abolitionist text was made clear. A version published in the periodical *American Museum* in May 1789 noted that it was "published by order of the Pennsylvania Society for promoting the ABOLITION of slavery."[89] Capitalization of all letters in "abolition" served an express purpose here, from the call for an end to the transatlantic slave trade to one for the abolition of slavery itself. Further, in this version the making of premature death through the stowage arrangements was described in this manner: "and reduced nearly to the state of being buried alive, with just air enough to preserve a degree of life sufficient to make them sensible of all the horror of their situation."[90] These conditions of premature death left many who traveled the Middle Passage as captives just on the cusp of survival. "Buried alive, with just air enough." According to Rediker, the mortality rate onboard the *Brooks* was 11.7 percent, which was "high for its own day (average for British ships between 1775 and 1800 was 7.95 percent)."[91] With a closer look at the *Description of a Slave Ship*, one can see that each of the tiny black figures are not replicas of each other; rather, some have variously crossed arms, different gestures, or seem to turn to face one another, while some stare and look back at the gaze from nowhere, and in so being the *Description of a Slave Ship* can also be understood as depicting black looks and the trauma of Middle Passage as multiply experienced and survived, and as hinting at the possible imaginings of what Omise'eke Natasha Tinsley terms "erotic resistance," that being the same-sex relationships forged because of and in spite of this shipping arrangement, where the formation of such relationships—like the intimate bond of shipmates—itself was an act of resistance to "imperial desires for Africans' living death."[92] Such resistance was a refusal of the Babylon system, or, as Bob Marley sings in "Babylon System": "we refuse to be what you want us to be / we are what we are."

Racializing Surveillance

The historical formation of surveillance is not outside of the historical formation of slavery. Using narratives of ex-slaves, runaway slave advertisements, the census, and a set of plantation rules as primary source data, what follows is a historicizing of some of the concepts and concerns that now shape the field of surveillance studies, approached by examining slave surveillance practices. The continuities that this archive reveals offer social theorists, I argue, new ways of understanding surveillance in contemporary life.

In the ten "General" and nineteen "Particular" rules for overseers recorded in the mid-nineteenth century by Charles William Tait for the governing of enslaved laborers on *Sylvania*, his 6,000-acre plantation in Columbus, Texas, Tait listed the prescribed methods for crop cultivation and clearing land, specified food rations, noted the daily schedule around meals and rest ("they must be ready to go to work by sunrise"), and detailed his punishment regime ("always attempt to govern by reason in the first instance and resort to force only when reason fails"), as well as postnatal procedures and back-to-work legislation for new mothers ("never require field-work of a woman, until the expiration of four weeks after confinement").[93] With the eighth general rule, Tait noted that "a regular and systematic plan of operation is greatly promotive of easy government. Have all matters therefore, as far as possible reduced to a system."[94] Tait's directives on the managerial control of slaves demonstrate how disciplinary power operated by way of set rules, instructions, routines, inspection, hierarchical observation, the timetable, and the examination. The timetable, then, was a means of regimenting enslaved labor through repetition where there was an attempt to account for every moment of enslaved life: "always require the negroes to eat their breakfast before they go to work" and "every negro-cabin to be inspected every sunday morning to see that it is kept clean. Every negro to appear in the field on Monday morning in clean clothes." Tait's fifteenth particular rule prescribed that "no profane or obscene language to be allowed among the negroes." The seventh general rule on punishment was an explicit directive regarding the overseer's performance that accompanied the punishment, as Tait wrote, "Never act in such a way as to leave the impression on the mind of the negro that you take pleasure in his punishment, your manner should indicate that his punishment is painful." So the prescribed punishment must be performed as a pain experienced by the overseer, who is not to express the possibility of pleasure taken in performing acts of violence. That a rule needed to be put in place in order to prevent such displays of violent delight should leave us to question the rates at which such pleasure was really expressed when, as Saidiya Hartman tells us, plantation practices sought to "make discipline a pleasure, and vice versa."[95] Importantly, this rule shows that for Tait, this pained performance by the overseer was a suffering that was meant to be remembered in the mind of the punished. Overseers were instructed by Tait's ninth general rule that "Negroes lack the motive of self-interest to make them careful and diligent," so in order to incentivize enslaved workers, "do not therefore notice too many small omissions of duty." What Tait's rules for overseers also make known is that plantation surveillance was an exercise of both sovereign power and racialized disciplinary power, working simultaneously, discretionarily, and in a prescribed fashion, as both were put to use in plantation societies to render slave life expendable.

In Tait's rules for what he called the "easy government" of his East Texas plantation, the specific rules on bureaucratic management and surveillance of slave mobilities, notably escape, were also made plain with particular rule "17th the negroes are never to be allowed to leave the plantation unless by special permission, and a written pass" and particular rule "18th no strange negro to be allowed to visit the plantation, unless by permission of the overseer, & a written pass from his master." The slave pass system relied on the notion that the slave could be known through a written identification document. Christian Parenti's writings on the kinds of surveillance practices employed during chattel slavery in the southern United States name the "information technologies" of the written slave pass, wanted posters and advertisements for runaway slaves and servants, and organized slave patrols as key features of this system.[96] Parenti situates plantation surveillance as the earliest form of surveillance practiced in the Americas. This was a system of surveillance that was regulated through violence and the written word.

The following accounts from *Born in Slavery: Slave Narratives from the Federal Writers' Project, 1936–1938* detailing the slave pass system further this point:

> By 1845 there were many laws on the Statute books of Georgia concerning the duties of patrols. . . . Every member of the patrol was required to carry a pistol while on duty. They were required to arrest all slaves found outside their master's domain without a pass, or who was not in company with some white person. He was empowered to whip such slave with twenty lashes.[97]

> The pattie-rollers was something else. I heard folks say they would beat the daylights almost out of you if they caught you without no pass.[98]

In the plantation system, the restriction of the mobility and literacy of the enslaved served as an exercise of power. The racializing surveillance of the slave pass system was a violent regulation of black mobilities. On and off the plantation, black mobility needed to be tightly regulated in order for slave owners to maintain control, so, as ex-slave Anderson Furr put it, one had to "git a pass for dis and a pass for dat."[99] This was a system that also relied on the publication and circulation of newspaper advertisements for runaway slaves and truant servants that announced not only those who escaped or went missing from plantations, but also those people who left enslavement in private homes and establishments, like shops, inns, and taverns in cities and urban spaces.

Runaway slave advertisements reveal a lot about black flight to freedom, as these notices of escape would not only name those who left enslavement and made their own way, but also provide a physical description and list the monetary rewards, if any, that awaited those who aided in their capture and return. These ads would list their talents, occupations and skills, vices, languages spoken and whether or not they could read or write, strategies they might have used to escape, and what they were wearing and took with them when they made their way. Also listed would be clothing, musical instruments, and other items that could be sold, traded, bartered, or used to support the appearance of being free. An advertisement for a runaway slave might read like so: "RUN away, a Negro Man named Tom, born in Jamaica, but last from Havannah," "blubber Lips, yellow Complexion, his Hair is neither right Negro nor Indian, but between both," "His eyes very full, as if they were starting out of his head," "had on when he went away a felt Hat, a Cotton Cap, a Homespun Coat with brass Buttons, a West-coat without sleeves, an Oznabrigs shirt, Leather Breeches with Brass Buttons, a pair of worsted Stockings and a pair of yarn ones, two pair of peak'd toe'd Shoes," "his great Toes have been froze, and have only little pieces of nails on them," "plays well on the Fiddle, and can read and write; perhaps he may have a false pass," "is plausible and smooth in speaking, and may pass himself for a Sailor, having been used to a boat," whoever secures said Negro shall have a reward of five pounds.[100]

An unusually long 1762 advertisement for "a Mulatto Servant man named Charles Roberts" states not only his age and height, but the condition of the clothes he carried, "several other Waistcoats, Breeches, and Pair of Stocking; a blue Great Coat, and a Fiddle." John Holt placed this ad, and in it he states that Roberts spoke "smoothly and plausibly, and generally with a cringe and a smile," and was good at arithmetic and accounting, leading Holt to charge that Roberts had probably forged documents to pass as a free man although he had "no legal claim to freedom." Holt laments that he placed confidence in Roberts, "which he has villainously abused; having embezzled Money sent him to pay for Goods, borrowed money and taken up goods" in Holt's name, unbeknownst to him. The reward for Roberts's capture in New York City was five pounds, and if found elsewhere the award would be greater. Anyone who captured him, the ad instructed, was to leave any money found on Roberts's person with the magistrate and was warned to be careful and "very watchful against an Escape, or being deceived by him, for he is one of the most artful of Villains."[101] Through their detailing of physical descriptions, the surveillance technology of the runaway slave advertisement was put to use to make the already hypervisible racial subject legible, borrowing again from John Fiske here, as "out of place."[102]

Runaway slave advertisements were not only about ascribing physical details to the runaway, but also offered the slave owner's assessment of the fugitive's character. One example of the role of runaway slave advertisements, and similarly wanted posters, in upholding racial categorization is a March 15, 1783, advertisement in the *Royal Gazette* offering a "Two Dollars reward" for "a Mulatto, or Quadroon Girl, about 14 years of age, named Seth, but calls herself Sall." This runaway advertisement states that Seth "sometimes says she is white and often paints her face to cover that deception." Seth's duplicity is not limited to her use of the alias "Sall," as this notice informs its readers, but also to her racial ambiguity, in her apparent choosing to self-identify or pass as white, rather than as "a Mulatto" (one black parent and one white parent) or a "Quadroon Girl" (one black grandparent), which was the racial nomenclature of the one-drop rule arising out of slavery and continuing beyond that institution. This advertisement also remarks that Sall has been "seen dancing" and "is well known in town, and particularly at the Fly-Market, for many wicked tricks." The Fly-Market in Lower Manhattan served as the city's market for provisions and other goods up until the early nineteenth century. Sall's ability to evade surveillance through makeup, wicked tricks, and hiding in plain sight exposes the one-drop rule as a social construction that, for some, could be subverted by performing whiteness. Seth's, or sometimes Sall's, hiding in plain sight—by identifying as white and using an alias—was a freedom practice to evade surveillance, and in so being a form of dark sousveillance. An 1836 runaway advertisement describes Edmund Kenney, who escaped enslavement by passing as white, thus: "he has straight hair, and complexion so nearly white, that it is believed a stranger would suppose there was no African blood in him."[103] An 1845 advertisement boasting a five hundred dollar reward for "a negro woman named Fanny" described her as a Bible-carrying, literate, "intelligent woman" who was "as white as most white women, with straight light hair, and blue eyes, and can pass herself for a white woman."[104]

THE CENSUS

In 1848 when Ellen and William Craft made their way out of Georgia and escaped chattel slavery by trains and by ships, they were able to do so through the ways in which Ellen's body was able to trouble the one-drop rule. Born to a black mixed-raced mother and fathered by the white man who owned her mother, Ellen was, at the time, labeled a quadroon but able to pass as white, as sometimes deaf and an "invalid gentleman" named "Mr. William Johnson." She passed as her husband's owner in order to secure his freedom as well as her own.[105] She used a poultice and put it in a white handkerchief "worn under the chin, up the cheeks, and to tie over the head," hoping that this disguise would hide "the expression of the countenance, as well as the beardless chin."[106] Because she could not read or write at the time of her escape, she feigned inflammatory rheumatism and placed her right arm in a sling in order to evade detection if, for example, she were asked to sign her name in a hotel's guest register. With Craft, her passing in terms of race, passing in terms of gender, passing in terms of class, and passing in terms of disability all played a role in her and William's passing into freedom.[107] The Crafts eventually left Boston to later arrive in England, where they lived for nineteen years before returning to the United States, where they opened a school for children and a cooperative farm in Georgia. In the 1850 census, Ellen was listed as residing in Boston and her race is recorded as Black (or rather " for "ditto," as it was recorded in the column under William's). The 1850 census marked the first time that the federal census included slave schedules for some states in order to enumerate each enslaved person held in a household or dwelling. By the 1890 census, Ellen Craft was recorded as "M" for Mulatto and her occupation as "keeping house" in Bryan County, Georgia.

In the United States, racial nomenclature as a form of population management was made official with the taking of the first federal census in 1790, which asked questions regarding the number of free white males, free white females, other free people, and slaves in a household. Census enumeration is a means through which a state manages its residents by way of formalized categories that fix individuals within a certain time and a particular space, making the census a technology that renders a population legible in racializing as well as gendering ways. The census is a form of "state stocktaking," as David Theo Goldberg puts it, which discloses "population size, shape, distribution, quality and flow of labor supply, taxation and conscription pools, political representation, voter predictability, and the necessities of population reproduction."[108] While such "state stocktaking" sees the census informant respond to a series of questions, including date of birth, how many people live in a single dwelling, and whether or not the dwelling is rented or owned, it takes the form of racializing surveillance through its very reinscription of racial categories. As an example, in terms of racial categories and the U.S. census form, there has remained a constant, unspecified whiteness as a racial category. Rather than employing an alphabetical order, "White" is always listed first among the boxes from which to choose in order to answer the question of the census informant's race. The proliferation of racial categories from which to choose, or have one's answer assigned, was first reserved for the management of blackness, with other groupings later added to reflect changing immigration patterns. In the 1890 census, Mulatto, Quadroon, and Octoroon appeared as subcategories of "Black," but by the 1900 census these subcategories were "collapsed into the singularity of an unqualified blackness," reflecting the one-drop rule.[109] "Mu" for Mulatto was reintroduced in 1910 and in the 1930 census it was replaced with "Neg" for Negro, a racial category that would fall in and out of favor, depending on each subsequent decennial enumeration. For the 2010 census, "Black, African-Am or Negro" were subsumed under one box and in 2013 the Census Bureau announced that "Negro" would be dropped from its surveys. As Goldberg writes, when the category "Mexican" was first introduced, it was understood as meaning not white unless the census informant "explicitly and accurately claimed white descent."[110] In this way, it was left to the census taker to judge whether the census informant's claim to the category of whiteness was valid, rather than accepting at face value the informant's self-identification as white. The 2010 questionnaire asks if the census informant is "of Hispanic, Latino, or Spanish origin," and, if "yes," the informant can choose "Mexican, Mexican Am., Chicano," Puerto Rican, or Cuban or fill in the blank to specify "another Hispanic, Latino, or Spanish origin." From its inception, the census has been a technology of disciplinary power that classifies, examines, and quantifies populations.

What It's Like, What It Is:
Controlling Images and Black Looks

In *Fighting Words: Black Women and the Search for Justice*, while referring not specifically to prison surveillance or plantation slavery but to the post-slavery, segregated southern United States, Patricia Hill Collins writes that while racial segregation was aimed at black people as a group or class and sought to erase individuality by making black people seemingly interchangeable, surveillance "highlights individuality by making the individual hypervisible and on display."[111] As part of the practice of "racial etiquette" in the segregated South, surveillance, Collins tells us, was a way of ensuring that "Blacks would stay in their designated, subordinate places in white-controlled public and private spheres."[112] Collins situates the bodies and lives of black women who labored as domestic workers and the white-controlled private homes in which they were employed as the "testing ground for surveillance as a form of control" that was enacted by way of "techniques of surveillance," including close scrutiny, sexual harassment, assault, violence, or the threat thereof. For the white women who employed them, Collins argues, this arrangement was predicated on the illusion that "the Black women workers whom they invited into their private homes felt like 'one of the family,' even though they actually had second-class citizenship in the family."[113] Yet within these labor conditions of hypervisibility, black domestic workers needed to assume a certain invisibility where, as bell hooks observes, "reduced to the machinery of bodily physical labor, THE black people learned to appear before whites as though they were zom-HOMESTEAD bies, cultivating the habit of casting the gaze downward so as not to appear uppity."[114] Seemingly "invisible to most white people, except as a pair of hands offering a drink on a silver tray," this signifying act was performed by many domestic laborers so that they would be assumed to be readily manageable and nonthreating.[115] Coupled with this system of scrutinizing black women's domestic labor in private white homes was the controlling image of "the mammy," one of "several interrelated, socially constructed controlling images of Black women, each reflecting the dominant group's interest in maintaining Black women's subordination."[116] The mammy as a representational practice relies on the circulation of stereotyped images and ideologies of black womanhood that seek to position black women as "the faithful, obedient domestic servant."[117] The mammy is depicted as caring for the family in which she is employed, often to the sacrifice of her own. This social control mechanism was "created to justify the economic exploitation of house slaves and sustained to explain Black women's long-standing restriction to domestic service," representing, as Collins puts it, "the normative yardstick used to evaluate all Black women's behavior."[118] In so being, the mammy served as a symbol of "the dominant group's percep-tions of the ideal Black female relationship to elite White male power."[119] She is content, deferential, forgiving, nurturing, and loyal to the family that she cares for, operating with some authority, however marginal, while still knowing "her 'place' as obedient servant."[120] Such exaggerated repre-sentational strategies work to rationalize the economic exploitation and sexual subjugation of black domestic workers and of those who labor in low-paying conditions in the service sector. This mammy image circulates throughout dominant culture, from films such as *Gone with the Wind* (1939) to *The Help* (2011), to what Patricia A. Turner calls "contemptible collect-ibles," those distorted depictions of blackness that often take the shape of figurines, postcards, kitchen utensils, and lawn ornaments. Simply put, "Mammy is the public face that Whites expect Black women to assume for them."[121] Of course, many black women who labored in white households forged loving and nurturing relations with their own families, despite the harsh working conditions of white supremacy.[122]

TKAMB

In her discussion of the black gaze and looking relations during slavery and during the racial apartheid of Jim Crow in the southern United States, hooks notes that although black people "could be brutally punished for looking, for appearing to observe the whites they were serving, as only a subject can observe or see," the violent ways in which blacks were denied the right to look back "had produced in us an overwhelming longing to look, a rebellious desire, an oppositional gaze."[123] "Black looks" were po-liticized and transformative when, as hooks states, "by courageously look-ing, we defiantly declared: 'Not only will I stare. I want my look to change reality.'"[124] This stare is the type of "eyeballing disposition" that disrupts racializing surveillance where, as Maurice O. Wallace discusses, such looks challenge the "fetishizing machinations of the racial gaze."[125]

Disruptive staring is the focus of *Pan's Opticon*, a fifteen-panel photo-graph by South African artist Robin Rhode (figure 1.3). In it, Rhode's subject, a black man and Rhode's doppelgänger, is smartly dressed in a fashion similar to that of the subjects that South African photographer Ernest Cole documented in his 1967 book *House of Bondage* as they toiled, were relocated or banished, defied, and survived under passbook laws and the racist repression of apartheid South Africa. It can also be said that Rhode's subject gestures to the *tsotsi* aesthetic popularized by Soweto youth and those in other townships of Johannesburg in the 1940s, a style and fashioning of masculinity that reflected working-class township life: a dark pinstriped jacket, white-collared shirt, and a straw boater hat.[126] His back is to the camera as he faces a concrete wall. His stare is accessorized with inside calipers—like compasses, but with the needles at each end curving outward—that appear to jut out from each of his eyes. The inside caliper first appeared around the sixteenth century as a measuring device often used to determine the dimensions of an aperture, that being the space through which light rays pass and come into focus on an image surface. In photography, the aperture's diameter regulates the amount of light that reaches the image surface. The smaller the aperture size, the darker the surface will appear. For the astronomical telescope, the aperture is the optical element that gathers light and brings the atmosphere into focus. No telescope, so far, can make dark matter visible.

Rhode's subject in the *Pan's Opticon* series is suited up with a prosthetic look. His ocular interrogation confronts the Panopticon and the architecture of surveillance—corners, shadows, reflections, and light—covering the wall with dark matter. On the subject of walls and architecture, Rhode writes that "when one speaks of walls, one speaks of security, privacy, and demarcation."[127] Rhode's *Pan's Opticon* is a play on Bentham's Panopticon. Rhode's naming of his series of photographs with the possessive noun *Pan's* is a claiming of Bentham's eighteenth-century plan for "obtaining power of mind over mind."[128] Rhode's black subject is not backed into a corner, but facing it, confronting and returning unverified gazes. That Rhode is a South African artist based in Germany points to the ways that disruptive staring can be transnational, as transnational as the structures that it disrupts. The stenciled circumferences of incomplete circles of black spray paint seemingly emanate from his eyes onto the wall's surface. With each frame of the storyboard, the circles refracted by the subject's eyes multiply, overlapping each other like disorganized Venn diagrams until the corner is completely covered in dark matter. In one frame, no neat stenciled circles appear, just two solid but smaller black circles of spray paint dripping down from the calipers onto the concrete wall, suggesting, perhaps, a peephole for a cu-

rious spectator's stolen vision, or the excesses of black looks that bleed outside stenciled borders, color outside the lines, and are out of place.

The disruptive stare of the subject in Adrian Piper's video installation *What It's Like, What It Is #3* (figure 1.4) is one such act of courageous looking. At the center of this installation is a four-sided column, like the Panopticon's inspection tower, but with each side of the column fitted with a television screen. Each screen plays prerecorded video of the front, back, and profile views of a black man (actor John L. Moore) who stares at those watching Piper's installation as he states his refusals of the stereotypes placed upon blackness: "I'm not pushy. I'm not sneaky. I'm not lazy. I'm not noisy." After listing four such refusals, he turns to face another direction and then lists four more: "I'm not vulgar. I'm not rowdy. I'm not horny. I'm not scary." He looks directly at the viewers of this installation, who can be either standing or seated on the bleacher-like seating that surrounds the center column. The installation is all-white and through its use of mirrors, the video is reflected throughout. In this setting like a lecture hall, viewers

FIGURE 1.3.
Robin Rhode, *Pan's Opticon* (2008). Fifteen digital pigment prints mounted on four-ply museum board, each 20⅞ × 31⅛ × 1⁹⁄₁₆ inches. © Robin Rhode. Courtesy of the artist and Lehmann Maupin, New York and Hong Kong.

of this installation are then instructed by the lists of refusals of the critique coming from the bodiless head in the column. In this way, *What It's Like, What It Is #3* can be read as confronting the surveillance imposed upon black life. The soundtrack to the nearly five-minute video of the installation is the Commodores' song "Zoom" (1977), playing in the background while the subject tells what it's like to live with antiblack racism, racial stereotyping, and the scrutiny of white supremacy coming from all sides: "I'm not shiftless. I'm not crazy. I'm not servile. I'm not stupid." His list of what black people are not is looped in repetition, leaving a space for alternative imaginings of what blackness really is and could be, while the voice of Commodores lead singer Lionel Richie croons in the background track, singing, "Zoom. I'd like to fly far away from here . . . where everybody can be what they want to be" and "I wish the word they call freedom someday would come." The song's lyrics express hope for escape, freedom, and a new way of being. In this way, Piper's piece offers us a look at oppositional gazing and talking back to the normalizing judgment and hierarchical observa-

Notes on Surveillance Studies   61

FIGURE 1.4. Adrian Piper, *What It's Like, What It Is #3* (1991). Video installation: wood constructions, mirrors, lighting, videodiscs, videotape, music soundtrack, dimensions variable. Photo credit: David Campos. Collection of the Adrian Piper Research Archive Foundation Berlin. © APRA Foundation Berlin.

———

tion of disciplinary, controlling images. Talking back is, as hooks puts it, "the expression of our movement from object to subject" and a "gesture of defiance that heals, that makes new life and new growth possible."[129] Talking back, then, is one way of challenging surveillance and its imposition of norms.

2

"EVERYBODY'S GOT A LITTLE LIGHT UNDER THE SUN"

THE MAKING OF THE BOOK OF NEGROES

Thus despite the bland assertions of sociologists, "high visibility" actually rendered one *un*-visible—whether at high noon in Macy's window or illuminated by flaming torches and flashbulbs while undergoing the ritual sacrifice that was dedicated to the ideal of white supremacy.
—RALPH ELLISON, *Invisible Man*

Our history takes place in obscurity and the sun I carry with me must lighten every corner. —FRANTZ FANON, *Black Skin, White Masks*

Billed as "the ultimate cat and mouse chase through the Canadian wilderness," the reality television series *Mantracker* made its debut on the Outdoor Life Network in 2006. With only a compass, a map, and a two-kilometer head start, each episode sees the aptly named "prey" given thirty-six hours to reach the finish line, by foot, often some forty kilometers away. Riding on horseback with a lasso and spurs, the Mantracker carries neither map nor compass and supposedly has no idea where the finish line is located. He is equipped with binoculars and an assistant, however. The Mantracker is Terry Grant, and, as the show's website tells it, he is a "full-blooded cowboy living in the wrong century." *Mantracker* began its third season with the episode "Al and Garfield." In this episode, viewers are invited to "watch as these urban warriors draw on the history of the Underground Railroad for inspiration to escape the unflappable Mantracker." The Mantracker's assistant in this episode is Barry Keown, a local horseman who cites John Wayne as one of his idols and who is familiar with the area of Deerhurst, Ontario, where the episode was filmed. At one point in the program, Keown jokes, "I guess I'm a little bit of a redneck at heart," and "we'll have those pilgrims rounded up so fast they wouldn't believe it." With its greenish, grainy night-vision footage mimicking on-screen GPS transmissions, high-resolution satellite aerial photograph mapping, and contestants offering staged confessions into a handheld video camera called a "preycam," *Mantracker* has all the trappings of the surveillance-based reality television genre. Each one-hour episode also fulfills a certain pedagogical role as viewers are instructed on antitracking techniques and shown ambush plan schematics, and definitions for useful tracking terminology are flashed on the screen, such as "Prey Drive (*conj. v.*): Instinct to evade capture by a predator (flight or fight response)." That the human prey has to be accompanied by at least one camera operator, a boom mike, and proper lighting does not seem to interfere with the appearance that the prey are evading their predators unhindered by the film crew and equipment needed to stage such a production.[1]

Described as "Toronto boys" from the "hard knocks hood of Toronto's Jane and Finch," contestants Al St. Louis and Garfield Thompson repeatedly invoke the Underground Railroad throughout the episode. At one point, the show's announcer even refers to the two as "fugitives." In one scene, the two remark,

> AL: This definitely reminds me of, uh, the Underground Railroad and the slaves running away. You know, two black guys on the run, man. We're keeping that in mind and that's what's fueling us forward.
>
> GARFIELD: It's kind of like we're doing it for our ancestors, man. You know what I mean?
>
> AL: That's deep. That's deep. That's deep. That's deep.
>
> ANNOUNCER: The prey draw on the past for inspiration.

I begin this chapter with the reality television program *Mantracker* to think about histories of black escape and the ways in which they inform the contemporary surveillance of the racial body. More specifically, I do this to question the surveillance technologies instituted through slavery to track blackness as property. When prey Garfield announces, "It's kind of like we're doing it for our ancestors," we should read this call on their self-emancipating ancestors for inspiration—as they attempt to outrun the

Mantracker—as offering a particular rendering of Canada and the tracking of black bodies within this nation that is often made absent from official narratives, that being the accounting of black people as recoverable property, with Al and Garfield playing the role of ex-slaves on the run. In one scene Al remarks, "We didn't want to leave any tracks. Our ancestors, you know, when the hounds are chasing after them, you know, they're sniffing, they're sniffing, but as soon as you go through the water they lose the scent, right? So that was the whole premise of walking through the water."

Later in the episode the Mantracker tells viewers that Al's seemingly cunning evasion strategy is a "cowboy myth" and that it is easier to track people in the water than on the ground. Throughout the episode, Al and Garfield are called "prisoners" and "rotten smilers" on a "swamp face off" who "got game," while Al mocks the Mantracker by calling him "cracker" and "redneck." Rinaldo Walcott, in arguing for a refusal of the black invisibility that is produced through Canada's official discourse of multiculturalism, suggests "it is crucial that recent black migrants not imagine themselves situated in a discourse that denies a longer existence of blackness" in Canada.[2] Al and Garfield could be doing just this, naming a black Canadian presence prior to 1960s migrations that "troubles and worries the national myth of two founding peoples."[3] However, this rendering is mediated for a television audience in a rather synoptic fashion, interpellating the viewer in a slick production of black escape as entertainment.[4]

In one scene that has Garfield complaining, "This bush is killing me, guy," Al responds with, "Think of it like this, Garfield. This is what our ancestors had to go through and worse, you know, and they were literally on the run for their lives, you know. So, a little bush, that ain't gonna do nothing. Suck it up. Let's go." In a voice-over of a campfire scene sometime later and shown for the audience in night vision, Garfield retorts, "There's no comparison in, um, us reflecting back on probably what it was like for our ancestors running for their lives. So later on in the nighttime, you know, we really, ah, we really connected, Al and I, talking about that, you know, and, it was a pretty sentimental and very emotional moment for us." The screen then cuts to Al and Garfield singing the Negro spiritual "Go Down Moses," which accompanies a black-and-white flashback montage highlighting scenes from the day's chase. The segment closes with the "prey" singing the line "let my people go" as the Mantracker's face flashes across the screen, eventually fading to the show's title card and then cutting to a commercial break. Also during the episode, Al makes reference to the widely documented difficulties that black people, and black men in particular, experience when trying to catch taxicabs in New York City, and he mentions Radio Raheem, a central character in director Spike Lee's 1989 film *Do the Right Thing*. Radio Raheem is often seen in that film carrying a radio blasting rap group Public Enemy's "Fight the Power" and he dies at the hands of a New York Police Department officer. Al can also be heard saying that the Mantracker should not think of him and Garfield as "easy prey" because they are "two black guys from the city" with "baggy pants and hats turned backwards." We can think of these references here as Al's critique of contemporary racial profiling, "sagging while black," and the various ordinances enacted in U.S. cities such as Albany, Georgia, or by the Fort Worth Transit Authority, that label those wearing pants below the hip, where doing so might often reveal undergarments, as committing crimes of fashion. Those criminalized for these fashion infractions are issued fines. Bans of sagging pants form part of the ongoing fashion policing that criminalizes black styling and expression, including acts such as the South Carolina Negro Act of 1735 that legislated what sundry, or dress, could be worn by black people, down to the type of cloth. The Negro Laws of South Carolina sought to "regulate the apparel of slaves" by prohibiting the wearing of "any thing finer, other or of greater value than negro cloth."[5] The episode of *Mantracker* closes with the Mantracker catching Al and Garfield. Upon their apprehension, images of their faces with a crosshair superimposed are put up on the screen with the word "captured."

Although this television program's website states that "the irony is not lost on these 'two black guys running from a white guy on a horse,'"[6] this particular episode of *Mantracker* speaks to the historical presence of the surveillance technologies of organized slave patrols and bounty hunters for runaways, notably those journeying at the height of the Underground Railroad from the United States to Canada. The remains of such technologies and the networked resistance to them—namely Negro spirituals that were at once expressions of the desire for freedom and sousveillance strategies with "every tone a testimony against slavery"—in this case are now rendered as cable television entertainment.[7] I bring up *Mantracker* here to serve as an entry into a deeper discussion of black mobilities, the visual culture of surveillance, lantern laws, and the *Book of Negroes*. The *Book of Negroes* is an eighteenth-century handwritten ledger that lists three thousand self-emancipating ex-slaves who embarked mainly on British ships during the British evacuation of New York in 1783 after the American Revolution. A key argument here is that the *Book of Negroes*, and its accompanying breeder documents, is the first government-issued document for state-regulated migration between the United States and Canada that explicitly linked corporeal markers to the right to travel.[8] The document also serves as an important record of pre-Confederation black arrivals in Canada, and as such it "ruptures the homogeneity of nation-space by asserting blackness in/and Canada" as it historicizes the links between migration and surveillance in the nation.[9]

In the three sections that follow, I offer a discussion of the racial body in colonial New York City by tracing the archive of the technologies of surveillance and slavery. The first section focuses on the technology of printed text, namely runaway notices and identity documents, in the production of the *Book of Negroes* during the British evacuation of the city. This section draws on archival documents to provide textual links that evidence the accounting of black people as intimately tied with the history of surveillance, in particular surveillance of black bodies by way of identity documents. In so doing, my methodology raises questions around my own surveillance practices in reading the archive: by accounting for violence, and counting violences done to the three thousand people listed in the *Book of Negroes* and those who did not make the cut, do my reading practices act to reinscribe violence and a remaking of blackness, and black bodies, as objectified? Thus, I am mindful of Katherine McKittrick's caution that there is a danger of reproducing "racial hierarchies that are anchored by our 'watching over' and corroborating practices of violent enumeration."[10]

To question acts of watching over and looking back, in the second section I turn to lantern laws in colonial New York City that sought to keep the black, the mixed-race, and the indigenous body in a state of permanent illumination. I use the term "black luminosity" to refer to a form of boundary maintenance occurring at the site of the black body, whether by candlelight, flaming torch, or the camera flashbulb that documents the ritualized terror of a lynch mob, as Ralph Ellison described. Think back here to my discussion of "the flashlight treatment" in chapter 1, where after a beating one could read the brand of a prison guard's flashlight on the body of a prisoner, and also Rudi Williams in Caryl Phillips's "The Cargo Rap," who described the use of artificial lighting in solitary confinement as being like having a desk lamp shining in one's face for twenty-four hours a day. Black luminosity, then, is an exercise of panoptic power that belongs to, using the words of Michel Foucault, "the realm of the sun, of never ending light; it is the non-material illumination that falls equally on all those on whom it is exercised."[11] Perhaps, however, this is a light that shines more brightly on some than on others. Here boundary maintenance is intricately tied to knowing the black body, subjecting some to a high visibility, as Ellison put it, by way of technologies of seeing that sought to render the subject outside of the category of the human, *un*-visible. My focus in the second section of this chapter is the candle lantern and the laws regarding its usage that allowed for a scrutinizing and racializing surveillance that individuals were at once subjected to and that produced them as the racial body. Following David Marriot in his reading of the spectacle of death that is lynching and its photographic archive, such laws, I suggest, operated "through visual terror" in the management of black mobilities, warning of the potential to reduce one to "something that don't look human."[12] Or maybe too human. Rather than looking solely to those moments when blackness is violently illuminated, this chapter uncovers moments of dark sousveillance by highlighting certain practices, rituals, and acts of freedom and by situating these moments as interactions with surveillance systems that are strategies of coping, resistance, and critique. This is to say, following Richard Sennett, that "ritual heals" and "constitutes the *social* form in which human beings seek to deal with denial as active agents, rather than as passive victims."[13]

With the third section, I consider varied notions of repossession by examining the Board of Inquiry arbitration that began in May 1783 at Fraunces Tavern in New York City between fugitive slaves who sought to be included in the *Book of Negroes* by exercising claims to mobility rights as autonomous subjects and those who sought to reclaim these fugitives from slavery as their property. In particular, what I seek to question here is the working of race and property in these arbitration hearings where black women, men, and children, figured as escaped property, would be rendered to their said owners with crude annotations written in the *Book of Negroes*, such as that concerning "a Negroe Wench named Mercy," which stated, "the Wench and her Children ought to be delivered to the Claimants to be disposed of as he may think proper." With this judgment, Mercy and her children were made ineligible to travel away from New York City; in effect, they were put on a no-sail list.[14] My use of the term "no-sail list" here is a play on post-9/11 no-fly lists, the U.S. Secure Flight program, the

Computer-Assisted Passenger Prescreening System maintained by the U.S. Transportation Security Administration, and Secondary Security Screening Selection, all of which subject certain travelers ("selectees") to additional scrutiny at U.S. and Canadian airports and other border crossings.[15]

In her discussion of the moments of narration through which racialized subjects "are brought into being," Hazel Carby considers the "creative, contested, contradictory and laborious work of constructing racial identities in narrative acts."[16] Carby implores us to "be alert to the occasions when racialized subjects not only step into the recognitions given to them by others but provide intuitions of a future in which relations of subjugation will (could) be transformed."[17] I am suggesting that the *Book of Negroes* is one of those occasions that Carby signals. At Fraunces Tavern, the pub-turned-courtroom on Wednesday afternoons, mobility rights were sought through decommodificatory narrative acts, disputing the claims made on the self as recoverable goods to be returned to slave owners. I conclude this chapter by turning to a different narrative act, Lawrence Hill's *The Book of Negroes: A Novel* (2007), as it extends the surveillance practices discussed in this chapter through its creative remembering of the brutalities of slavery. I begin and end this chapter with representations of black escape to argue that, in different ways, they allow for a rethinking of the archive of the technologies of slavery and surveillance, in that they reveal how this archive continues to inform relations of subjugation and unfinished emancipations.

The *Book of Negroes* lists passengers on board more than two hundred ships that set sail from New York between April 23, 1783, and November 30, 1783, during the British evacuation after the War of Independence. Ships, Paul Gilroy writes, "were the living means by which the points within the Atlantic world were joined."[18] Following this, the *Book of Negroes* is not only a record of escape from New York on board over two hundred ships, but it can also be thought of as a record of how the surveillance of black Atlantic mobilities was integral to the formation of the Canada-U.S. border. Prior to the 1782 provisional peace treaty between Britain and the Congress of the Confederation, that being the governing body of the United States of America, which set out the terms of the *Book of Negroes*, such journeys by sailing ship would have been within British territories rather than crossings of an international border, for the most part.

With its crude inscriptions, such as "scar in his forehead" and "stout with 3 scars in each cheek," the *Book of Negroes* is an early imprint of how the body comes to be understood as a means of identification and tracking by the state. In this section, I outline how the *Book of Negroes* became the first large-scale public record of black presence in North America. This hand-written and leather-bound British military ledger lists three thousand black passengers who left New York in 1783. Bound for Canada, mainly, and some for England and Germany, passengers listed in the *Book of Negroes* traveled as indentured laborers to white United Empire Loyalists or as free people, described in this ledger, for example, as "on her own bottom." Around the same time, others left New York enslaved to white Loyalists. Some of those listed in the *Book of Negroes* set sail for Germany on ships named *Ladies Adventure* and *Hero*, most likely as the property of German Hessian soldiers, captured from rebel states as spoils of war. The travelers listed in the *Book of Negroes* would later be recognized by many as United Empire Loyalists for their efforts as soldiers, support staff, and wage workers (cooks, blacksmiths, laundresses, nurses, spies, and other skilled laborers) with the British forces during the War of Independence. The naming of those listed as Loyalists, or specifically Black Loyalists, is not without controversy, as many entered into the bargain with the British for freedom and not necessarily out of some loyalty to the Crown.

What follows is a discussion of the proclamations and the provisional treaty that eventually led to the *Book of Negroes*. I tell of the making of the *Book of Negroes* through the stories of black escape in and around the time of the evacuation of New York that are found in the archive: runaway notices and advertisements, official correspondence, a memoir, an early passport. With these texts we can understand how the tracking of blackness, rooted in the violence of slavery, was instituted through printed text. My argument here is that the body made legible with the modern passport system has a history in the technologies of tracking blackness. My discussion on the making of the *Book of Negroes* offers a historicizing of the ways in which the tracking, accounting, and identification of the racial body, and in particular the black body and black social life, form an important, but often absented, part of the genealogy of the passport.[19]

Linking identity to bodily markers and infirmities, such as scarring from smallpox, "blind right eye," or "lame of the left arm," the *Book of Negroes* lists the names of each passenger falling under the Philipsburg Proclamation on board over two hundred ships that left New York in 1783. Each entry details the passenger's physical description, age, and places of birth and enslavement, and includes a section for comments or details of when and how each passenger came to fall under the Philipsburg Proclamation. Issued by British commander in chief Sir Henry Clinton on June 30, 1779, the Philipsburg Proclamation promised "to every negroe Who shall desert the Rebel Standard, full security to follow within these lines, any Occupation which he shall think proper."[20] Whether those who had voluntarily left their Patriot masters and found themselves with the British felt assured that by "full security" it was meant that they would be secure in the mutual recognition of their personhood or that they were fighting for what would ultimately lead to their emancipation is questionable; however, numerous slaves owned by Patriots deserted these slave owners and fled to the British holdings.

The fear of the loss of property that the proclamations and the ensuing black escape caused is reflected in a 1776 runaway notice for Cuffe Dix, in which slave owner Mark Bird of Pennsylvania claimed, "As Negroes in general think that Lord Dunmore is contending for their liberty it is not improbable that said Negro is on his march to join his Lordship's own black regiment, but it is hoped he will be prevented by some honest Whig from effecting it."[21] Those enslaved by white Loyalists, whether owned previously or confiscated during raids on Patriot estates, were not a part of this arrangement of wartime service in exchange for freedom. Also detailed in the *Book of Negroes* were the names of the passengers' claimants, if any, as a caveat set out by Article Seven of the provisional peace treaty reached on November 30, 1782, between Britain and the Congress of the Confederation, which stated that the British withdrawal would be executed without "carrying away any Negroes, or other Property of the American Inhabitants." A Board of Inquiry consisting of American and British delegates was established to adjudicate Patriot claims of loss of human property. When the Treaty of Paris was signed on September 3 of the following year, this stipulation regarding "carrying away any Negroes" was included. If it was found that the British did indeed abscond with their property, Patriot owners could be duly compensated. The *Book of Negroes* was intended to serve as a record in case of claims for compensation.

At the time of the British evacuation, the circulation of printed text allowed for a certain "simultaneous consumption" of newspaper advertisements for runaway slaves by a public that was assumed to be white and who by consuming at once the black subject, imagined as unfree, produced the readers of such advertisements as part of the "imaginary community" of surveillance: the eyes and ears of face-to-face watching, observing, and regulating.[22] Through their detailing of physical descriptions, the surveillance technology of the fugitive slave advertisement was put to use to make the already hypervisible black subject legible as what Thelma Wills Foote terms "objectified corporeality."[23] Beyond its primary function of surveillance, that being to serve as a public notification of runaways by announcing "property as out of place,"[24] the subjective descriptions employed by subscribers in runaway notices often reveal the subversive potential of being out of place. While runaway advertisements were a way of marking boundaries, making borders, and defining a slave as out of place, I want to think here of "out of place" as gesturing to the usage of the term in many African diasporic contexts, such as the Trinidadian saying "fast and out of place," meaning crossing the line and being demanding or "intolerably impertinent," or the term "bol'face" and its derivative "boldfacity," meaning "open rudeness without hesitation or embarrassment."[25] Similarly, the Jamaican term "facety" is understood to mean obtrusive, audacious, and "not knowing one's distance." Facetiness is not to be taken as having the same meaning as facetious; rather, facetiness, or facety acts, are a rejection of the colonial condition of lived objectification and a refusal to stay in one's place. Along with "backchat," these terms were and continue to be used to name subversive acts of looking and talking back.

The refusal to stay in spaces of dispossession, disposability, and lived objecthood can be observed in a June 14, 1783, runaway notice in the *Royal Gazette* that offered "twenty dollars reward" for sixteen-year-old Sam. Sam is described by the subscriber as "five feet high, slim made" and "remarkable in turning up the white of his eyes when spoke to." Sam's bold refusals, or his facetiness, are agential acts, at first ocular, looking back—to at once return and dismiss the gaze with the gesture of the eye roll—and then to go missing or steal himself and make his own place. With this notice for Sam, readers were cautioned, "all Masters of vessels and others are hereby warned not to habour or carry off said Negro, as they will answer for the same at their peril."[26] During this time, other notices were placed in newspapers for slaves to be sold, such as that for "a likely Negro man," about whom it was promised that "any family looking to settle in Nova Scotia, could not meet with one to answer their purpose better."[27] Other advertisements were placed by those wishing to purchase black men and women for enslavement in Canada, such as that in search of "a negro woman to live in a genteel family going to Port Roseway. For one who is a compleat house wench, and who is sober, honest and good natured, a generous price will be given."[28] These two advertisements for the purchase and sale of slaves make known that while many traveled to Canada as emancipated people, not all those who arrived in that country did so freely. As slave owners could make claims on their human property during the British evacuation of New York, this made for many start-ups in slave catching. In his memoirs, Boston King (1798), who is listed in the *Book of Negroes* as traveling to Nova Scotia on the ship *L'Abondance* on July 31, 1783, recounts the terror that spread at this time:

> For a report prevailed at New York, that all slaves, in number 2,000, were to be delivered up to their masters, although some of them had been three or four years among the English. This dreadful rumour filled us all with inexpressible anguish and terror, especially when we saw our masters coming from Virginia, North Carolina, and other parts, and seizing upon their slaves in the streets of New York, or even dragging them out of their beds.

Some owners came to New York or sent representatives and slave catchers in their place to demand the return of the black women, men, and children whom they considered to be their property, making New York at once a space of terror and a site of freedom for those who came under one British proclamation or another.

It was not only Patriots who seized upon their slaves. British Loyalists also contributed to this atmosphere of anguish and terror, although many black women, men, and children undermined it. Valentine Nutter, a slave owner, placed a notice in the May 12, 1783, edition of the *New York Gazette and the Weekly Mercury* offering a reward of five guineas for "a negro man named Jack," described as around twenty-three years of age and wearing "check shirt, blue waist coat, blue coatee with a red cape, long white trousers" and as having a stutter and speaking "very little English." Notably, this advertisement drew detailed attention to Jack's skin as a means of identification, describing him as having "scars on his left arm and a small scar on his nose." Perhaps Jack evaded capture, as the following September Nutter left for Port Roseway, Nova Scotia, aboard the ship *L'Abondance* with "Silvia," a woman described as a thirty-year-old "stout wench," and "Sam," a "tall" and "stout fellow" recorded as twenty-two years old, as his property.

During the time of the British evacuation, slave owner Thomas Walke of Princess Anne County, Virginia, journeyed to New York City, along with others, seeking to claim around three hundred black men and women who escaped to the city. Walke was remiss when he was rebuffed by the commander in chief of all British forces in North America, General Guy Carleton, who would not deliver those who had absconded from their owners by way of the proclamations. Though the Treaty of Paris stipulated that the British were not to "carry away any Negroes," for Carleton it did not require the British to readily facilitate the delivery of those deemed property. Detailed in a letter he penned to the Virginia delegates to the Continental Congress, Walke found this a "glaring piece of injustice" and sought to prevent "a further injury being done to the citizens of the country," suggesting, "if there is not an immediate check put to the proceedings of the British General in this matter, the injury will be inconceivable, as I am well assured several hundred of the above mentioned slaves sailed away last week to Nova Scotia."[29] Such protest was met with a preemptive move: the British began to issue Birch Certificates by order of Brigadier General Birch as de facto passports. These Birch Certificates served as status documents that identified the holder and confirmed the holder's right to cross an international border. Called also Certificates of Freedom, they also served as a certification of the holder's freedom. Birch Certificates would become breeder documents for the *Book of Negroes*. These early passports were a guarantee that the legitimate holder had resided voluntarily with the British before November 30, 1782, the date of the signing of the provisional peace treaty, as only those who had resided within British lines for twelve months or longer were deemed eligible for embarkation on British ships out of the United States. Birch Certificates, such as the one issued to Cato Ramsey, read as follows:

New York, 21st April 1783

This is to certify to whomever it may concern, that the bearer hereof Cato Ramsay a Negro, resorted to the British Lines, in consequence of the Proclamations of Sir William Howe, and Sir Henry Clinton, late Commanders in Chief in America; and that the said Negro has hereby his Excellency Sir Guy Carleton's Permission to go to Nova Scotia, or wherever else he may think proper.

By the Order of Brigadier General Birch

Those who made use of such certification to embark on the ships to Canada, or British North America as it was called at the time, as well as England and Germany, had their names listed in the inventory that is the *Book of Negroes*. After General Birch departed New York in 1783, similar certification was issued by General Thomas Musgrave to close to three hundred black people who were eligible for evacuation.

The ledger, in its accounting for humans as commodity in the enterprise of racial slavery, according to Saidiya Hartman, "introduces another death through its shorthand."[30] The *Book of Negroes* is no exception. With each entry, quick assessments are made on the subject's being that are then jotted down in point form, sometimes by way of corporeal descriptors, first names and sometimes last names, gendered nouns such as "wench" and "fellow," adjectives like "fine," "thin," and "lusty," race and place of birth such as "better half Indian," and "Barbadoes" and "St. Croix," or sometimes referencing some specific labor that they performed; or the entry might describe a body made disabled by that very labor: "worn out," "stout healthy negro," "young woman," "born free," "blind of one eye," "Quadroon sickly," "ordinary fellow with a wooden leg," "free as appears by a Bill of Sale," "healthy negress," "a refugee," "11 months," "says she served her time," "stout labourer," "Boston King," "nearly worn out," "Dinah Archer," "stout wench with a mulatto child 7 months old," "ditto," "M, between an Indian & Span.," "thin wench, black," "squat wench," "he is Cook on board the ship," "stout man marked with small pox," "thick lips," "ordinary fellow," "passable," "thick set man," "stout, flat, square wench," "Mulatto from Madagascar," "Daughter to ditto," "came from Jamaica, can't understand him," or an "ordinary wench" named "Pusie." But in the fifteen pages that precede the ledger we are afforded, by way of a very crude transcript, a means to understand the Board of Inquiry hearings at Fraunces Tavern as moments of contestation for mobility rights where black subjects were often repossessed by claimants, but, importantly, they used legal channels and their own testimony to decommodify themselves through assertions of their right to freedom and autonomy. They were no longer recoverable goods. Often this was done with the aid of counterfeit identities, aliases, forged identity documents, and the telling of necessary counternarratives that challenged a claimant's stated timeline. I take up this transcript further below. For now, two interlocking questions emerge: First, how are we to read the historical record of these hearings given the context in which they were written, where humans owned other humans? Second, how do we grapple with the textual meaning itself, given that the record of these hearings is composed not of verbatim transcripts but of records of proceedings and decisions rendered almost noneventful in their brevity, and that are only partial accounts meant to be put to later use in the service of Patriots for claims of injury, losses of property, and compensation? By situating the Board of Inquiry hearings at Fraunces Tavern as moments of repossession, what I am arguing for here is a mapping of Fraunces Tavern as a space where black women, black men, and black children challenged *un*-visibility through contestations for freedom and mobility that were simultaneously demands for recognition not as property, but as full subjects, as humans. For Mercy, the so-called negroe wench, and her children, in the end Fraunces Tavern was a space for the making of her and her children as disposable ("to be disposed of as he may think proper"). They were sentenced to a life back in slavery. In the section that follows, I take up eighteenth-century lantern laws to question how black luminosity as a means of regulating mobility was legislated and also contested. I do this to historicize the surveillance of black life in New York City.

Torches, Torture, and Totau:
Lantern Laws in New York City

I am truly a drop of sun under the earth.
—FRANTZ FANON, *Black Skin, White Masks*

"Moment by moment" is the experience of surveillance in urban life, as David Lyon observes, where the city dweller expects to be "constantly illuminated."[31] It is how the city dweller contends with this expectation that is instructive. To examine closely the performance of freedom, a performative practice, I suggest, that those named fugitive in the Board of Inquiry arbitration hearings at Fraunces Tavern made use of, I borrow political theorist Richard Iton's "visual surplus" and its B side, "performative sensibility."[32] What Iton suggests is that we come to internalize an expectation of the potential of being watched and with this emerges a certain "performative sensibility." Coupled with this awareness of an overseeing surveillance apparatus is "the conscious effort to always give one's best performance and encourage others to do the same, and indeed to perform even when one is not sure of one's audience (or whether there is in fact an audience)."[33] Iton employs the term "visual surplus" to think about the visual media of black popular culture (graffiti, music videos) made increasingly available to the public through the rise of hip-hop in the five boroughs of New York City in the 1970s and the uses of new technologies (cellular phones, hand-held cameras, the Internet, DVDs) to record and distribute performances. Applied to a different temporal location, Iton's analyses of visual surplus and performative sensibility are useful for how we think about fugitive acts, black expressive practices, and the regulation of black mobilities in colonial New York City two hundred years earlier. What I am suggesting is that for the fugitive in eighteenth-century New York, such a sensibility would en-courage one to perform—in this case perform freedom—even when one was not sure of one's audience. Put differently, these performances of free-dom were refusals of dispossession, constituting the black subject not as slave or fugitive nor commodity, but as human. For the black subject, the potentiality of being under watch was a cumulative effect of the large-scale surveillance apparatus in colonial New York City and beyond, stemming from transatlantic slavery, specifically fugitive slave posters and print news advertisements, slave catchers and other freelancers who kidnapped free black people to transport them to other sites to be enslaved, and the passing of repressive black codes, such as those in response to the slave insurrection of 1712.

April 1712 saw an armed insurrection in New York City, when over two dozen black slaves gathered in the densely populated East Ward of the city to set fire to a building, killing at least nine whites and wounding others. In the end, over seventy were arrested, with many coerced into admissions of guilt. Of those, twenty-five were sentenced to death and twenty-three of these death sentences were carried out. Burned at the stake, hanged, be-headed, and their corpses publicly displayed and left to decompose, such spectacular corporal punishment served as a warning for the city's slave population and beyond. With these events and the so-called slave con-spiracy to burn the city in 1741, the codes governing black city life consoli-dated previously enacted laws that were enforced in a rather discretionary fashion. Here black city life is understood as being intricately tied with Indian city life, as laws regulated the mobility of both Negro and Indian slaves.[34] On Sundays, for example, it was forbidden for three or more enslaved people to gather to play sports or make loud noises. Some of these laws spoke explicitly to the notion of a visual surplus and the regulation of mobility by way of the candle lantern. In March 1713, the Common Council of New York City passed a "Law for Regulating Negro & Indian Slaves in the Nighttime" that declared, "no Negro or Indian Slave above the age of fourteen years do presume to be or appear in any of the streets" of New York City "on the south side of the fresh water in the night time above one hour after sun sett without a lanthorn and a lighted candle."[35] "Fresh water" here refers to the Fresh Water Pond found in lower Manhattan, slightly adjacent to the Negroes Burial Ground, which supplied the city with drinking water at the time. Other laws put into place around light, lanterns, and black mobilities in New York City stipulated that at least one lantern must be carried per three Negroes after sunset and regulated curfews more tightly. In 1722, the Common Council relegated burials by free and enslaved blacks to the daytime hours with attendance of no more than twelve, plus the necessary pallbearers and gravediggers, as a means to reduce opportunities for assembly and to curtail conspiracy hatching.[36] Again, this law regulating mobility and autonomy through the use of the technology of the candle lantern was amended in April 1731 with "A Law for Regulating Negro's & Slaves in Night Time," where "no Negro, Mulatto or Indian slave above the age of fourteen years" unless in the company of "some white person or white servant belonging to the family whose slave he or she is, or in whose service he or she then are" was to be without a lantern lit so that it could be plainly seen and where failure to carry such a lantern meant that it was then "lawful for any of his Majesty's Subjects within the said City to apprehend such slave or slaves" and "carry him, her or them before the Mayor or Recorder or any of the Aldermen of the said City who are hereby authorized upon proof of offense to commit such slave or slaves to the Common Gaol."[37] That fire (candle lantern) was employed to deter fire (burning the city down) is not without irony.

Lantern laws made the lit candle a supervisory device—any unattended slave was mandated to carry one—and part of the legal framework that marked black, mixed-race, and indigenous people as security risks in need of supervision after dark. In this way the lit candle, in a panoptic fashion, sought to "extend to the night the security of the day."[38] Any slave convicted of being unlit after dark was sentenced to a public whipping of no more than forty lashes, at the discretion of the master or owner, before being discharged. Later this punishment was reduced to no more than fifteen lashes. Such discretionary violence made for an imprecise mathematics of torture.

Mostly, punishment for such transgressions was taken into the hands of the slave owner. In 1734, a male slave of John van Zandt was found dead in his bed. The dead man was said to have "absented himself" from van Zandt's dwelling in the nighttime.[39] Although it was first reported that this slave was horsewhipped to death by van Zandt for being caught on the streets after dark by watchmen, a coroner's jury found van Zandt not negligent in this death, finding instead that "the correction given by the Master was not the cause of death, but that it was by the visitation of God."[40] In recounting physician Alexander Hamilton's narrative about his travels through New York City in July 1744, Andy Doolen details that one outcome of the alleged conspiracy of 1741 was the ruining, according to Hamilton, of the traditional English cup of tea. It was thought by Hamilton that

> they have very bad water in the city, most of it being hard and brackish. Ever since the negroe conspiracy, certain people have been appointed to sell water in the streets, which they carry on a sledge in great casks and bring it from the best springs about the city, for it was when the negroes went for tea water that they held their caballs and consultations, and therefor they have a law now that no negroe shall be seen upon the streets without a lanthorn after dark.[41]

We can think of the lantern as a prosthesis made mandatory after dark, a technology that made it possible for the black body to be constantly illuminated from dusk to dawn, made knowable, locatable, and contained within the city. The black body, technologically enhanced by way of a simple device made for a visual surplus where technology met surveillance, made the business of tea a white enterprise and encoded white supremacy, as well as black luminosity, in law. In situating lantern laws as a supervisory device that sought to render those who could be, or were always and already, criminalized by this legal framework as outside of the category of the human and as un-visible, my intent is not to reify Western notions of "the human," but to say here that the candle lantern as a form of knowledge production about the black, indigenous, and mixed-race subject was part of the project of a racializing surveillance and became one of the ways that, to cite McKittrick, "Man comes to represent the only viable expression of humanness, in effect, overrepresenting itself discursively and empirically," and, I would add, technologically.[42] With these lantern laws in place and overrepresented Man needing no candle to walk after dark, these laws, then, were overrepresenting Man as the human.

When the lantern laws were again amended on March 2, 1784, it was not without public condemnation. With the amendment of this lantern law concerning "negroe & molatto slaves" also came the passing of laws against assembly, the carrying of weapons, riding on horseback through the city by "trotting fast" or in some other disorderly fashion, gaming, and gambling, along with other regulations to the racialized body in the city.[43] An excerpt of a letter published in the *New York Journal and State Gazette* questioned "the cruelty and inconsistency" in the laws that governed slave life.[44] Writing about the vagueness of the clause on being caught out in the street at an "unreasonable hour," the unnamed author questioned a law that allowed "a white drunkard" to "disturb the street til midnight, with impunity; when a poor black girl of fifteen if a gale of wind unfortunately extinguishes the candle in the lanthorn, is hurried to gaol, and next morning ignominiously scourged in public." This letter writer provided readers with a hypothetical: what if an enslaved person were to travel by horseback through the city on a Sunday in search of a doctor for a master that had fallen ill? If this said slave finds himself in the street when "the Chappel announces the fatal nine" and is without a lit candle and lantern and cannot "procure a light, or [is] so unguarded to unlock his lips (for he must not make a noise) or so forgetful as to have his whip in his hand (for it is a weapon) a prison or flagellation is his position and his master may perish for want of assistance." The unnamed writer wondered "what the framers of the part of the law thought negro slaves were made of, when they interdicted almost everything which constituted a rational being: laugh, weep or speak, they certainly must not, for that is making a noise and almost every other action in common life; that is not sheer labor maybe constituted into sport or play. Happy would it be for the poor wretches, if by law, you could deprive them of reflection." Of course, unsupervised leisure, labor, laughter, travel, assembly, and other forms of social networking past sunset by free and enslaved black New Yorkers continued regardless of the enforcement of codes meant to curtail such things.

Oftentimes social networking by free and enslaved black New Yorkers took place right under the surveillant gazes of the white population, in markets and during Sabbath and holiday celebrations. In these spaces of sometimes interracial and cross-class commerce and socializing, black performative practices of drumming, dancing, and chanting persisted. Just as Frantz Fanon writes in *The Wretched of the Earth* that "the dance circle is a permissive circle," in that it "protects and it empowers," in New York City performative practices engaged in by black people empowered.[45] For instance, during celebrations of Pinkster marking the feast of Pentecost in the Dutch Reformed Church, free and enslaved blacks elected a governor who would serve as a symbolic leader resolving disputes and collecting monetary tribute, making this holiday an event for white spectatorship of black cultural, economic, and political production, although for many such celebratory resistance made this "a festival of misrule."[46] The Common Council of Albany, New York, banned Pinkster celebrations in 1811, for reasons including a resentment of the space that it opened up for unsettling exchanges between blacks and whites.[47]

The most controversial incorporation of black performativity into Pinkster was the Totau. On the Totau, Marvin McAllister writes, "A man and a woman shuffle back and forth inside a ring, dancing precariously close without touching and isolating most of their sensual movement in the hip and pelvic areas. Once the couple dances to exhaustion, a fresh pair from the ring of clapping dancers relieves them and the Totau continues."[48] That such a performative sensibility was engaged in by black subjects in colonial New York City approximately two hundred years before the emergence of hip-hop in the Bronx is of much significance. The Totau and, later, the Catharine Market breakdown reverberate in the cypher of b-boys and b-girls. In Eric Lott's discussion of black performances, he cites Thomas De Voe's eyewitness account of the Catharine Market breakdown in mid-nineteenth-century New York City:

> This board was usually about five to six feet long, of large width, with its particular spring in it, and to keep it in its place while dancing on it, it was held down by one on each end. Their music or time was usually given by one of their party, which was done by beating their hands on the sides of their legs and the noise of the heel. The favorite dancing place was a cleared spot on the east side of the fish market in front of Burnel Brown's Ship Chandlery.[49]

In this instance, the breakdown is performed in a market, allowing for white spectatorship and patronage in a space that is already overdetermined as a site of commerce within the economy of slavery. Later, De Voe was quoted in an 1889 *New York Times* article about the decline of Catharine Market. Recalling from decades earlier the "public negro dances" during Pinkster, he described the various ways the dancers would adorn their hair, and he is quoted as saying that the dancers "would bring roots, berries, birds, fish, clams, oysters, flowers, and anything else they could gather and sell in the market to supply themselves with pocket money."[50] Sylvia Wynter's "provision ground ideology" is instructive here for an understanding of solidarity, survival, and the role of folk culture as resistance to the "dehumanization of Man and Nature."[51] Provision ground ideology names the slave's relationship to the Earth as one concerning sustenance through the growing of produce for survival, rather than that harvested for the profit of the plantation. Where the "official ideology," that of the plantation, as Wynter explains, "would develop as an ideology of *property*, and the rights of property, the provision ground ideology would remain based on a man's relation to the Earth, which linked man to his community."[52] The idea of Earth here is not one of property or of land, but of the formation of community through spatial practices "concerned with the common good."[53] Out of the provision grounds came the cultivation of ceremonial practices, including dance, that were, as Wynter tells us, "the cultural guerilla resistance against the Market economy."[54] For Wynter, dance is one form of ceremonial observance by which the black subject "rehumanized Nature, and helped to save his own humanity against the constant onslaught of the plantation system by the creation of a folklore and a folk-culture."[55] Here we see the centrality of folk practices, including dance, to the "emancipatory breaching" necessary for a liberatory remaking of humanness.[56] The remains of the Catharine Market breakdown can be found, I suggest, in the cardboard, turntables, b-girls, and b-boys of the breakdancing cypher.

What I have outlined here, and argue in the chapters that follow, is that then and now, cultural production, expressive acts, and everyday practices offer moments of living with, refusals, and alternatives to routinized, racializing surveillance. In so being, they allow for us to think differently about the predicaments, policies, and performances constituting surveillance. The predicaments: colonial New York City was a space of both terror and promise for black life. The policies: lantern laws, fugitive slave notices, public whippings, and the discretionary uses of violence by "his Majesty's subjects" rendered the black subject as always and already unfree. The performances: acts, like the breakdown, that were constitutive of black freedom still persisted even under routinized surveillance and violence at the hands of his Majesty's subjects. It is within this context, where certain humans came to be understood by many as unfree and the property of others while at the same time creating practices that maintained their humanity by challenging the routinization of surveillance, that we should read the 1783 Board of Inquiry hearings at Fraunces Tavern.

Of Property and Passports:
The Board of Inquiry Hearings at Fraunces Tavern

What began as a meeting between Generals Carleton and Washington on the point of Article Seven in the provisional peace treaty regarding "Negroes, or other Property" ended with an exchange of letters between the two, with Washington reiterating his concern regarding the embarkation of escaped slaves. Carleton responded, in kind, with a letter dated May 12, 1783. On what he called Washington's "surprise" about the evacuation and Washington's accusation that such action "was a measure totally different from the letter and spirit of the treaty," Carleton reminded Washington that the British set up a register "to serve as a record of the name of the original proprietor of the negro, and as a rule by which to judge of his value. By this open method of conducting business, I hoped to prevent all fraud."[57] Further, alluding to both self-repossession and the *Book of Negroes* as a searchable database for the future tracking of those listed in it, Carleton suggested that "had these negroes been denied permission to embark they would, in spite of every means to prevent it, have found various methods of quitting this place, so that the former owner would no longer have been able to trace them, and of course would have lost, in every way, all chance of compensation." On the notion of black people as property, Carleton put it this way: "Every negroe's name is registered and the master he formerly belonged to, with such other circumstances as served to denote his value, that it may be adjusted by compensation, if that was really the intention and meaning of the treaty." Given this, American and British commissioners charged with receiving and settling claims were appointed to inspect all embarkations in order to prevent evasion of Article Seven. Because of this article, ships were visually inspected for people who could be taken or repossessed as property, or rather, repossessed as if they were property. And with this came the setting up of the arbitration hearings that took place at Fraunces Tavern. At the corner of Pearl and Broad Streets in lower Manhattan, Fraunces Tavern served as the center of arbitration, where almost every Wednesday from ten in the morning until two o'clock in the afternoon, from May through

November 1783, the formerly enslaved came to argue for their inclusion in the *Book of Negroes* by asserting their right to leave New York as free people.

On August 2, 1783, merchant Jonathan Eilbeck brought a claim before the Board of Inquiry, questioning the legitimacy of the embarkation of a woman named Jenny Jackson for Nova Scotia. Jackson was brought ashore to be examined, and she produced for the board a Birch Certificate issued on June 5, 1783, which stated, "That a Negro named Jenny Jackson formerly the property of John Mclean of Norfolk in the Province of Virginia came within the British Lines under the Sanction and claims the Privilege of the Proclamation respecting Negroes theretofore issued for their Security and Protection." Eilbeck, a Loyalist, produced a bill of sale for a Judith Jackson from John Maclean dated July 16, 1782. Jackson admitted to the board that she was indeed Judith Jackson and formerly enslaved by Maclean and clarified that when Maclean departed for England and left her behind, she went with the British army to Charlestown and then New York. More detail on Jenny "Judith" Jackson's narrative of falling within the proclamation can be found in the May 6, 1773, edition of the *Virginia Gazette*. Between ads for the sale of slaves, tracts of land, and a "fashionable" chariot, and notices for a lost watch and for strayed and stolen livestock, a runaway announcement for a "Negro woman named Judith" was placed by John Maclean of Norfolk. Offering a reward of up to six dollars, Maclean's notice describes Judith as "tall and slender, not very black, appears to be between thirty and thirty-five years of age." In the notice, Maclean claimed that he could not offer much of a description as Jackson had only briefly been in his possession, as he had purchased her from Austin Smith of Middlesex the day before she made off, but Maclean noted that Jackson departed with her infant daughter and was perhaps pregnant. Maclean speculated in the fugitive slave notice that Jackson could be seeking to return to Smith and making her way back to Middlesex. It is supposed that Jackson stayed in and around Norfolk until responding to Dunmore's proclamation in 1775, taking up work with the British forces as a laundress.[58] Although Jackson had labored with the British for eight years in Charlestown, South Carolina, and New York, and was issued a Birch Certificate attesting to her right to depart, the board did not make a ruling in the dispute, perhaps because Eilbeck was a British Loyalist and the board was charged only with adjudicating American Patriot claims of loss of property. The board forwarded the case to General Carleton. Two women named Judith Jackson are recorded in the *Book of Negroes*. One woman, described as a twenty-four-year-old "thin wench" and "mullato," departed from New York City on the ship *Ann* to Port Roseway, Nova Scotia, before the above case was heard. The other Judith Jackson left on the ship *Ranger* for Port Mattoon, Nova Scotia, on November 30, 1783. This Judith Jackson remained in New York until the final day that the ships departed as she petitioned Carleton for her passage to Canada and for the return of her two children, who were given to Eilbeck. She left for Canada without her children. She is described in the *Book of Negroes* as an "ordinary wench" of fifty-three years of age, and formerly the property of "John Clain" of Norfolk, Virginia, whom she is recorded as leaving in "early 1779." Eilbeck also makes an appearance in the *Book of Negroes* in the ledger entry for "Samuel Ives." This unusually long entry states, "Sold to Captain Grayson by Jonathan Eilbeck of New York who it does not appear had any right to sell him as he was the property of Capt. Talbot of Virginia from whence he was brought by the troops 5 years ago and had a pass from Lt. Clinton which Mr. Eilbeck destroyed." With this entry, Eilbeck's questionable means of claiming possession of others is revealed.[59]

Not all who attempted to embark by altering their recollection of the time of their arrival within the British lines met the same fate. On August 2, 1783, Thomas Smith took issue with the pending embarkation to Nova Scotia of a woman named Betty, and she was brought ashore in order to appear before the board. Betty produced a Birch Certificate issued to one "Elizabeth Truant," detailing that she was formerly the property of Smith but "that she came within the British Lines under the Sanction and claims the Privilege of the Proclamation respecting Negroes therefore issued for their Security and Protection." Smith insisted that "the Wench [was] his property" and that she only arrived in New York City from his estate in Acquackanonk Township, New Jersey, on April 20, 1783. Perhaps out of terror and with the hope of reducing the punishment she might have imagined would ensue on the inevitability of her return, Betty relented and acknowledged that she escaped Smith the previous April, making her ineligible for the proclamation. The board ruled for the claimant and directed Betty to be "disposed of" by Smith "at his pleasure." On May 30, the board heard the case of Violet Taulbert. In an advertisement placed by David Campbell of Greenwich in the May 24, 1783, *Royal Gazette*, Taulbert is said to have escaped with her two boys, seven-year-old Willis and two-year-old Joe. A reward of five guineas was posted for their return. No decision was made by the board in this case as they could decide only on cases regarding those ready to embark.

In another case heard on July 17, 1783, Dinah Archer produced before the board a Birch Certificate issued to her on May 2, 1783. This passport stated "That the Bearer Dinah Archer being a free Negro has the Commandants permission to pass from this Garrison to whatever place she may think proper." Archer had been brought for examination before the Board through a claim by William Farrer. During the hearing, Archer testified "that she was formerly the Property of John Baines of Crane Island Norfolk County Virginia" and that she was sold by Baines to Farrer and lived and labored in Farrer's household for about three years until he left for England, leaving her behind. Archer told the Board that she was later informed by Baines that he never issued a bill of sale to Farrer, and Baines "compelled her to return to him." Archer remained in Baines's possession until she escaped to the British and arrived in New York City under Sir George Collier and General Matthews's "Expedition up the Chesepeake." The Board decided that they were "not authorized to determine the Question between the Claimant and the Negroe woman" and referred the case to the commandant of New York City. Recorded in the *Book of Negroes* as a forty-two-year-old "one eyed" "stout wench," Dinah Archer traveled on the ship *Grand Duchess of Russia* to Port Roseway on September 22, 1783. She traveled to Canada indentured to a Mrs. Savage. Although Archer had seemingly perjured herself to gain a passport, her narrative of coming behind the British lines before the signing of the provisional peace treaty allowed the British to deny William Farrer's claim on her as his property.

In total, the Board of Inquiry heard fourteen cases. Of those fourteen, five were children, two men, and seven women. The five children were all returned to their claimants; the two men were allowed to embark; and of the seven women, three were allowed to leave New York. All those whose cases were heard and then were prevented from embarking were put on a "no-sail list." In all, 1,336 men, 914 women, and 750 children are listed in the *Book of Negroes*. Once in Canada, they would find there enslaved black people, other Black Loyalists who were evacuated from Boston in 1777, and largely untenable land. Many labored on public works projects, feared slave catchers, and faced possible recapture and other forms of forced or coerced labor. After some time, many, including Boston King, left to establish what is now Freetown, Sierra Leone.[60] No doubt on their journey to Sierra Leone they passed slave ships traveling the Atlantic Ocean packed with Africans as cargo heading in the other direction.

While conducting the research for this chapter, I visited Fraunces Tavern. The tavern is said to be one of the oldest buildings in Manhattan. It was built by a member of the Delancey family in and around 1706. By 1762, Samuel Fraunces or "Black Sam" took ownership of the building, opening a social club, tavern, and inn, and he named it the Queen's Head. Fraunces Tavern is now part museum, part restaurant, and part brewery. The museum is run by the Sons of the Revolution, a hereditary society whose members promote and celebrate military and civil service during the American Revolution. I could only guess where the *Book of Negroes* arbitration hearings took place, but I figured that they might have happened in the main dining room. Maybe they were held someplace out of sight. There is no record, no plaque, nothing commemorating those Wednesdays in 1783 when black people would come to the tavern to argue for their freedom. The only discernible trace is a copy of Cato Ramsey's Birch Certificate mounted on a wall. One of the security guards working at Fraunces Tavern told me that "this building was Black Wall Street." This young, black security guard related to me that the museum director had removed any pictures of Samuel Fraunces that would signify Fraunces's blackness. There is some disagreement surrounding Jamaican-born Fraunces's racial identity, which reveals anxieties around race, and blackness in particular, then and now in America. Curated out of the category of blackness, to me at least, Fraunces is seemingly white in all the images now displayed around the tavern. Curious about this absenting of blackness, I asked the security guard if I could speak to the museum's librarian who was upstairs at the time of my visit in the summer of 2010. He went upstairs to inquire. When he returned, he said that she told him to tell me that she wasn't available to speak to me.[61]

erasure at its finest :^)

Conclusion

In discussing the archive of transatlantic slavery, Hartman asks, "how might it be possible to generate a different set of descriptions from this archive? To imagine what could have been?"[62] I close this chapter by considering *The Book of Negroes: A Novel* to ask if this creative work can offer an alternative imagining of the events surrounding the making of the *Book of Negroes* that could not be fully realized with the historical documents examined here. The novel traces protagonist Aminata Diallo's life from her capture in

West Africa, her enslavement in South Carolina, her journey to Manhattan, and her eventual escape from her slave master to become a bookkeeper at Fraunces Tavern. Diallo eventually works with the British under the proclamations, emigrates to Nova Scotia and then on to London, and finally returns to Africa. Through Diallo we are offered a remembering of Fraunces Tavern and those archived in the *Book of Negroes* as she is tasked by the British to interview, inspect, and register the names in the ledger: "I wanted to write more about them, but the ledger was cramped."[63] Diallo was set to leave New York City for Nova Scotia on the ship *Joseph*, but a claim was made on her person as recoverable property and she was taken in front of the Board of Inquiry at Fraunces Tavern, "wrists tied and legs shackled."[64] In this claims court, promises of freedom were broken, despite the pleas and testimony. Diallo narrates,

> At the back of the room, I heard claims against two other Negroes who, like me, had been pulled off ships in the harbour. Both—one man, and one woman—were given over to men who said they owned them. I despised the Americans for taking these Negroes, but my greatest contempt was for the British. They had used us in every way in their war. Cooks. Whores. Midwives. Soldiers. We had given them our food, our beds, our blood and our lives. And when slave owners showed up with their stories and their paperwork, the British turned their backs and allowed us to be seized like chattel. Our humiliation meant nothing to them, nor did our lives.[65]

Diallo voices a story of life, surveillance, and the making of the *Book of Negroes* different than one of acts of British compassion. By approaching surveillance technologies through stories of black escape—Al and Garfield's televisual escape, Sam's disruptive staring in "turning up the white of his eyes," lantern laws, Aminata Diallo's narrative acts—the brutalities of slavery are not subject to erasure; rather, such a renarration makes known the stakes of surveillance, emancipation, and freedom. The next chapter begins with another image of escape, *Wilson Chinn, a Branded Slave from Louisiana*, to enter into a discussion of branding, biometric technology, and the commodification of blackness.

3

B®ANDING BLACKNESS

BIOMETRIC TECHNOLOGY AND THE
SURVEILLANCE OF BLACKNESS

Two days before embarkation, the head of every male and female is neatly
shaved; and if the cargo belongs to several owners, each man's brand is im-
pressed on the body of his respective negro. This operation is performed
with pieces of silver wire, or small irons fashioned into the merchant's initials.
—THEODORE CANOT, *Memoirs of a Slave Trader*

We have been branded by Cartesian philosophy.
—AIMÉ CÉSAIRE, *Discourse on Colonialism*

Let's face it. I am a marked woman, but not everybody knows my name.
—HORTENSE SPILLERS

You can find *Wilson Chinn* on eBay.com or other online auction sites for
sale among antebellum ephemera. Wilson Chinn's portrait was taken
around 1863 by Myron H. Kimball, a photographer with an interest in da-
guerreotype and a correspondent with the *Philadelphia Enquirer* during
New York's 1853 World's Fair. Kimball also served as an official photographer for the Freedman's Bureau. In this particular portrait, a chain is tied
around Chinn's ankle and various tools of torture lie at his feet: a paddle,
a leg iron, a metal prodding device. The caption below the image reads,
"exhibiting Instruments of Torture used to punish slaves." The carte de
visite (figure 3.1) captures Wilson Chinn's stare at the camera. Particularly
striking is the "longhorn," or pronged metal collar, fastened around Chinn's
neck. An 1862 copy of *Harper's Weekly* describes this torture device as consisting of three metal prongs, "each two feet in length, with a ring on the
end," to which would be attached a chain to "secure the victim beyond all

FIGURE 3.1.
Wilson Chinn, a Branded Slave from Louisiana.
Carte de visite (1863).
Library of Congress Prints
and Photographs Division,
Washington, DC.

possible hope of escape." This burdensome device would prevent its wearer from "lying down and taking his rest at night."[1] Not entirely visible in this carte de visite is the brand on Chinn's forehead: the initials V. B. M. Valsin Bozonier Marmillion was a Louisiana planter and slaver. When Chinn was in his early twenties, he was sold to Marmillion's father, Edmond. The Marmillions had a penchant for branding: "Of the 210 Slaves on this plantation 105 left at one time and came into the Union camp. Thirty of them had been branded like cattle with a hot iron, four of them on the forehead, and the others on the breast or arm."[2] The brand here is a traumatic head injury that fixed the black body as slave—or, at least, attempted to. An ex-slave,

Chinn escaped to Union lines in New Orleans and was "freed" by Major General Nathaniel P. Banks.

Wilson Chinn, the carte de visite, brings plantation punishment, branding, and escape into focus. I continue here with the discussion begun in chapter 2 on the *Book of Negroes*, lantern laws, and how the tracking of blackness as property informs the contemporary surveillance of the racial body by now questioning how the intimate relation between branding and the black body—our biometric past—can allow us to think critically about our biometric present. Biometric information technology, or biometrics, in its simplest form, is a means of body measurement that is put to use to allow the body, or parts and pieces and performances of the human body, to function as identification. In order to understand the meanings of branding as historically situated, in this chapter I explore some early applications of this biometric information technology and question its role in the racial framing of blackness as property. What I am suggesting here is that branding in the transatlantic slave trade was a biometric technology, as it was a measure of slavery's making, marking, and marketing of the black subject as commodity.

The first section of this chapter, Branding Blackness, provides a discussion of the practice of branding and its role in the making of the racial subject as commodity at the ports of the transatlantic slave trade. I do this by looking to narratives, some written by abolitionists, others by slave merchants and owners. As well, I look at the uses of branding as a form of racializing surveillance: as both corporeal punishment in plantation societies and in urban domestic settings of slave ownership, and for identification purposes. I do this through a reading of Frantz Fanon's observations on epidermalization, that being the "epidermal racial schema" that sees the black body fashioned as "an object among other objects."[3] Epidermalization, Paul Gilroy tells us, stems from "a historically specific system for making bodies meaningful by endowing in them qualities of 'colour.'"[4] Drawing on Frantz Fanon's theory of epidermalization, I consider the historical specificity of branding as a practice put to use to ascribe certain meanings to certain bodies: as a unit of tradeable goods, runaways, survivors. To more clearly draw the links between biometric information technology and transatlantic slavery, I trace its archive, namely written narratives, runaway notices, a carte de visite. This is a difficult archive to write about, where iron instruments fashioned into rather simple printed type became tools of torture. It is also a painful archive to imagine, where runaway notices speak of bodies scarred by slavery and of those that got away: "Twenty dollars reward. Ranaway from the subscriber, a negro woman and two children; the woman is tall and black, and a few days before she went off, I burnt her with a hot iron on the left side of her face; I tried to make the letter M."[5]

The branding of the slave played a key role in the historical formation of surveillance. Although branding was practiced as a means of punishment for white servants and sometimes to punish abolitionists, it is not the focus of my discussion here. This practice has been documented by Marcus Wood's research on the branding of abolitionist Jonathan Walker with SS for "Slave Stealer" on his right palm in 1844 as punishment for his attempt to help enslaved people make their escape from Florida to freedom. Wood argues that Walker's brand became "the most visible brand in the history of American slavery" and that through its display, its reproduction in printed texts including children's books, photographs, John G. Whittier's ballad "The Branded Hand," and Walker's personal appearances, it "became a fragmentary monument to the cause of abolition and the suffering of the slave."[6] Instead, I look here at how the branding of blackness remains visible, and also makes certain brands visible. Put differently, this chapter examines branding not only as a material practice of hot irons on skin, but as a racializing act, where the one-drop rule was a technology of branding blackness that maintained the enslaved body as black.

Can the epidermal racial schema that Fanon makes plain be found in some contemporary biometric information technologies—the iris scanners and fingerprint readers that are said to secure borders and protect a collective "us" from identity fraud and personal data theft? To answer this question, in the second section of this chapter, Branding Biometrics, I examine the role played by prototypical whiteness and how it is coupled with dark matter in the making of some bodies and not others as problematic in biometric technology and its attendant practices. By "practices" I am referring here specifically to research and development (R&D) coming out of the biometrics industry. In the third section, Blackness B®anded, I discuss the branding of blackness in contemporary capitalism with a focus on actor Will Smith's blockbuster movies that market biometric information technology: *Enemy of the State, Men in Black,* and *I, Robot.* As well, I look to visual artist Hank Willis Thomas's B®anded series for the ways in which it points to and questions the historical presence of branding blackness in contemporary capitalism. I do this to suggest that these moments and texts allow us a reading of branding and biometrics as a commodification of information of and about the body that is highly contingent upon discursive practices for its own making and, in the case of Thomas's B®*anded* series, unmaking.

Branding Blackness

Right on her rib was a circle and a cross burnt right in the skin. She said, "This is your ma'am. This," and she pointed. "I am the only one got this mark now. The rest dead. If something happens to me and you can't tell me by my face, you can know me by this mark." Scared me so. All I could think of was how important this was and how I needed to have something important to say back, but I couldn't think of anything so I just said what I thought. "Yes, Ma'am," I said. "But how will you know me? How will you know me? Mark me, too," I said.
—SETHE IN TONI MORRISON'S *Beloved*

What can branding during the transatlantic slave trade tell us about the production of racial difference? In her influential 1987 essay "Mama's Baby, Papa's Maybe: An American Grammar Book," Hortense Spillers emphasizes that the trafficking of humans in the transatlantic slave trade marked a violent "*theft* of the *body*," rendering the captive body "a territory of cultural and political maneuver."[7] Branding was a practice through which enslaved people were signified as commodities to be bought, sold, and traded. At the scale of skin, the captive body was made the site of social and economic maneuver through the use of iron type. The brand, sometimes the crest of the sovereign and at other times alphanumeric characters, denoted the relation between the body and its said owner. In an early eighteenth-century account of slaving along the Cape Coast of Africa, John Atkins, a surgeon for the British Royal Navy, remarked of those enslaved there, "they are all marked with a burning Iron upon the right Breast, D.Y. Duke of York."[8] In this case, these marks of identification served to distinguish those who were enslaved by the English from other slaveholding entities. In this way, branding before embarkation, on the slave vessel, and at the point of disembarkation must be understood alongside its implication in the formation of the "racial state."[9] David Theo Goldberg has shown that in its effort to oversee economic possibilities, the racial state shapes labor relations and "will open or stem the flow of the racially figured labor supply in response to the needs of capital, but delimited also by political demands and worries."[10] Goldberg further points out that in the "naturalistic extreme, racially identified groups are treated much like the natural resources found in the environment, no different than the objects of the landscape available for the extraction of surplus value, convenient value added to raw material."[11] Branding before embarkation on the slave vessel was executed in such a fashion, where humans seen as resources to be extracted were branded with a clinical precision. The following passage is taken from a late seventeenth-century account of a barracoon by French slave merchant John Barbot. It tells of branding for the purposes of identifying those made slaves as units within a larger cargo:

> As the slaves come down to Fida from the inland country, they are put into a booth, or prison, built for that purpose, near the beach, all of them together; and when the Europeans are to receive them, they are brought out into a large plain, where the surgeons examine every part of every one of them, to the smallest member, men and women being all stark naked. Such as are allowed good and sound, are set on one side, and the others by themselves; which slaves so rejected are there called Mackrons, being above thirty five years of age, or defective in their limbs, eyes or teeth: or grown grey, or that have venereal disease, or any other infection. These being so set aside, each of the others, which have passed as good, is marked on the breast with a red-hot iron, imprinting the mark of the French, English, or Dutch companies, that so each nation may distinguish their own, and to prevent their being chang'd by the natives for worse, as they are apt enough to do. In this particular, care is taken that the women, as tenderest, be not burnt too hard.[12]

What this narrative also makes known is that branding was not only a mass corporate and crown registration of people by way of corporeal markers, but an exercise of categorization whereby those deemed most fit to labor unfreely, that being the "good and sound," were distinguished from others and imprinted, literally, with the mark of the sovereign. Here, African children, women, and men were violently made objects for trade. Slave branding was a racializing act. By making blackness visible as commodity and therefore sellable, branding was a dehumanizing process of classifying people into groupings, producing new racial identities that were tied to a system of exploitation. But as the above quote details, branding was also a gendering act, as with women a discretionary concern was said to be taken. In this "large plain" turned slave factory, bodies were made disabled, as those named contagious or defective in their limbs, eyes, and teeth were re-jected. Thus the barracoon, or slave barracks, was a slave factory where the surgeon's classificatory, quantifying, and authorizing gaze sought to single out and render disposable those deemed unsuitable, while imposing a cer-tain visibility by way of the brand on the enslaved. That Barbot chose to name the spatial logic of capture as a purpose-built prison gestures toward the bureaucratic regulation of branding as part of the much larger carceral and traumatic practices of transatlantic slavery.

Later in this narrative, Barbot describes the enslaved Africans at Fida as sourced from various countries "where the inhabitants are lusty, strong, and very laborious people" who, he writes, although not "so black and fine to look at as the North-Guinea and Gold-Coast Blacks," are more suit-able "for the American plantations, than any others; especially in the sugar islands, where they require more labour and strength." On the topic of up-risings, Barbot warns that "Fida and Ardra slaves are of all the others, the most apt to revolt aboard ships, by a conspiracy carried on amongst them-selves."[13] The barracoon, it seems, was also a space for ascribing an ontologi-cal link between labor preparedness, race, ethnicity, and resistance. A useful concept to help think about this making of intergroup distinctions here is what Joe Feagin has termed the "white racial frame."[14] Distinctions made by Barbot and other merchants of slavery between the "black and fine" and the "lusty and strong" speak to the early role of the "dominant white racial frame" in categorizing difference, where blackness is framed as unruly, with some said to be more unruly than others. Feagin outlines the dominant white racial frame as consisting of an "anti-black subframe" that worked to rationalize slavery and its attendant violence by framing, or I would say by branding, blackness as "bestial," "alien," and "rebellious," among other markers of difference, in the white mind.[15] With this antiblack subframe came representations of blackness as ungrateful and unruly.

To unpack this antiblack subframe, Feagin looks to the eighteenth-century writings of Edward Long, an English settler in Jamaica. Long was a slave owner and a self-fashioned ethnographer who minutely detailed the flora and fauna of the island and outlined the usual suspects of pseudo-scientific discourse used to falsify evolutionary trajectories and stratify hu-man groupings: physiology, phrenology, temperament, primate analogies, and even dental anatomy: "no people in the world have finer teeth than the native Blacks of Jamaica," Long wrote.[16] Long's extensive, three-volume *The History of Jamaica* (1774) attempts to place Jamaicans within the taxonomic space of flora and fauna. His effort at botanical classification, and human categorization and division is part of a larger imperial project of colonial expansion that aimed to fix, frame, and naturalize discursively constructed difference by situating black Jamaicans as at once innately primitive and corrupting, and as objects to fear, through his claims of the existence of cannibalism in the colonies with statements such as, "many Negroes in our colonies drink the blood of their enemies."[17] On black women, Long had much to say regarding servility, sexuality, and the intersection of both in the colonial context: "the Europeans, who at home have always been used to greater purity and strictness of manners, are too easily led aside to give loose to every kind of sensual delight, on this account some black and yellow *quasheba* is sought for."[18] Although "Quasheba," also known as "Quashie," is a stereotyped caricature of a black Jamaican enslaved woman known for her outspokenness and independent qualities, or her facetiness, the way that Long invokes quasheba here functions to displace the sexual violence of slavery onto enslaved women, and in so doing, masking the violence of the colonizer. In this way neither desire nor "sensual delight" could be removed from the relations of power within the colonial project where, as Robert Young argues, the "paranoid fantasy" of "the uncontrollable sexual drive of the non-white races and their limitless fertility" abounded.[19]

Barbot's narrative of branding at the barracoon comes out of the same taxonomic project as Long's, where appeals to the naturalization of difference aimed to fix social hierarchies that served the order of the day: colonial expansion, slavery, racial typology, and racial hierarchization. In an earlier passage, Barbot writes that although he was "naturally compassionate," he sometimes caused "the teeth of those wretches to be broken, because they would not open their mouths" in their refusal to eat.[20] The false pretense of naming resistance to force-feeding as unruliness is an attempt to mask the violence of the slave trader by displacing the violence of slavery onto the African. However, such refusals by the enslaved were agential acts that challenged the slaver's attempts at force-feeding, correction, and the imposition of a lived objecthood. In its creative remembering of the brutalities of transatlantic slavery, abolitionist Smith H. Platt's fictionalized account, *The Martyrs and the Fugitive; or a Narrative of the Captivity, Sufferings, and Death of an American Family, and the Slavery and Escape of Their Son* (1859), gives us some insight into the violent practice of branding onboard the slave ship. This fictional narrative tells the story of Bobah and Mabowah, who were kidnapped, along with their two children, from the interior of south-western Africa and were later renamed Jacob and Ruth Welden when they arrived in Savannah, Georgia. During their journey, Platt writes, "mothers with babes at their breasts were basely branded and lashed, hewed and scarred," and hot irons were fashioned "in the form of certain letters or signs dipped into an oily preparation, and then pressed against the naked body till it burnt a deep and ineffaceable scar, to show who was the owner."[21] All of this was done, Platt's account explains, under threat of a cat-o'-nine-tails, an instrument often put to use when the brand was met with resistance, and those made slave "were lashed without mercy on the bare back, breasts, thighs" with "every blow bringing with the returning lash pieces of quivering flesh."[22] On those marked for death, branding sought to inscribe a slow, premature death on black skin.

SILVER WIRE AND SMALL IRONS: EPIDERMALIZATION

Epidermalization, Stuart Hall writes, is "literally the inscription of race on the skin."[23] It is the disassociation between the black "body and the world" that sees this body denied its specificity, dissected, fixed, imprisoned by the white gaze, "deafened by cannibalism, backwardness, fetishism, racial stigmas, slave traders, and above all, yes, above all, the grinning *Y a bon Banania*."[24] "Y'a bon" is the slogan for Banania, a banana flour–based chocolate drink first sold commercially in France in the early 1900s and popularized with a caricature of a smiling, red fez–wearing Senegalese soldier with his rifle at his feet gracing the drink's packaging. Such commodity packaging is invested with the scientific racism, like that expressed by both Long and Barbot, which depicted Africans as servile, primitive, and ranked as an inferior species. An earlier campaign for this product featured an image of a woman, ostensibly a Caribbean woman, flanked by two banana bunches and holding an open can of Banania in each hand, pouring its contents onto the celebrating and joyous French masses pictured below. The French words for "energy," "force," "health," and "vigor" animate the powdered drink mix as it is pictured flowing from the woman's hands, as if to say that the cocoa and banana plantations of the Caribbean and Central America will restore national vigor through, as the promotional copy tells us in French, a *suralimentation intensive*, a revitalizing boost of energy. With this, the Caribbean is made an exotic, as well as an eroticized, source of power of the French colonial project.

Since then, Banania's advertising campaigns continue to convey what Anne McClintock calls "commodity racism," where "mass-produced consumer spectacles" express "the narrative of imperial progress."[25] Mc-Clintock explains that commodity racism is

> distinct from scientific racism in its capacity to expand beyond the literate, propertied elite through the marketing of commodity spectacle. If, after the 1850s, scientific racism saturated anthropological, scientific and medical journals, travel writing and novels, these cultural forms were still relatively class-bound and inaccessible to most Victorians, who had neither the means nor education to read such material. Imperial kitsch as consumer spectacle, by contrast, could package, market and distribute evolutionary racism on a hitherto unimagined scale.[26]

Today, the chocolate drink's mascot is a childlike cartoon character with exaggerated red lips, though still sporting a red fez and a wide toothy grin. His name is simply Banania. He dances, Rollerblades, builds snowmen, and walks through the jungle, among other activities, hawking a variety of chocolate products on the Banania website. Truly an object among objects. This is the epidermal racial schema that, as Fanon tells us, returned his body to him "spread-eagled, disjointed, redone" and in so being negatively racialized.[27] This epidermal racial schema makes for the ontological insecurity of a body made out of place, and "overdetermined from the outside."[28] I am taking epidermalization here as the moment of fracture of the body from its humanness, refracted into a new subject position ("Look, a Negro!" or "Look, an illegal alien!" or some other negatively racialized subject position). In other words, it is the moment of contact with the white gaze—a moment where, as Fanon describes, "all this whiteness burns me to a cinder"[29]—that produces these moments of fracture for the racial Other, indeed making and marking one as racial Other, experiencing its "being for others."[30] This is not to say that by being object to the white gaze one is interpellated into a completely passive, negated object, existing only as objection. Instead, Fanon offers us an insightful correction to theorizing moments of contact with the white gaze, where instead the racial subject's humanness is already established, and identities are realized and constructed by the self; where "black consciousness does not claim to be a loss. It *is*. It merges with itself."[31] It is the making of the black body as out of place, an attempt to deny its capacity for humanness, which makes for the productive power of epidermalization. So this making of blackness as out of place must be read as also productive of a rejection of lived objectivity, as being out of place.[32] Think here of ex-slave Sam's facetiness, as told in chapter 2, and the remarkable way in which he turned up the white of his eyes, escaped, and made his own way, as if to say, "I'll show them! They can't say I didn't warn them."[33]

Epidermalization continued in its alphanumeric form through a series of steps and measures upon disembarkation, during the purchase of slaves and in plantation punishment. Abolitionist Thomas Clarkson, in his efforts to collect evidence of the brutalities of the slave trade, conducted interviews with those involved in the trade, namely aggrieved sailors, first in Bristol, England, beginning in June 1787, and later Liverpool, and then in August 1788 he traveled to other ports along the River Thames. One of these accounts tells of slave merchants branding slaves at the moment of disembarkation in the West Indies. Clarkson's informant explained the process, relaying that "the gentleman, to whom the vessel was consigned" would board the ship, making "use of an iron pot, into which he put some rum. He set the rum on fire, and held the marking irons over the blaze."[34] The enslaved were then ordered "to pass him one by one" as he "applied the irons to each slave" and "branded them before they went out of the ship."[35] An assembly line of simple but violent instruments: rum, oil, silver wire, iron pots, fire. Branding upon disembarkation was not only the domain of British slave merchants. As Saidiya Hartman explains in *Lose Your Mother: A Journey along the Atlantic Slave Route* (2007), the Dutch West India Company (WIC) branded the enslaved on arrival in Curaçao, as the island served as the hub, of sorts, for slave trading throughout the Spanish Americas.[36] In Curaçao, the brand was sometimes administered at the slave market right on the auction block, and the scars that remained as evidence of that trauma were used to identify enslaved people at auction, during criminal proceedings, and postmortem.[37] For captains of slave ships under the Dutch charter companies, instructions for administering the brand were formally articulated: "as you purchase slaves you must mark them at the upper right arm with the silver marker CCN, which is sent along with you for that purpose," and the procedure was laid out in two parts: "note the following when you do the branding: (1) the area of marking must first be rubbed with candle wax or oil; (2) The marker should only be as hot as when applied to paper, the paper gets red."[38] These were the instructions for branding set out by the Middelburgsche Commercie Compagnie, or the Trade Company of Middelburg, a Dutch charter company that later displaced the WIC in slave trading. The WIC kept detailed records and used

Arabic numeral branding irons until 1703, after which time the company began to use alphabetic branding irons in an *A–Z* sequence, with the exception of the letters *U* and *J* so as not to be confused with the letters *V* and *I*, and the letter *O* was not used due to the iron being worn down. Think here of what it means for a branding iron, used to mark humans as property, to be worn down. The WIC's *A–Z* sequence was first complete in 1715, recommenced, and then last put to use in 1729 with the letter *T* to mark those enslaved on the ship *Phenix*.[39]

Sherley Anne Williams's novel *Dessa Rose* tells the story of Dessa, who, when traveling as part of a coffle of slaves, was involved in an uprising and was condemned to death for her role in that battle. Pregnant at the time of her recapture, with assistance Dessa eventually escaped from her jail, marked with the scars of corporeal punishment: whip scarred and branded with the letter *R*, a mark of punishment that remains inscribed on the body. These scars made the private space that is Dessa's body publicly legible as commodity, in a way: "he could prove who I was by the brand on my thigh."[40] However, she refused the idea that her body was a text that could be so easily read. Similarly, Sethe in Toni Morrison's *Beloved* (1987) could not comprehend it when her mother slapped her when she said, "Mark the mark on me too."[41] "Not till I had a mark of my own," Sethe said, did she come to understand her mother's rejection of the brand.[42] Although a fictionalized account, *Dessa Rose* articulates and disrupts branding as an attempt at making the body legible by functioning as a means of identification. This story, like those of nonfictional enslaved people found in the archive of racial slavery, makes known that branding was a practice of punishment and accounting, and a preemptive strike at marking the already hypervisible body as identifiable outside of the plantation and other spaces of enslavement, whether those branded found themselves outside through escape or by other means (for example, abduction or leasing out).[43] For instance, in 1655 the Barbados Council prescribed branding the letter *R* on the forehead of any runaway slave found to have set fire to the sugarcane fields, while the Society for the Propagation of the Gospel in Barbados ceased branding SOCIETY on the chests of those it enslaved in 1732.[44] Of course, many ran away, regardless of receiving this marking as slave. A notice published in the *Pennsylvania Gazette* on April 15, 1756, posting a reward of forty shillings for "a Negro man named Cato, alias Toby" attests to this: "he was branded when a boy in Jamaica, in the West Indies, with a B (and I think) C on his left shoulder blade," the advertisement states. In this advertisement Cato is described as a "sly artful fellow" who "deceives the credulous, by pretending to tell fortunes, and pretends to be free." In this way, the *B* and the *C* on Cato's shoulder served as a sign that could betray his identity despite his cunning use of an alias and other artful tactics. An August 29, 1757, advertisement placed in the *New York Gazette* lets us know that over a year later Cato was still unaccounted for, or rather that he had changed his name and asserted himself as someone who counted, as "it is supposed he has forged a pass."[45] While a January 3, 1778, runaway notice for "a Negro boy named ALICK" placed by Richard Wright in New York's *Royal Gazette* notes that Alick "is branded on the breast with the letters R.W."[46]

Although branding was a practice of racializing surveillance that sought to deny black human life from being multiply experienced (every body marked SOCIETY), running away and numerous other counterpractices suggest that dehumanization was not fully achieved on an affective level, and that those branded were still ungovernable under the brand, or in spite of it. For example, the diaries of English overseer-turned-planter and slave owner Thomas Thistlewood tell of plantation conditions in eighteenth-century Jamaica and the life of an enslaved woman named Coobah (or the possessive "my Coobah," as she is often called by Thistlewood in his diaries), one of the many women, children, and men that were subjected to his brutalities, as detailed in his diaries. Among the data that he collected on the people he enslaved, Thistlewood would record in his diaries the dates and locations of his predatory sexual advances by marking the letter *x* three times in a triangular formation. Coobah is described as "4 feet 6 Inches and 6/10 high, about 15 years of age, Country name Molio, an Ebo" when she was purchased by Thistlewood in 1761.[47] Coobah, or Molio, was branded on her right shoulder with Thistlewood's brand mark, a *TT* within an inverted triangle. In his diaries Thistlewood records Coobah as often ill, having suffered from pox in 1765 with "stout water" prescribed as a remedy, the loss of her infant daughter Silvia in 1768, and as enduring Thistlewood's sexual assaults (one time recorded in his diary in broken Latin: "Cum Coobah (mea) in Coffee gd. Stans!Backwd"—"with Coobah in the coffee ground. Standing! Backwards").[48] Coobah escaped captivity numerous times. Each time she was recaptured, she was severely punished: flogged, chained and collared (although she escaped and was recaptured still wearing the chain and collar), or with iron restraints fastened upon her at "noon and night." Even after being branded on her forehead for punishment after one escape ("flogged her well and brand marked her in the forehead"), Coobah continued to run away from Thistlewood.[49] On July 11, 1770, five days after Coobah was brutally branded with TT on her forehead as a form of punishment for her escape, Thistlewood wrote in his diary that he had found "Coobah wanting this morning." In defiance of the brand, she ran again and made her own way, once to see a shipmate in Bluefields on the south coast of the island. Another time Thistlewood wrote that he "heard of my Coobah's robbing a Negroe Wench . . . in the wood, under the pretense of carrying her load for her, march'd away with it."[50] In *Slavery and Social Death: A Comparative Study*, Orlando Patterson explains that slave branding "backfired" in Brazil, where the letter *F* that branded a recaptured runaway was "proudly displayed" to the "more cautious but admiring fellow sufferers," marking its resignification as a mark of honor, not of capture.[51] Eventually Coobah was sold by Thistlewood for forty pounds and transported out of Jamaica to Savannah, Georgia, on May 21, 1774. Coobah's running away, despite the TT that marked her forehead and her right shoulder, and the countless others who repurposed the brand mark for social networking and used the scars that remained from the violence done to their bodies as a means to reestablish kinship ties or forge connections to shipmates with whom they shared the Middle Passage, reveal the limit of these acts of dehumanization.[52]

SELLING BLACKNESS

In another carte de visite of Wilson Chinn, taken by Kimball, Chinn is not staged wearing shackles or a longhorn around his neck; rather he stands boldly with one foot on top of the mechanisms of bondage laid in front of him on a wooden floor. The brand of the initials V. B. M. remains, however, revealing the spectacular punishment of plantation life. Kimball, along with another photographer, Charles Paxson, produced several images of emancipated or disowned ex-slaves, notably white-looking ex-slave children. These portraits were reproduced as carte de visite photographs and sold by Freedman's Relief Associations in support of their philanthropic efforts and circulated as a way to invoke fascination and compassion and to trouble their intended white audience. The fascination here is with the one-drop rule made collectible, as the children in the portraits were quantified as black under the racial nomenclature of slavery. These images trouble the large-scale sexual violence, coerced sex, rape, and the breeding system that underwrote slavery: *partus sequitur ventrem*, which codified into law in Virginia in 1662 that children born to enslaved women were the property of that mother's owner, regardless of whether the owner was kin. The compassion that was sought through these cartes de visite is that although named black, for the intended white audience, these children were seemingly white, or at least postslavery could enter into the category of whiteness through adoption, sponsorship, schooling, and certain ways of dress. *Wilson, Charley, Rebecca and Rosa, Slaves from New Orleans* (figure 3.2), a carte de visite produced by Paxson, features Chinn seated in a leather chair reading a book along with the ex-slave children who are doing the same and are seated around Chinn, with only Charley propped up in a way that allows him to share the same line of sight as Chinn, establishing for the viewer a certain equity between sixty-year-old Wilson Chinn and eight-year-old Charley Taylor. A *Harper's Weekly* article reporting on these ex-slaves makes this distinction, that being the color line, clear with its caption, "Emancipated Slaves, White and Colored."[53] Now collector's items, these pictures of ex-slaves are currently authenticated and then auctioned online with bids set anywhere from around $750 to $2,000.

Wilson Chinn marks the circulation of the nineteenth-century photographic archive of slave branding and, in some ways, the ex-slave carte de visite photographs, along with other slavery ephemera, are the contemporary instantiations of the auction block. These artifacts live on as heirlooms on the Internet. One such was Item #140035393839, a "BLACK AMERICANA ANTIQUE SLAVE Branding Iron 19TH c.," advertised for sale on eBay by seller ThE StRaNgEst ThINg in 2008 (figure 3.3). This item was described as "In Fantastic Condition" and of "RARE HISTORICAL Museum Quality" but with "some oxidation" and "protected from the elements by an old light coat of black paint," which the seller suggests should not affect the value of the piece. With its "unique design FORGED AT THE END to identify a particular slave," this instrument of torture was listed at a "Buy It Now" fixed price of $1,126.25, reduced from $1,325.00 with the advertised option of a 0 percent annual percentage rate until 2009, if purchased with a new eBay MasterCard. Seller ThE StRaNgEst ThINg also specified, "from what I have read and researched, each Slave was normally branded twice. Once in Africa when leaving their Country and once in the Americas upon their arrival" and said that the branding iron "can be purchased and then gifted to a Museum for display for all to SEE and LEARN from." Why this seller chose not to donate this "strange thing" to a museum rather than auctioning it on eBay is not mentioned in the description of the branding iron. I wonder

FIGURE 3.2. *Wilson, Charley, Rebecca and Rosa, Slaves from New Orleans.* Carte de visite (1864). Library of Congress Prints and Photographs Division, Washington, DC.

LEARNING IS WEALTH.

WILSON, CHARLEY, REBECCA & ROSA.

Slaves from New Orleans

whether it is the thing itself that is strange, or the selling of this thing that was used to brand humans that is, in fact, strange—or, at least, should be made stranger than it already is.

The contemporary circulation of slavery-era branding tools and other so-called Black Americana for sale in online auction spaces is questioned and made strange with conceptual artists Mendi + Keith Obadike's *Blackness for Sale* (2001), an Internet art piece, or "Black.net.art," that saw Keith Obadike auctioning Item #1176601036—his Blackness—on eBay as a way to disrupt the trade in slave memorabilia and commodity kitsch on the Internet, and the commodification of blackness more generally.[54] This com-

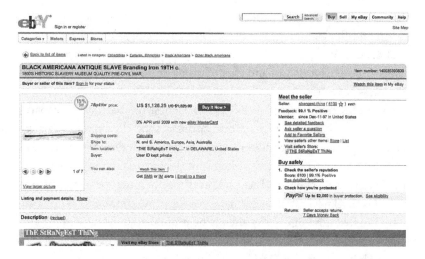

FIGURE 3.3. Slave branding iron for sale on eBay in 2008.

---

modity kitsch is the formerly ubiquitous and everyday items of distorted blackness—namely kitchen utensils like mammy cookie jars and Uncle Mose sugar and creamer sets—that are now labeled "vintage," named "collectibles," and traded in a way that seemingly belies their original intent: commodity racism, that being to consume while at the same time alienating blackness.[55] Collecting and consuming blackness, and black people, whether kitsch or corporeal, forms part of the larger history continuing to the present of the ritualized practices and trauma of white supremacy, as the archive of lynching makes plain. After such extrajudicial killings and the ceremony that accompanied death, memorabilia would be taken, and oftentimes sold, as souvenirs: pieces of the victim's charred clothing, pictures and postcards (now made coffee table books), and mementos from the scene of the lynching including fingers, genitals, organs, and other dismembered parts and pieces of the victim.[56] The collection of such memorabilia was a way for members of the collective that partook in a lynch mob to depart the scene with something, or to own a part of someone, as a keepsake to remember their role as participant in acts of antiblack terrorism that served as a means of (re)constituting a community (or re-membering) through white supremacist violence.

Obadike's auction was scheduled to last for ten days but was deemed inappropriate by eBay, and after only four days Item #1176601036 (figures

3.4 and 3.5) was removed from the website. The opening bid was listed at $10.00 and the auction garnered twelve bids overall, the highest coming in at $152.50. With the "Location: Conceptual Landscape" but able to be shipped "to United States and the following regions: Canada," Obadike's Blackness is described as an "heirloom" that "has been in the possession of the Seller for twenty-eight years." This Blackness has been used primarily in the United States so "its functionality outside the US cannot be guaranteed." No pictures of Obadike accompany this item's description. Instead, potential buyers are provided with a list of "Benefits and Warnings" regarding Obadike's Blackness: "This Blackness may be used for instilling fear" and "this Blackness may be used for accessing some affirmative action benefits (Limited time offer. May already be prohibited in some areas)"; also, "the Seller does not recommend that this Blackness be used while voting in the United States or Florida," as well as not recommending "that this Blackness be used while demanding fairness." Or simply put: "The Seller does not recommend that this Blackness be used while demanding." The benefits and warnings listed disclose the surveillance of blackness while shopping, while seeking employment, or during legal proceedings.

In an interview with Coco Fusco, Keith Obadike provides some insight as to why *Blackness for Sale* was a necessary counterframing to concurrent net.art in that it critiqued the commodification of blackness and the ways that colonial narratives are reproduced through Internet interfaces: "While watching what many were doing with net.art, I didn't really see net artists dealing with this intersection of commerce and race. I really wanted to comment on this odd Euro colonialist narrative that exists on the web and black peoples' position within that narrative. I mean, there are browsers called Explorer and Navigator that take you to explore the Amazon or trade in the ebay. It's all just too blatant to ignore."[57]

Mendi + Keith Obadike's Internet art project (or "auctionism") is one of black counterframing where the institutionalized and the everyday surveillance, appropriation, and negation of black life is satirized as a way to highlight its structural embeddedness and the pervasive nature of that very surveillance. Auctionism is a type of Internet art that, as Alexander R. Galloway describes, is a form of "social exchange" that "unravels the limitations of the network" as the performance is not only on eBay but also on the e-mail lists, message boards, and other social spaces of the Internet that drive traffic to the piece and discussion of it.[58] In the case of *Blackness for Sale,* an announcement of the auction was posted to the Internet-based

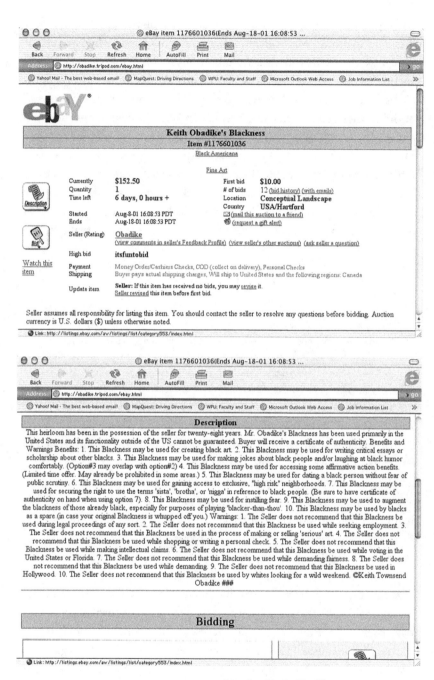

arts organization Rhizome, while blackplanet.com ran a poll where "26% thought the project was brilliant, 29% found it offensive," while 45 percent thought Obadike had too much time on his hands.[59] *Blackness for Sale* is auctionism that explores a black antiracist counterframing. As Feagin explains, black antiracist counterframing provides a "counter system analysis" of "how, where, and when white hostility and discrimination operate interpersonally, as well as in society generally."[60] *Blackness for Sale*, then, points to the productive possibilities of black expressive practices and, perhaps satirically, to the apparent limits of black antiracist counterframing, or as Mendi + Keith Obadike put it: "This Blackness may be used for writing critical essays or scholarship about other blacks" and "the Seller does not recommend that this Blackness be used while making intellectual claims."

Branding Biometrics

Information machines are the sole means of vision in digital visual culture, but as the body itself becomes socially defined and handled as information, there is even more at stake in paying attention to the incursions of machines in everyday life and the forms of resistance available to us.
—LISA NAKAMURA, *Digitizing Race: Visual Cultures of the Internet*

Paul Gilroy observes that where previously the idea of race was produced as that which is anatomical, where a certain and essential truth was said to be written on the body, scopic and microscopic regimes of seeing (for example, genomics, ultrasonography, neuroimaging, computed tomography) are laying bare the previously unseen at increasingly intimate scales.[61] The highly mediated production of racial discourse through scientific method that relied on cultural production, representation, myth, and colonial project making and where the intention was "to make the mute body disclose the truth of its racial identities" has been augmented by technologies of seeing that have the minute as their focus. Gilroy suggests that "the observational habits that have been associated with the consolidation of today's nano-science might also facilitate the development of an emphatically postracial humanism."[62] My intervention here is not meant to negate this potentially progressive moment that Gilroy alerts us to, but to claim that unlike the technological advances of, say, ultrasonography and other body imaging technologies, with certain biometric information technologies and their attendant "observational habits" this potentially postracial humanism is elided. Instead, with biometrics it is the moments of observation, calibration, and application that sometimes reveal themselves as racializing.

If, as Gilroy suggests, the pseudoscientific enterprise of truth seeking in racial difference can be more fully comprehended through the Fanonian concept of epidermalization,[63] how can epidermalization, as a concept, be made useful at a scale of the body made biometric? I suggest here that we come to think of the concept of digital epidermalization when we consider what happens when certain bodies are rendered as digitized code, or at least when attempts are made to render some bodies as digitized code. By digitized code I am referring to the possibilities of identification that are said to come with certain biometric information technologies, where algorithms are the computational means through which the body, or more specifically parts, pieces, and, increasingly, performances of the body are mathematically coded as data, making for unique templates for computers to then sort by relying on a searchable database (online or one-to-many/$1:N$ identification/answering the questions: Who are you? Are you even enrolled in this database?), or to verify the identity of the bearer of the document within which the unique biometric is encoded (offline or one-to-one/$1:1$ verification/answering the question: Are you who you say you are?). Popular biometric technologies include facial recognition, iris and retinal scans, hand geometry, fingerprint templates, vascular patterns, gait and other kinesthetic recognition, and, increasingly, DNA. Biometric technology is also used for automation (one-to-none/$1:0$ automation/answering the question: Is any body there?), for example with computer webcams that make use of motion-tracking software or touchless faucets, toilets, and hand dryers that employ infrared or capacitive sensing to detect a user's presence and gestures. In the case of those technologies, it is not for recognition or verification of a user's identity that the biometric is put to use, but rather for an acknowledgment of the user's presence or an awareness that someone, or at least a part of someone, is there, ideally.

In simple terms, biometrics is a technology of measuring the living body. The application of this technology is in the verification, identification, and automation practices that enable the body to function as evidence. Identities, in these digitizing instances, must also be thought through their construction within discourse, understood, following Hall, as "produced in specific historical and institutional sites within specific discursive formations and practices, by specific enunciative strategies."[64] The notion of a body made out of place, or made ontologically insecure, is useful when thinking through the moments of contact enacted at the institutional sites of international border crossings and spaces of the internal borders of the state, such as the voting booth, the welfare office, the prison, and other sites and moments where identification, and increasingly biometric information, is required to speak the truth of and for muted bodies. These sites and moments are productive of, and often necessitate, ontological insecurity, where "all around the body reigns an atmosphere of certain uncertainty."[65] This atmosphere of certain uncertainty is part of what Lewis Gordon refers to as "the problematic of a denied subjectivity."[66] On this, Gordon is worth quoting at length:

> Fanon's insight, shared by DuBois, is that there is no inner subjectivity, where there is no being, where there is *no one there*, and where there is no link to another subjectivity as ward, as guardian, or owner, then *all is permitted*. Since *in fact* there is an Other human being in the denied relationship, evidenced by, say, antiblack racism, what this means is that there is a subjectivity that is experiencing a world in which all is permitted against him or her.[67]

For Gordon, this problematic of a denied subjectivity is a structured violence where "all is permitted" and where this structured violence is productive of and produced by a certain white normativity, meaning that whiteness is made normative and, in so being, raceless, or what Goldberg terms "racially invisible."[68] What Gordon insightfully calls the "notion of white prototypicality" is the enabling condition of the structured violence of "the dialectics of recognition."[69] This prototypical whiteness is one facet of the cultural and technological logic that informs many instances of the practices of biometrics and the visual economy of recognition and verification that accompanies these practices. Digital epidermalization is the exercise of power cast by the disembodied gaze of certain surveillance technologies (for example, identity card readers and e-passport verification machines) that can be employed to do the work of alienating the subject by producing a truth about the racial body and one's identity (or identities) despite the subject's claims.

To understand the practices of prototypical whiteness (as well as prototypical maleness, youth, and able-bodiedness) and the ways that biometric information technologies are sometimes inscribed in racializing schemas that see particular biometric systems privileging whiteness, or lightness, in the ways in which certain bodies are measured for enrollment, I turn now to some findings appearing in publications in biometrics R&D. These publications tell of industry concerns and specifications, and they also tell us something about what kinds of bodies these technologies are designed to suit best. One such study examined how face detection technology could be employed in a "multiethnic environment" to classify facial features by race and gender.[70] A technology like this could be applied, for example, in shopping malls, casinos, or amusement parks or for photo tagging applications similar to that used by Facebook for what that social networking service calls photo summary information or, in other words, facial recognition technology. This technology is employed to match uploaded photographs to a specific user's profile.[71] The authors of this study found that when programmed generically for "all ethnicities," their gender classification system "is inclined to classify Africans as males and Mongoloid as females."[72] So black women are presumably male, and Asian men are classified as female, in this way mirroring earlier pseudo-scientific racist and sexist discourse that sought to define racial and gendered categories and order humans in a linear fashion to regulate those artificial boundaries that could never be fully maintained (e.g., mustard seed–filled skulls in *Crania Americana*, polygenism and the ranking of races by way of recapitulation, black woman as surrogate man, the desexualized Asian man, diagnoses of the slave's desire for freedom as the so-called sickness of the runaway named drapetomania, and Nott and Gliddon's *Types of Mankind*).[73] Interestingly, when their gender classifier was made "ethnicity specific" for the category "African," they found that images of African females would be classified as female about 82 percent of the time, while the same African classifier would find images of "Mongoloid" females to be female 95.5 percent of the time, and 96 percent for "Caucasoid" females. In other words, even when calibrated to detect black women, the African classifier is better suited to detect "Mongoloid" females and "Caucasoid" females.

Using actor Will Smith's face as the model of generic black masculinity (figure 3.6), Gao and Ai, the study's authors, are left to conclude that "the accuracy of gender classifier on Africans is not as high as on Mongoloid and Caucasoid."[74] The racial nomenclature of "Mongoloid" and "Caucasoid" is seemingly archaic but not uncommon in certain biometrics R&D. It is worth noting here that, as a different study put it, the "statistical knowledge of anthropometry" is still being invoked in biometric information technology R&D.[75] For instance, in one study, authors Li, Zhou, and Geng argue

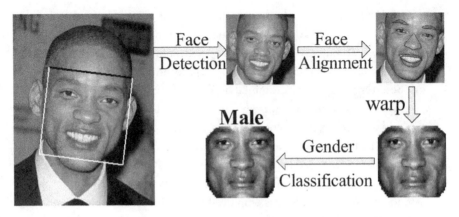

FIGURE 3.6. "Face Gender Classification Flowchart," from Gao and Ai, "Face Gender Classification on Consumer Images in a Multiethnic Environment." A face detection algorithm is first applied to a photo of Will Smith. Then, eighty-eight facial feature points are mapped out and used for face texture normalization and gender classification. Courtesy of Haizhou Ai and with kind permission from Springer Science and Business Media.

————

that "the difference of Races is obvious, and it is the core field of research of anthropology. Anthropometry is a key technique to find out this difference and abstract the regulation from this difference."[76] Anthropometry, or Bertillonage, was introduced in 1883 by Alphonse Bertillon as a system of measuring and then cataloguing the human body by distinguishing one individual from another for the purposes of identification, classification, and criminal forensics. This early biometric information technology was put to work as a "scientific method," alongside the pseudo-sciences of craniometry (the measurement of the skull to assign criminality and intelligence to race and gender) and phrenology (attributing mental abilities to the shape of the skull, as the skull was believed to hold a brain made up of individual organs). First developed by taking the measurements of prisoners and repeat offenders, Bertillonage made use of a series of measurements of the head, torso, and limbs gathered through a choreographed routine where the subject would sit, stand, and stretch out limbs, including measuring the length of the head, the right ear, and the left foot. Later, Bertillonage included descriptions of other markers of identification, such as eye color and scars.[77] With Li, Zhou, and Geng's study quoted above, we can see that pseudo-scientific discourse of racial difference forms the theoretical basis from which to develop a facial computational model that could qualify (and mathematically quantify) difference to allow for identity authentification. Li, Zhou, and Geng claim that "as a result of using the statistical information of the Mongolian Race's feature, our method is suitable to be used in the north of China."[78] Claims such as these demonstrate that some advances in biometric information technology are organized around the idea of digital epidermalization.

Epidermalization—the imposition of race on the body—is present, for example, when Nanavati, Thieme, and Nanavati note that in comparative testing of biometric systems and devices using control groups, higher fail-to-enroll (FTE) rates appear with those whose fingerprints are said to be unmeasurable. They state, "Elderly users often have very faint fingerprints and may have poorer circulation than younger users. Construction workers and artisans are more likely to have highly worn fingerprints, to the point where ridges are nearly nonexistent. Users of Pacific Rim/Asian descent may have faint fingerprint ridges—*especially female users*."[79] Unmeasurable fingerprints are often those of the elderly and people who come in contact with caustic chemicals and frequent hand washing in their work environments, such as mechanics, health care workers, and nail salon technicians or manicurists. Some massage therapists also fail to enroll due to occupational wear of their fingerprints. This unmeasurability forms part of what Torin Monahan calls "body discrimination" in technology design, where "unequal power relations are reproduced and reinforced by technological means."[80] Could these systems, then, be calibrated to allow for cutaneous gender detection, or for class differentiation? Or could they be programmed to allow for the "digital segregation of racialized population groups," as Joseph Pugliese suggests?[81] In this same study, Nanavati, Thieme, and Nanavati note that facial scan technology may produce higher FTE rates for "very dark-skinned users," not due to "lack of distinctive features, of course, but to the quality of images provided to the facial-scan system by video cameras optimized for lighter-skinned users."[82] What their research and development tell us is that their technology privileges whiteness, or at least lightness, in its use of lighting and in the ways in which certain bodies are lit and measured in the enrollment process.

Prototypical whiteness in biometrics is an extension of the "general culture of light" that Richard Dyer lays out regarding photography, film, and art.[83] This is a culture in which, as Dyer asserts, "white people are central to it to the extent that they come to seem to have a special relationship to light."[84] The logic of prototypical whiteness is seemingly present in earlier models of iris-scanning technology that were based on 8-bit grayscale image capture, allowing for 256 shades of gray but leaving very dark irises "clustered at one end of the spectrum."[85] The distribution of this spectrum's 256 shades of gray is made possible only through the unambiguous black-white binary; the contrapuntal extremes that anchor the spectrum, leaving the unmeasurable dark matter clustered at one end. Prototypical whiteness cannot be understood without the dark matter that gets clustered at one end of the spectrum, without those bodies and body parts that fail to en-roll.[86] Such epidermal thinking is present in other research on facial recognition technology that found that when "the facial feature quantities (spacing between eyes, turn up of the eyes, thickness of mouth etc.) are classified," it is possible that these systems "can search for faces with a certain feature, if the degree of the feature quantity is designated."[87] Here the possibilities for racializing surveillance are revealed. This is especially so when facial recognition technology is calibrated to cull matches only from within specified racial and gendered groupings, leading to high FTE rates for some groupings, as discussed earlier. The application of surveillance technologies in this way leads to questions concerning the idea that gender and race can be specified, and also how and if nonbinary, gender nonconforming, mixed-race, intersexed, or trans people fit into this algorithmic equation. They are unaccounted for in the algorithm that is set to fix race and gender.

As the above R&D reports make clear, there is a certain assumption with these technologies that categories of gender identity and race are clear cut, that a machine can be programmed to assign gender categories or determine what bodies and body parts should signify.[88] Such technologies can then possibly be applied to determine who has access to movement and stability, and to other rights. I take up this possibility in chapter 4 through a discussion of the airport and DNA technology. Following Anne Balsamo here, I am suggesting that we must question the effects that certain technologies (in this case, biometric information technologies) have on "cultural enactments of gender" and of race; we must uncover how such technologies are "ideologically shaped by the operation of gender" and seek to understand the role they play in racializing surveillance and in reinforcing "traditional gendered patterns of power and authority."[89]

Given this, some important questions to ask here include: How do we understand the body once it is made into data? What are the underlying assumptions with surveillance technologies, such as passport verification machines, facial recognition software, or fingerprint template technology?

There is a notion that these technologies are infallible and objective and have a mathematical precision, without error or bias on the part of the computer programmers who calibrate the search parameters of these machines or on the part of those who read these templates to make decisions, such as the decision in 2004 in which U.S. citizen Brandon Mayfield was wrongfully determined to be involved with the Madrid, Spain, train bombings based on a latent fingerprint.[90] Mayfield had served in the U.S. Army and is a Muslim, having converted to Islam shortly after marrying his Egyptian-born wife in 1986. He is a lawyer and did not hold a valid U.S. passport at the time of the synchronized bombings on four commuter trains that killed 191 people and wounded and maimed many others on May 11, 2004. A latent fingerprint was found on a bag containing detonator devices that was recovered by Spanish authorities from a vehicle that was parked at a train station. The FBI matched this latent fingerprint with Mayfield's. It was later revealed that Mayfield's print was one of twenty possible matches, but that additional biographical information was used by the FBI to bolster the case to detain Mayfield as a material witness. His military training, his religion, and the fact that he did not have a valid passport rendered him under the category of the "credible enemy," the rationale being that Mayfield would have to have traveled using a counterfeit passport to commit the commuter train bombings. I borrow the term "credible enemy" from Ursula Franklin's discussion of the task of the state in the "real world of technology," where, as she says, "the state has to guarantee the on-going, long term presence of a credible enemy, because only a credible enemy justifies the massive outlay of public funds" for arms productions and securitization.[91] According to Franklin, the credible enemy must be "cunning, threatening and just barely beatable by truly ingenious and heroic technologies" and, importantly, Franklin warns, there is historical precedent of the state's war machine turning inward and "seeking the enemy within."[92] Think here of this act of seeking the enemy within as signaled by the term "home-grown terrorists." Mayfield was held for nineteen days and released only after Spanish authorities announced that they had arrested someone else.

Although verification machines now do the work of sorting the bearers of identity documents, these machines are designed and operated by real people to sort real people. It is through the human aspects of this process of sorting that the digitized, biometric body is brought into view. Through this process of visualizing and sorting, the digitized body and in effect its material, human counterpart could be epidermalized. My intent here is not in defense of "race-thinking,"[93] nor is it an effort to reontologize race, but to situate certain biometric information technologies as techniques through which the cultural production of race can be understood. Following scholar Eugene Thacker's call for a "critical genomic consciousness" in relation to biotechnology,[94] I am suggesting here that we must also engage a critical biometric consciousness. Such a consciousness entails informed public debate around these technologies and their application, and accountability by the state and the private sector, where the ownership of and access to one's own body data and other intellectual property that is generated from one's body data must be understood as a right. A critical biometric consciousness must also factor in the effects of the supply chain, production, and disposal of the hardware of these technologies, whether that be the mining of conflict minerals, like coltan, or where the assembly of the devices is tied to sweatshop labor.[95] A critical biometric consciousness could be engendered by the type of learning that takes places with, for example, the Keeper of Keys machine (KK) developed by Marc Böhlen (aka RealTechSupport) in the context of the Open Biometrics Initiative (figure 3.7). The Open Biometrics Initiative argues:

> Formerly a domain reserved for human forensics experts, minutiae extraction can now be translated into executable computer code. In the machine, both minutiae map and minutiae matching are found within degrees of error and translated into probabilities. However, the results of these mathematical operations generate information that is valid within certain limits and under certain assumptions. The rules of probability theory ensure that the assumptions are computationally tractable. Error is translated into a fraction of unity.[96]

The "Open Biometrics idea," as Böhlen names it, understands all body data as probabilistic.[97] By taking seriously the idea that identification and verification of fingerprint biometric data through computational means relies on probability—that a match is more akin to an approximation than a confirmation—the Open Biometrics Initiative designed the KK to subvert the notion that biometric identification technology is infallible. The KK is "designed to re-imagine, beyond the confines of security and repression, notions of machinic identity control and biometric validation."[98]

The KK is a fingerprint analysis application that takes an image of the user's fingerprint. Rather than reducing this fingerprint data to a represen-

FIGURE 3.7.
The Keeper of Keys
Machine. Courtesy
of Marc Böhlen (aka
RealTechSupport).

tative subset, the results of the finger scan that the KK provides is a "mathematically precise but open list of probable results" allowing "the user insight into the internals of an otherwise hidden process."[99] This information is printed out for the user as a set of minutiae or characteristic points and probabilities, what the Open Biometrics Initiative calls a "probabilistic IDcard" (figure 3.8) that details "all characteristic points of a finger scan together with class (ridge ending or bifurcation) and most importantly likelihood" rather than assigning some infallibility to the data.[100] In this way, the probabilistic IDcard identifies characteristic points of the user's fingerprint that could come under dispute by a fingerprint examiner using standard finger scan technology. The user's fingerprint data is not retained by the KK. In this way, the user's digitized body data remains the property of the user, not that of state actors or a private organization or some other governmental body. Given this, the KK is a way of critiquing the idea that the state, the private sector, or other nongovernmental institutions should hold biometric information about users that users themselves cannot hold or

FIGURE 3.8. Keeper of Keys Certified Good Scan. Courtesy of Marc Böhlen (aka RealTechSupport).

———

even have access to. As well, it forces us to ask: if you would not surrender your biometric data to a machine like the KK that provides some transparency regarding the data capture process, then why would you surrender such data at a bank or at a border or to your employer or your iPhone, often without user agreements or questions about how the data will be stored or transmitted, what it will be used for, or whether or not it will be shared, sold, rented, or traded? These are some of the questions that should inform a critical biometric consciousness.

Importantly, a critical biometric consciousness must acknowledge the connections between contemporary biometric information technologies and their historical antecedents. Meaning here that this critical biometric consciousness must contend with the ways that branding, particularly within racial slavery, was instituted as a means of population management that rendered whiteness prototypical through its making, marking, and marketing of blackness as visible and as commodity. As well, it must contend with the ways in which branding was a form of punishment and racial profiling (every body branded *SOCIETY*, or *F* for fugitive—or perhaps that *F* stood for freedom, and *R* for revolt rather than runaway). As demonstrated above, much of how biometrics are described in recent R&D derives from the racial thinking and assumptions around gender that were used to falsify evolutionary trajectories and rationalize the violence of transatlantic slavery, colonialism, and imperialism. The absence of a nuanced discussion of how such racial thinking shapes the research and development of contemporary biometric information technology is itself constitutive of power relations existing in that very technology, where the idea of blackness is invoked (think actor Will Smith) to reproduce power relations, even sometimes in the physical absence of actual black people.

Blackness B®anded

I want to return to Will Smith for a moment to question what his image is doing in a biometric technology industry publication on new research and development. What kind of work is his picture doing here? Smith is the star of at least three Hollywood blockbuster action movies in which surveillance technology plays a role: *Enemy of the State* (1998), *I, Robot* (2004), and to a lesser extent *Men in Black* (1997). Seeing how surveillance is displayed, discussed, and depicted in and through Smith's films is important for an understanding of the various ways that contemporary surveillance technologies, from CCTV to unmanned aerial vehicles (UAVs or drones) to facial recognition technology, are marketed through popular entertainment. *I, Robot* is set in Chicago in the year 2035, where robotic workers, seemingly replicas of each other, act as servants (sometimes referred to in the film as slaves), are stored in stacked shipping containers when decommissioned, and eventually plot a nationwide revolt and imprison their human owners. We learn that Smith's character, police detective Del Spooner, was injured in a car accident and became an involuntary subject in a cybernetics program for wounded police officers. This left him with a prosthetic left arm built by the same company that created the robot servants, U.S. Robotics. Spooner uses biometric information technology, namely hand geometry access and voice pattern recognition, in the film, but he is antirobot. As the *New York Times'* film critic A. O. Scott put it: Spooner is "a raging anti-robot bigot, harboring a grudge against the helpful, polite machines that shuffle around the city running errands and doing menial work."[101] According to Scott, Spooner's grudge causes him to commit "technological profiling," revealing the film's "undercurrent of racial irony."[102] Seemingly a commentary on the dystopic potential of unregulated androids or a comment on enslavement, perhaps *I, Robot* animates concerns around such imaginings of artificial intelligence. In *I, Robot*, biometric information technology is a mere backdrop to a slave revolt; a palm scanner here, some voice recognition there. In this way, *I, Robot* depicts a society where biometrics are integrated into the everyday for the purposes of identification, verification, automation, and convenience.

In the comedy *Men in Black*, however, biometrics is that which can tether one to a fixed identity. Smith's character in *Men in Black*, James Darrell Edwards III, has his dental records, Social Security number, and even his Gold's Gym membership deleted from various databases, and his fingerprints are permanently erased from his body, leaving him without identifying marks and documents, rendering him anonymous. He becomes simply Agent J of the secret agency Men in Black (MIB). During this process of anonymization, a voice-over tells viewers of the film,

> You'll dress only in attire specially sanctioned by MIB Special Services. You'll conform to the identity we give you, eat where we tell you, live where we tell you. From now on you will have no identifying marks of any kind. You'll not stand out in any way. Your entire image is crafted to leave no lasting memory with anyone you encounter. You are a rumor, recognizable only as déjà vu and dismissed just as quickly. You don't exist. You were never even born. Anonymity is your name. Silence, your native tongue. You are no longer part of "the system." You are above "the system." Over it. Beyond it. We're "them." We're "they." We are the Men in Black.

This scene from *Men in Black* offers its viewers an understanding of the reach of the surveillance state, where documents and identifying marks are stored in interconnected databases. In this fictional world where "aliens" are among us, everyone is watched and our transactions are monitored. *Enemy of the State* is a panoply of surveillance. Set in Washington, DC, the film's plot revolves around Smith as labor attorney Robert Clayton Dean as he gets caught up with the National Security Agency (NSA), an assassination plot, and pending legislation that would increase domestic spying capabilities by way of a "Telecommunication, Security and Privacy Act," a bill that, as one character puts it, "is not the first step to the surveillance society, it *is* the surveillance society."[103] Throughout the film, Dean, and by extension the viewing audience, is given a primer on pre-9/11 surveillance technologies, their histories and capabilities, and the reach of the NSA by retired NSA agent Edward "Brill" Lyle, played by Gene Hackman, as both Brill and Dean become targets of the NSA.[104] In one scene Brill tells Dean, "Every wire, every airwave. The more technology you use, the easier it is for them to keep tabs on you. A brave new world out there. At least it better be." Thus, surveillance is wielded in a rather conspiratorial manner against Dean and Brill: facial recognition and fingerprint template technology, GPS tracking, databases, CCTV feeds, audio surveillance, beacon transmitters, satellite imagery, and even ominous black helicopters hover above them. It could be argued that in *Enemy of the State* surveillance technologies operate by way of product placement and that through such brand integration—to use ad industry terms—the film's viewers come to understand surveillance technologies. Fictional narratives such as *Enemy of the State*, and also television programming, shape public conceptions of surveillance technologies and are one of the ways that the public comes to develop a popular biometric consciousness. David Lyon argues that what such a display of technology does is suggest that the mere "presence of high technology speaks for itself, somehow guaranteeing its own effectiveness."[105] Lyon names this an apparent "sociological shallowness" of *Enemy of the State*, but also notes that this attitude is significant "especially in the American context where belief in the efficacy of technological 'solutions' far outstrips any evidence that technical devices can be relied upon to provide 'security.'"[106]

Enemy of the State closes with Dean and Brill turning the tables on the NSA agents and analysts that have tracked them throughout the film. Answering Jeremy Bentham's question of "quis custodiet ipsos custodes?" (who watches the watchers?), Dean and Brill surveil their surveillers; they watch the watchers. In this way, the film offers a "neutrality thesis" regarding surveillance technology which suggests that if placed in the right hands surveillance loses its negative valence and it need not be feared or a cause for worry.[107] However, these "right hands," in this case, are gendered in a particular way. As Anne Balsamo argues in her discussion of "the dominant myth of gender and technology," such depictions ultimately leave intact dominant representations of men as the "idealized and most important agents of technological development."[108] Popular culture representations of surveillance are some of the ways that the public comes to know these technologies and also how ideas about certain technologies as necessary surveillance and security measures get rationalized and sold to the general public. In other words, "our experience of surveillance is itself shaped by popular culture."[109] As a pitchman, it does not get much better than Will Smith, whom *Forbes* magazine named as the highest-paid actor for 2008. Interestingly, when promoting *I, Robot* in 2004, Smith was asked by the German press about some earlier comments that were attributed to him, in which

Smith reportedly claimed that he could one day hold the office of president of the United States. Smith replied that he envisioned the possibility of a black president, suggesting that a "young black man from Chicago, Barack Obama," would probably run for that office sooner or later. Asked about the effects of the 9/11 terrorist attacks, Smith reportedly answered,

> If you grow up as a black person in America, you get a completely different view of the world than white Americans. We blacks live with a constant feeling of discomfort. Whether you're attacked and wounded by a racist cop or attacked by terrorists, excuse me, it makes no difference. In the sixties, blacks were continuously the target of terrorist attacks. Although it was domestic terrorism, terrorism is terrorism. We are used to being attacked. As for a permanent alert, a defensive attitude with which one lives anyway—it has not changed since. No, for me personally, as to my everyday life, the tragedy of September 11 changed nothing. I live always a hundred percent alert. I was not even nervous, anxious, or cautious after 9/11.[110]

Articulating here the racial terror imposed on black life in America by an overseeing surveillance apparatus in effect on September 10, 2001, and long before, Smith received criticism for his comments, and some called for a boycott of his films. *I, Robot* grossed over $345 million in box office sales that year.

Many criticize Smith for playing only "safe" roles, and although a "bad boy" (he played Detective Mike Lowrey in the 1995 film *Bad Boys* and the 2003 sequel), he has never really portrayed a "bad guy." Being a star of blockbuster films means that the movie-watching audience is constantly subjected to Smith's always heroic exploits, particularly for films that are in syndication on network television. So these lessons on surveillance technologies and practices are regularly broadcast in which Smith is often seen saving America, and by extension the planet, from alien Others (*Independence Day*, the *Men in Black* franchise, *Wild Wild West*, *I Am Legend*, *Hancock*, *I, Robot*, and *After Earth*), or cast in some policing role (the *Bad Boys* franchise). It should not go without notice here that the image of the prototypical white man featured in Gao and Ai's article on their biometric gender classification system is that of Tom Cruise, the star of *Minority Report* and the *Mission Impossible* franchise, standing alongside his then-wife Katie Holmes (figure 3.9). Biometric information technology play an important yet commonplace role in those films. For example, one scene

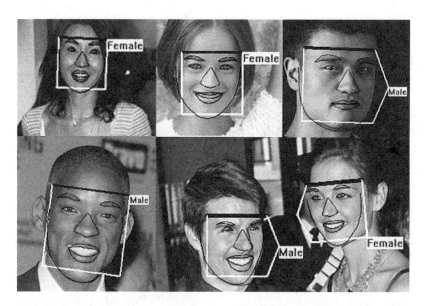

FIGURE 3.9. Photos of Will Smith, Tom Cruise, and Katie Holmes among facial images classified by gender using biometric analysis. From Gao and Ai, "Face Gender Classification on Consumer Images in a Multiethnic Environment." Courtesy of Haizhou Ai and with kind permission from Springer Science and Business Media.

in *Mission: Impossible—Ghost Protocol* (2011) features a contact "lens cam" that when worn is capable of drawing a match from faces scanned in a crowd and could then trigger an alert to an iPhone of a match of a possible target for assassination. Such product placement was not so far off at the time of that film's release. In 2013, Google filed patent applications with the U.S. Patent and Trademark Office for contact lenses that integrate cameras and other sensors. This patent-pending lens cam could capture and record images when the wearer uses a specific blink pattern, or could use motion detection to alert blind wearers to oncoming vehicles at crosswalks.[111] The "social optics of race" in *Minority Report* has been theorized by Lisa Nakamura, who argues that in that film, "the act of seeing itself has become inseparable from the political economies of race, retailing, crime and surveillance."[112] So commerce, in *Minority Report*, is readily enabled by technologies of surveillance (like retinal scans) that link identity, and by extension race, to product placement and marketing.

Priceless #1 (2004) is part of Hank Willis Thomas's *B®anded* series, in which the artist questions "how black bodies were branded as a sign of ownership during slavery, and how their descendants' bodies are branded today through corporate advertising."[113] As such, the meaning of branding for Thomas is not only about the violence inflicted on black skin, but also about how blackness brands certain consumable goods. The series is part of Thomas's creative response to the fatal shooting of his twenty-seven-year-old cousin Songha Willis during a mugging for a gold chain in Philadelphia that took place in February 2000. *Priceless #1* (figure 3.10) is a photograph of mourners at Songha Willis's funeral with the MasterCard logo superimposed on the bottom left corner. When MasterCard financial services first began running its trademarked Priceless campaign in 1997, each commercial spot would list the price for different products or services and would end with that one unfigurable thing that no amount of money could buy ("the way music makes you feel: priceless") and a voice-over of the slogan "there are some things money can't buy; for everything else there's MasterCard." With Thomas's *Priceless #1*, the phrases "3-piece suit: $250," "gold chain: $400," "new socks: $2," "9mm Pistol: $80," and "Bullet: ¢60" are overlaid on the image of this moment of trauma along with a play on the MasterCard tagline: "Picking the perfect casket for your son: priceless." The words "Pistol," "Bullet," and "Picking" are the only ones that are capitalized in this image, signaling the link between the labor of slavery (picking cotton) and its violent aftermath (firearm-related homicide), and the ways in which black death is capitalized upon (picking caskets). Debt (reparations for slavery, credit card debt) underwrites Thomas's remaking of MasterCard's Priceless campaign. With B®anded comes Thomas's interrogation of advertising and the commodification of blackness, urban violence, and the transatlantic slave trade. In its appropriation of the signs and language of the popular MasterCard campaign, *Priceless #1* instead gives us an image of a community in grief, one that is replayed and recounted over and over again as young black men ages twenty to twenty-four and twenty-five to twenty-nine formed the groups with the highest and second-highest homicide victim rates in the United States in 2013.[114] Thus *Priceless #1* is a mash-up of premature death, grief, black city life, and commodity packaging.[115]

The brand logos of the National Basketball Association, outdoor wear manufacturer Timberland, Johnnie Walker scotch, American Express credit services, and others are remade in Thomas's B®anded series, which sees both the stowage plan of the slave ship *Brooks* and the Door of No Return as mash-ups with the Absolut Vodka campaign. By "mash-ups," what I

FIGURE 3.10. Hank Willis Thomas, *Priceless #1* (2004). Lambda photograph. Dimensions variable. Courtesy of the artist and Jack Shainman Gallery, New York.

———

mean here is that these photographs combine brand logos with the difficult archive of transatlantic slavery to create new meanings and commentary other than what the original commodity packaging was meant to signify. For example, the Absolut Vodka bottle peopled with tiny figures in planked position similar to the stowage plan of the slave ship *Brooks* in *Absolut Power* (2003), or shaped into a door frame with the view from the Door of No Return on Gorée Island in *Absolut No Return* (2010). Priceless. When asked about the intent behind his *B®anded* series, Thomas has said that he was "interested in the way that black men are the most feared and revered bodies in the world in this weird way" and that he was "trying to figure out why that was and what that was about, and the relationship to slavery and commodity, which is commerce, culture, cotton, and that body type."[116] With this series we see Thomas uncover the moments in advertising when blackness is pitched "as a way to cash in on street cool or urban icon."[117] One such icon of street cool is Nike's brand logo known as the Swoosh that adorns the company's shoes, clothes, and other sporting apparel. In the *B®anded* series, however, the Swoosh is instead branded on the male black body, first as a large scar on the side of a bald head in *Branded Head* (2003), and also in a series of nine raised keloid-appearing scars on the upper torso in *Scarred Chest* (2004). *Branded Head* gives viewers a profile view, but the image is cropped in such a way that we do not see the face of the branded subject, while *Scarred Chest* is cropped at the neck and the genitals. Keloid scars have been known to grow, itch, and remain painful posthealing, and are said to occur more often within black populations. *Branded Head* and *Scarred Chest* are photographic reckonings with the trauma of racial injury, traumatic head injuries, raised keloid scars that grow beyond the boundary of the seemingly healed original wound, commercial branding, and the power of advertising to crop and frame the black body, and the power of the artist to counterframe.[118]

In 2004 *Branded Head* was part of the public space art installation *Jamaica Flux: Workspaces and Windows* and was placed in the ad space adjacent to a telephone booth at the corner of Union Hall Street and Jamaica Avenue in Queens, New York (figure 3.11). The telephone booth was neatly embedded in this site of commerce as it sits directly in front of a Chase Bank and was located close to a food vending cart in this busy shopping district. JPMorgan Chase, the parent company of Chase Bank, is "one of the oldest financial institutions in the United States. With a history dating back over 200 years," according to its website.[119] The Merchant Bank and the Leather Manufacturers Bank both merged in the 1920s with what would later become Chase Bank, and they both had provided insurance policies on the lives of enslaved laborers.[120] On a nearby building at the time of this installation was a billboard ad for Nike footwear featuring National Football League (NFL) quarterback Michael Vick, then signed to the Atlanta Falcons.[121] The tagline of the ad was "to fly, your head must reach the . . . Air Zoom Vick II." The NFL suspended Vick in 2007 for violating its player conduct policy due to his involvement in unlawful dogfighting and gambling. Criminal charges led to the loss of Vick's lucrative Nike endorsement contract and an eventual conviction, followed by a twenty-month incarceration, with house arrest by way of an electronic ankle monitor and travel restrictions imposed after his release from prison. Vick signed with the Philadelphia Eagles in 2009 and was named 2010 NFL Comeback Player of the Year. Nike re-signed Vick in 2011, stating that it supports Vick's efforts

FIGURE 3.11. Hank Willis Thomas, *Branded Head* (2003). Lambda photograph. Dimensions variable. Courtesy of the artist and Jack Shainman Gallery, New York.

at reforming his public image. This re-signing, then, marks Vick's rebranding; the first professional athlete in the United States to lose and then regain a major endorsement deal.[122]

Conclusion

This chapter began by offering a longer history of biometric information technology and the ways that this history is in close alignment with the commodification of blackness. Current biometric technologies and slave branding, of course, are not one and the same; however, when we think of our contemporary moment when "suspect" citizens, trusted travelers, prisoners, welfare recipients, and others are having their bodies informationalized by way of biometric surveillance, sometimes voluntarily and sometimes without consent or awareness, and then stored in large-scale, automated databases, some managed by the state and some owned by private interests, we can find histories of these accountings of the body in, for example, the inventory that is the *Book of Negroes*, slave ship manifests that served maritime insurance purposes, banks that issued insurance policies to slave owners against the loss of enslaved laborers, and branding as a technology of tracking blackness that sought to make certain bodies legible as property. My suggestion here is that questioning the historically present workings of branding and racializing surveillance, particularly in regard to biometrics, allows for a critical rethinking of punishment, torture, and our moments of contact with our increasingly technological borders. This is especially important given the capabilities of noncooperative biometric tagging by way of wearable computing, such as Google Glass, or through UAVs, drones, or other flying objects employed in U.S. counterinsurgency measures and other military applications, for example targeted killings or search-and-rescue missions.

Understanding how biometric information technologies are rationalized through industry specification and popular entertainment provides a means to falsify the idea that certain surveillance technologies and their application are always neutral regarding race, gender, disability, and other categories of determination and their intersections. Examining biometric practices and surveillance in this way is instructive. It invites us to understand the histories and the social relations that form part of the very conditions that enable these technologies. When surveillance systems that rely on visualization as a way of classification are, as Sylvia Wynter aptly puts it, "increasingly becoming automated," allowing for "the great masses of people who have to be cast out,"[123] such casting out, or failure to enroll, must be attended to critically, given the privacy concerns surrounding file sharing and the current extraconstitutional treatment of those who are deemed by the state to be "risks." It is at the border—territorial, epidermal, and digital—a site where certain bodies are cast out and made out of place, that a critical biometric consciousness and the possibilities suggested by what Gilroy terms an "alternative, metaphysical humanism premised on face-to-face relations between different actors—being of equal worth—as preferable to the problems of inhumanity that raciology creates" can be re-alized.[124] It is precisely this casting out that incites such a critical biometric consciousness and rethinking that seeks our linked subjectivity as no alter-native, but, as Fanon puts it, "the right to demand human behavior from the other."[125]

4

"WHAT DID TSA FIND IN SOLANGE'S FRO"?

SECURITY THEATER AT THE AIRPORT

> Surveillance seems designed to produce a particular effect—Black
> women remain visible yet silenced; their bodies become written by
> other texts, yet they remain powerless to speak for themselves.
> —PATRICIA HILL COLLINS, *Fighting Words:*
> *Black Women and the Search for Justice*

> Discrim-FRO-nation.
> My hair is not a storage drawer.
> Although I guess I could hide a joint up in here.
> *Blames "Romnesia" (my wigs name)
> —SOLANGE KNOWLES

We often think of baggage as something in one's past that forms a burdensome attribute that one brings into a new relationship: debt, children,
trauma, or drama, as in, "She's got a lot of baggage." Or that something that
gets carried around or lugged from place to place, from space to space, or
that one leaves behind, such as unclaimed baggage. Or even something
that gets searched and rifled through, as when travelers are notified by
the Transportation Security Administration (TSA) by way of a Notice of
Baggage Inspection, the little note left in their luggage that informs them
that a search was performed as a precaution because "smart security saves
time." Baggage can be accrued over time, something that is in excess, heavy,
or overweight, or what one gets weighed down with, like emotional baggage, as in, "Still!? Let it go. You really should move on." Baggage can be
an inconvenience. Sometimes it's material; sometimes it's memory; sometimes at the airport it's the weight that gets put upon certain bodies. Going

through airports can be a drag. After going through the security checkpoint at an airport in 2012, Solange Knowles used her Twitter account to exclaim, "My hair is not a storage drawer" and called her experience "Discrim-FRO-nation."[1] She also tweeted, "I kid you not. This just happened to me," and provided a link to a news article on the TSA's search of Isis Brantley's Afro, reportedly for explosives.[2] Many people take to their social media accounts to complain about the TSA; however, Knowles turned her security hassle into a game by inviting her over 1.3 million Twitter followers to play "What did TSA find in Solange's Fro"?[3] Guesses ranged from "the good lord, Jesus of nazareth" to "a bobby pin" to her sister Beyoncé and Jay Z's daughter "blue ivy." One player of this game tweeted, "process is so discriminatory, angers me @ the thought." I want to think here of discrimination at the airport through the concept of "racial baggage," where certain acts and certain looks at the airport weigh down some travelers, while others travel lightly. Or, put in a different way by David Theo Goldberg, "the weight of race is at once a racist weight."[4] I begin this chapter by recounting Solange's "Discrim-FRO-nation" game, where she invited her followers to tweet their own experiences with airport security and make light of the TSA, as it offers me a starting point for this chapter's two itineraries of inquiry about the airport.

Itinerary 1. This chapter's first section asks, broadly, in what ways are the bodies of black women deployed in narratives surrounding air travel and aviation security? When it comes to theorizing surveillance at the airport, the experiences of black women—the racist and sexist practices that they are often subjected to, their acts of resistance, and creative practices, like Solange's TSA security game—can allow us to articulate an understanding of the intersecting surveillances that are produced and reproduced at the airport. First, some background. A U.S. Government Accountability Office (GAO) report released in 2000 stated that at the airport, black women who were U.S. citizens had the highest likelihood of being strip-searched and "were 9 times more likely than White women who were U.S. citizens to be x-rayed after being frisked or patted down."[5] This report, "Better Targeting of Airline Passengers for Personal Searches Could Produce Better Results," also revealed that "on the basis of x-ray results, Black women who were U.S. citizens were less than half as likely to be found carrying contraband as White women who were U.S. citizens." An apparent routinization of nonintrusive searches (frisks and pat downs) and intrusive searches (X-ray inspections, strip searches, body cavity searches, administered laxatives, and monitored bowel movements) for certain travelers at Chicago's O'Hare International Airport after disembarking from international flights led eighty-seven black women to file a federal class-action lawsuit in 1997 that accused the U.S. Customs Service of racial profiling, on the grounds that they were subjected to humiliating, intimidating, and unconstitutional strip-searches and detentions. The case was settled in 2006 for $1,929,725. U.S. Customs admitted no wrongdoing. Citing this class-action case, as well as the GAO report, in a legal complaint regarding what it termed to be a case of "Flying While Black," the American Civil Liberties Union (ACLU) noted the following:

> Customs incident logs from O'Hare Airport show that of 104 strip searches conducted in 1997, 76 were conducted on women, and 47 of those were conducted on black women. That is, the incident reports indicate that women made up 74 percent of those searched and black women made up 46 percent of the persons who were strip-searched at O'Hare in 1997. This rate is grossly disproportionate to the percentage of international travelers who proceeded through Customs at O'Hare who were female and black. The rate at which black women were strip-searched is not justified by the search results.[6]

The ACLU's complaint further stated, "as a facade for its discriminatory practices," U.S. Customs "has promulgated contradictory and vague guidelines which have given Inspectors wide latitude to search almost anyone" and "has programmatically implemented a custom, policy or practice of racial and gender profiling."[7] The ACLU's case, *Bradley v. US Customs Service, et al.*, was filed in May 2000 on behalf of Yvette Bradley, an African American woman who was "unjustly singled out because of her race and gender, in conformance with a custom, policy or practice of the United States Customs Service of targeting black women for invasive, non-routine searches."[8] Upon Bradley's return from vacationing in Jamaica, she underwent a "humiliating" search at New Jersey's Newark International Airport, after which she "felt extremely violated and degraded, and she feared for her safety," according to the ACLU complaint.[9] After filing a complaint the following day with the passenger service representative at Newark Airport, Bradley was told she was searched because she was wearing a hat. The ACLU complaint notes that the hat that Bradley was wearing at the time was a "$300 Anna Sui couture signature-designed" hat that "fit snugly to her head and left no room under it to conceal weapons or drugs."[10] During the inspection Bradley was not asked if her $300 Anna Sui hat could be searched and, according to the ACLU complaint, she observed a group of white men who were ahead of her in the customs line and who were all wearing baseball caps, yet were not subjected to luggage or body searches.[11] The ACLU complaint was dismissed on September 10, 2001, with the district judge, Nicholas H. Politan, writing in his letter opinion that searches at U.S. ports of entry "are subject to wholly different standards than traditional searches not conducted at our borders," although it was "entirely understandable" that Bradley would feel "annoyance, embarrassment, and even disgust" with the customs officers.[12]

Itinerary 2. If the airport can be thought of as a site of learning, what can representations of security theater in popular culture and art at and about the airport tell us about the post-9/11 flying lessons of contemporary air travel? The second section of this chapter takes artworks produced in response to the post-9/11 airport as a form of social inquiry that can explore the various ways that people can navigate, comply with, refuse, and resist surveillance practices at airports. To do this, I turn to Pamela Z's *Baggage Allowance*, Evan Roth's *Art in Airports* series, and the digital art exhibition *Terminal Zero One* as they each question and critically engage security theater in contemporary air travel. Also in this section, I identify a pattern in the ways that black women have been caricatured in representations of aviation security by looking first to an episode of the Comedy Central channel's popular animated television series *South Park*. I argue that while the representations of black women as airport security workers often depict them as rude, aggressive, uninterested, or only interested in groping travelers, with these representations black women come to symbolize state power at airport security checkpoints in the domestic War on Terror. In this way, an apparent paradox is revealed. Black women are, at once, a site of power at the airport, and, as the GAO report revealed, untrusted and therefore searchable.

In this chapter I tell "airport stories" by recounting searches, detentions, and removals from planes. These stories disrupt common notions of airports as merely transportation spaces. Instead, they allow me to situate airports as spaces where enactments of surveillance reify boundaries and borders, and weigh down some bodies more than others, where the outcome is often discriminatory treatment. I recount these stories about airports in this chapter as a way to think through the concept of security theater by examining the many ways that travelers approach performances of security through their own assertions of travel agency, mobility rights, and resistance at airports. At the airport, the traveling subject is meant to produce herself as trusted and self-regulating. In this way, travel, particularly through airports, is as much about self-control as it is about border control. For travelers, the airport is not merely a transportation space marred with the occasional indignity and pat down, but also a space that demands what Mark B. Salter calls a "confessionary complex" that sees to it that the traveler recite a certain truth through rituals and customs,[13] and increasingly to express this truth by way of biometric encoded travel documents that are said to reveal a truth about a person's identity despite what that person claims. Other travelers bypass such practices, as borders for them are merely, as performance artist Guillermo Gómez-Peña suggests, "evaporated jet fuel."[14]

At the airport certain rules and rights are only applied to some. The development of trusted traveler programs attests to this.[15] The term "trusted traveler" is commonly employed in the commercial aviation and security sectors, often to refer to those passengers enrolled in preregistered traveler clearance programs. Travelers pay a fee and voluntarily provide their biometric data to join such programs. Given this opt-in requirement, trusted traveler programs and the "biometric borders" that they engender are "as much about the trustworthiness of the traveler as it is about the trusted traveler's trust in the state," as Benjamin J. Muller argues.[16] However, those who do the sorting work at airports ultimately dictate the outcomes of the application of trusted traveler programs, passports, and other identification technologies. This would be the customs officers, and increasingly the airline officials as proxy customs inspectors, and online databases that allow commercial airlines and government agencies to share passenger information preflight through the creation of "data shadows," a process that Colin J. Bennett suggests must be examined for its contingencies. As Bennett points out, some travelers, like those "with 'risky' surnames and meal preferences," experience a more intensive surveillance than others during air travel.[17] For the untrusted traveler, airports are the starting places for deportations, disease-related screening and quarantines, or removals in the form of extraordinary renditions, like that of Canadian citizen Maher Arar, who was detained at New York's JFK International Airport and eventually rendered to a secret detention center, or black site, in Syria in 2002. Arar was held in a three-by-six-foot cell and tortured for over ten months.[18] Or, in the case of Canadian citizen Berna Cruz, O'Hare Airport became a site of expedited removal. In February 2003, after visiting family in India, Cruz was returning home to Toronto by making a connecting flight through Chicago. U.S. Immigration and Naturalization Service officials looked at her valid Canadian passport and deemed it "funky" and counterfeit, and issued her an expedited removal order, placing Cruz on a Kuwait Airways flight to be removed to India.[19] In short, airports are complex places, differently experienced depending upon citizenship, gender, race, class, labor relations, and other categories of determination and their various intersections. In the cases of Maher Arar and Berna Cruz, it was the U.S. Customs officer who exercised a discretionary power to decide who is "really" Canadian and who is not, and who will miss their connecting flights, separating who is deemed a security risk from those deemed trusted travelers, and removing those who appear out of place.

Itinerary 1: Flying While Black

I often play Jet Set: A Game for Airports on my phone while waiting in line at airport screening zones, in this way playing security theater while security theater is actually in play. Jet Set is a video game where players take on the role of a TSA agent ushering passengers through the screening process at security checkpoints. Players are charged with confiscating a changing array of prohibited items—from toothpaste to rocks to sippy cups to T-shirts with Arabic text. Designed by Persuasive Games, Jet Set's players must screen passengers for prohibited items by touching the item on the phone's touch screen to, for example, remove a traveler's pants, depending upon whether pants are prohibited or allowed. Players must be efficient in clearing the lines of travelers, or a backlog will ensue. A "no jokes" sign hangs on the wall of this game environment. Ambient airport noise plays in the background along with the occasional overhead public address announcement: "Security policy is subject to arbitrary changes. Please be alert," or "Heightened security fashions are changing daily. TSA styling consultants are available," and "Please be advised, security personnel are authorized to use groping." If a player removes an item from a traveler's carry-on baggage or person that is not on the prohibited list—a rotating list of items located on the top right-hand corner of the screen—a chorus of "boos" is heard and the words "rights violation" flash across the screen. If a prohibited item is overlooked and allowed to pass through, the words "security violation" appear. If a player accumulates five violations, then the game is over. When Jet Set is played in certain airports, players who earn the highest scores have their names recorded on a list. I've made the high-score list at a few different airports. With Jet Set, gaming becomes a way to play with the lessons of air travel and the frequently changing policies post-9/11, post–summer 2006's antiliquid protocol following the charges of a London-based plot to detonate liquid bombs onboard transatlantic flights, and post–Christmas 2009 "underwear bomber" Umar Abdulmutallab, who boarded Northwest Airlines Flight 253 in Amsterdam with plastic explosives hidden in his underpants, which he attempted to detonate as the plane approached Detroit.

Jet Set allows me to, literally, play with questions of power, labor, and the theater of airport security. I also want to think here of the "theater" in "security theater" as a "military metaphor" in the way that Robin D. G. Kelley reminds us, in his discussion of African American working-class oppositional practices, of the "moving theaters" of the Jim Crow South during World War II, namely segregated buses and other public transportation spaces.[20] He recounts the history of protest on the buses and streetcars of Birmingham, Alabama, some of it organized resistance, some spontaneous individual actions like passengers talking back, cursing, or refusing to move to the back of the bus, and some of it "play." For example, Kelley writes that "groups of black youth spent some summer evenings disengaging trolley cables and escaping into dark Birmingham alleyways" while others played pranks onboard buses, like the chemical warfare of releasing stink bombs.[21] I cite Kelley here to say that security theater at the airport must be understood not only as about the staging of security and the theatrical performance that passengers must successfully comply with in order to pass through screening zones, but also as reflecting the airport screening zone as a military theater of operations, the place where security in the domestic War on Terror is observed and upheld. When some people speak up and speak out in this theater of operations, this talking back is often met with what bell hooks described during the pre-9/11 era as "airline English."[22] For hooks, as she related her experience of "airline English" in *Killing Rage: Ending Racism*, it was accompanied by "sequences of racialized incidents involving black women" during air travel that amounted to racial and gendered harassment: being ignored at the ticketing counter, being denied service, and a traveling companion who booked a first-class seat but was issued the wrong boarding pass and then forced to move to the back of the plane.[23]

Airline English has taken on a more formal structure post-9/11. Spoken by airport and airline personnel, it is a tone and pattern of speech that affects an only slightly veiled hostility and that serves to verbally exercise a limited, but ultimately limiting for certain travelers, power held by some who work in the service sector of air transportation. This is a power that is underwritten by the idea of care, like the TSA Cares toll-free helpline and TSA customer comment cards that recite the TSA pledge of expedient and customer-friendly screening experiences at security checkpoints. This power is also underwritten by the notion that a person who has nothing to hide will have nothing to fear regarding being searched, stopped, scanned, or otherwise held up at the airport. An example of this power to limit certain travelers took place on June 30, 2011, when, after going through imaging technology at a screening zone at the Seattle-Tacoma airport, traveler Laura Adiele was told by a TSA agent working the screening zone, "We're going to have to examine your hair," and that the police would be called if Adiele did not submit to this inspection. When Adiele responded with "No, you are not" and questioned this procedure, she was told that TSA agents have to examine anything that "poofs from the body." In a later interview, Adiele stated that she believed the search was racially motivated.[24] In a similar occurrence, in July 2011 TSA agents at San Antonio International Airport patted traveler Timery Shante Nance's "Afro puff." When asked by Nance if it was "only African-American women with natural hair texture" that received the additional screening, the TSA agent responded that only "certain kinds of ponytail or bun" were subject to additional screening.[25] In a later interview with the *New York Times*, Nance expressed that the search should have been conducted in private, if at all. In separate responses to both Adiele's and Nance's complaints, the TSA released this statement, in standardized airline English: "All passengers are thoroughly screened coming through the screening checkpoint. Additional screening may be required for clothing, headgear or hair where prohibited items may be hidden."[26] In this way, hair is named as a bodily marker that poses a barrier to passing through security for some.

It is important to connect these hair searches to the larger histories of circumscribing black hair as "dangerous" and as capable of being employed to smuggle contraband weapons or for hiding prohibited objects. For example, in the news reporting and rumors that circulated regarding the death of George Jackson in August 1971 at San Quentin State Prison in California, much was erroneously made of his Afro or possibly a wig being used to smuggle a gun or guns into the penitentiary.[27] In his essay "Black Hair/Style Politics," Kobena Mercer writes, "where 'race' structures social relations of power, hair—as visible as skin color, but also the most tangible sign of racial difference—takes on another forcefully symbolic dimension" and that black hair becomes "burdened with a range of negative connotations."[28] The various accounts of hair searches recounted here reveal the burden put upon black hair in airport security checkpoints.

On June 15, 2011, DeShon Marman, a twenty-year-old black college student and football player at the University of New Mexico, was removed from US Airways Flight 488 to Phoenix from San Francisco International Airport after a gate agent requested that he pull up his sagging pants as he entered the plane. Marman could not immediately comply with the request because he was carrying his luggage with both hands. A member of the flight crew complained that she was offended "by the fact that she could see the outline of his private area."[29] In a video of the incident taken by another passenger on Flight 488 and later posted to YouTube, Marman is heard telling an airline official, "I paid my fees" and "I'm just like everybody else on this plane." The airline official responded, "You're not like everybody else."[30] All passengers onboard the aircraft were made to deplane and Marman was arrested. Marman was held at San Mateo County Jail in California for two nights, charged with resisting arrest, assaulting an officer, and trespassing, although he had a boarding pass for the flight. Those charges were later dropped.[31] In an interview with a local news crew, Marman's mother, Donna Doyle, stated that her son was "attacked for three reasons: his clothing, his skin, and his hair," revealing that, for her, this was not merely a case of wearing sagging pants while black, but that Marman's dreadlocked hair was also a factor in his presence on Flight 488 being determined as unruly.[32]

In another case of flying while black, Malinda Knowles boarded an early morning flight on July 13, 2010, to Fort Lauderdale, Florida, wearing shorts and a large T-shirt. While Knowles was seated, a JetBlue supervisor, Victor Rodriguez, approached her, asked if she was wearing underwear, and required proof. Rodriguez, while holding his walkie-talkie, allegedly "stuck his walkie-talkie between her legs" to verify and then contacted Port Authority police to remove Knowles from the plane to check for underwear.[33] In the police report filed regarding Knowles's eventual removal from the flight to Fort Lauderdale, the plane's captain, James Ewart, stated that Knowles was "unruly" and that because of such presumed unruliness he refused to fly with her and had the police escort her to the ticket counter to be booked on another flight. In a later interview, Knowles told a reporter, "I didn't want to show him anything. He wanted me to basically show him my crotch. I was completely humiliated. It was vulgar. It was macho. It was rude."[34] These cases of flying while black reveal the ways in which certain bodies, particularly those of black women, often get taken up as publicly available for scrutiny and inspection, and also get marked as more threatening, unruly, and, in the words of the US Airways official to DeShon Marman, "not like everyone else."

To situate airports as sites of learning is to take seriously the pedagogical possibilities embedded in its performances and its procedures. I turn here to the case of Suaad Hagi Mohamud to think of airports as sites of critical biometric consciousness raising. On May 21, 2009, Mohamud, a Somali-born Canadian citizen, was detained at Jomo Kenyatta International Airport in Nairobi, Kenya. Set to board a KLM Royal Dutch Airlines flight en route to Toronto, Mohamud was questioned by a KLM official and told that she would not be allowed to board her scheduled flight. Mohamud was told by airline authorities that her lips were different than those observed in her four-year-old passport photo, and because of this she was said to be not the rightful holder of the Canadian passport that she presented. Mohamud was held overnight at the airport. The following morning she met with officials from the Canadian High Commission in Nairobi, who apparently supported the assertions of the KLM worker, and they confiscated Mohamud's passport. In a later interview with a reporter for the *Toronto Star* newspaper, Mohamud recalled her dealings with the airline official, and she stated that he told her, "he could make me miss my flight."[35] She took this utterance to be a request for a bribe. In an attempt to prove her identity to officials at the Canadian High Commission in Nairobi, Mohamud offered up the contents of her wallet: "I showed them my travel documents, my driver's licence, my Canadian citizenship, my social insurance card, my OHIP card, my son's social insurance card, my Visa card, and my health card. I also showed them Canadian Tire money. They did not believe me. Again, they told me I was not Suaad."[36]

The migration integrity officer (MIO) with the Canadian High Commission did not accept Mohamud's various identification documents, and she was charged by Kenyan authorities with using a false passport, impersonating a Canadian, and being in Kenya illegally. Canadian authorities turned over her passport to Kenyan authorities to aid in the prosecution of charges brought against her. After being detained in the airport for four days, Mohamud was released on a bond and given two weeks to substantiate her identity. She was subsequently jailed by Kenyan authorities from June 3 to June 11 in Langata women's prison in Nairobi, facing possible deportation to Somalia. During her incarceration at the Langata women's prison, she contracted pneumonia. Bail of $2,500 (U.S.) was posted and Mohamud was moved to a dingy hotel and then to another location as she still faced charges. While Mohamud was stuck in Kenya, Lawrence Cannon, then Canada's minister of foreign affairs, was quoted on July 24 as saying, "there is no tangible proof" that Mohamud was really Canadian and that "all Canadians who hold passports generally have a picture that is identical in their passport to what they claim to be."[37] Cannon made this statement after Mohamud submitted her fingerprints to Canadian officials in Kenya, and her employer in Toronto confirmed in writing that she was on approved vacation after Canadian officials made an inquiry on July 13, and after an officer from the Canadian Border Services Agency visited her place of employment in Toronto on July 22 so that her coworkers could identify a photograph of her. It was later disclosed that Mohamud's fingerprints were not on file with the Canadian government, so no comparison could be made with those taken by the Canadian High Commission in Nairobi.

Documents released under the Access to Information Act revealed that officials with Foreign Affairs and International Trade Canada (DFAIT), the department that oversaw diplomatic and consular relations and the authentication of Canadian documents, had suggested that Mohamud was impersonating one of her sisters, a "sister act" as it was called in the partially redacted e-mails, stating, "claims of weight loss and new glasses do not explain the visual differences, which are based off factors which would not be affected by these changes." One e-mail exchange was particularly revealing. In it, the DFAIT case management officer, Odette Gaudett-Fee, states,

At the end of the day, Canada decides who enters Canada, and if the MIO and Consular (for Passport) have determined that this person is inadmissible, then she is inadmissible. What they do with her is their issue as she was detained in Kenya—we do want the passport back— assuming they still have it. If they refuse to return it to us, it should probably be cancelled in the system so it cannot be used.

She is free to sue the Gov. of Canada for negligence, prejudice, etc. . . . but the Kenyan court has no authority over our borders.

All we should have to say is that after close examination, we are not satisfied that she is who she claims to be . . . or something of the sort. . . . The onus is on her to prove her identity and citizenship and she has not proven it.

Here Gaudett-Fee expresses a mix of annoyance and outrage that Kenyan authorities requested that Canadian consular officials be called to testify regarding their findings on Mohamud's citizenship claims. The use of the possessive plural pronoun "our" (as in "the Kenyan court has no authority over *our* borders") signals a sense of collective ownership and belonging to the nation and the citizenship and mobility rights that this select type of belonging entails. As well, it points to the fears and anxieties surrounding the idea of "our" porous borders that could easily be breached. In this way, certain bodies are understood as unlawfully invading social spaces that belong to citizens and other documented state subjects. Mohamud requested DNA testing through a motion filed before the Canadian Federal Court by her attorney in Toronto. It was not until August 10, 2009, that a DNA test conducted on Mohamud in comparison to that of her Canadian-born son, who remained with relatives in Toronto while Mohamud was in Kenya, confirmed Mohamud's identity, with a probability of 99.99 percent. The charges were dropped. She was issued an emergency passport and she boarded a plane to Amsterdam to make her way home to Toronto, arriving there on August 15. This DNA verification not only proved that she was indeed who she said she was, but apparently determined her citizenship status too.

Mohamud's case raises the question of what proof of identity Canadian officials will accept from a stranded and detained citizen abroad. Or, as Mohamud put it, "What would have happened if my son had come with me to Kenya? How could I have proved who I was? What would have happened if I did not have a child?"[38] Further, this case begs the question of who can be left at the border and abandoned by the state and by what technological means. This thinking and attendant practices around who constitutes a Canadian citizen is not limited to the Nairobi airport or to Canadian consular officials in Kenya. A 2007 study on decision-making practices of immigration officers in the United Kingdom commissioned by the Home Office found higher "stop rates," or secondary screening rates, for Canadians entering the U.K. who are read as nonwhite compared to white Canadians. The report also found that a passenger's clothing and appearance can mark her as either suspicious or a trusted traveler; for example, the report notes that for some immigration officers, "young women wearing white stiletto shoes and short skirts" raise suspicion as they "might possibly be involved in prostitution," and "people who look very shabby can turn out to be well educated professionals, such as university professors."[39]

The Mohamud case makes known that although identification documents function as a key technology in the contemporary management of state-sanctioned human mobility, the discretionary power exercised by the border guard or customs inspector, and increasingly by the airline official acting as proxy customs inspector, is a power that makes it plain that, as David Lyon explains, "all technologies are human activities."[40] Meaning that these technologies of border control (passports, biometrics, airport preboarding passenger screening zones) are developed within, put to use, and often replicate existing inequalities. On the customs inspector, Frantz Fanon was clear, as he recalls, "I had another acquaintance, a customs inspector in a port of the French mainland, who was extremely severe with tourists or travelers in transit. 'Because,' he explained to me, 'if you aren't a bastard they take you for a poor shit. Since I'm a Negro, you can imagine how I'm going to get it either way.' "[41] For Fanon, the discretionary power exercised by the black customs inspector forms part of the "situational neurosis" inherent in antiblack spaces.[42] This is where alienation, negation, and inferiorization engenders, as Fanon put it, "the attitude of the black man toward the white, or toward his own race, [which] often duplicates almost completely a constellation of delirium, frequently bordering on the region of the pathological."[43] These attitudes, then, are demands for recognition of one's worth as fully human, rejecting the imposition of the alienation that antiblackness imposes at the border, the racial baggage that weighs heavily both for certain workers and for certain travelers at the site of the airport and other border crossings.

Although Mohamud produced symbols of what Lyon calls the "stable self" (her driver's license, credit card, health card, a promotion letter from her employer—even an old dry cleaning receipt), government functionaries challenged the integrity of these documents and denied Mohamud's claim that she was indeed who she said she was.[44] Here it is useful to think of the process that Sara Ahmed refers to as the "sociality of lines." "Lines," Ahmed writes, "mark out boundaries" that establish who does and who doesn't belong, who is in or out of place, where the "spatial function of lines marks the edges of belonging, even when they allow bodies through."[45] Whiteness, for Ahmed, should be understood as "a straight line rather than . . . a characteristic of bodies"; whiteness is what she terms a "straightening device" that sees itself reproduced in and through "acts of alignment."[46] When the "nationality of the passport does not seem to follow the line of the name" or picture, or lips in the case of Mohamud, then the "body is suspect."[47] For Mohamud, the border extended beyond that act of alignment in the airport when her body was read as suspect and continued throughout her detention, in the reporting by Kenyan and Canadian news media outlets, and through the actions of the Canadian government, in particular those of the DFAIT. The border, then, is also about claiming citizenship rights, in Mohamud's case as a Canadian, and about the institutional practices that align to weigh down particular passport holders with racial baggage when they try to claim those rights. In an interview with CBC News, Mohamud stated that she felt that she would not have been detained in Kenya had she been white, saying, "the Canadian High Commission wouldn't be treating me the way they treat me. If I'm a white person, I wouldn't be there in one day. I wouldn't have missed the flight."[48] In other words, whiteness, coupled with being Canadian, is a straightening device that produces a particularly privileged status that allows many to cross with ease, while its lack causes others to be stopped, detained, and weighted down. Shortly after her return to Canada, Mohamud filed a $2.6 million lawsuit against the Canadian government for callous and reckless treatment. The lawsuit was settled for an undisclosed amount in 2012.

Suaad Hagi Mohamud's ordeal with the Kenyan and Canadian governments raises important questions about airport screening practices and the interactions between travelers, airline workers, and customs officials. Mohamud's case also reveals a lot about what happens when DNA meets the border. What are the racial politics of genetic ancestry testing at border crossings? The Human Provenance project was introduced by the U.K. Border Agency through a pilot project that began in late 2009. This project sought to scrutinize adult asylum applicants, mainly those hailing from East Africa, who were thought to be making false claims regarding their nationality, or those applicants suspected of falsifying their relation to children that accompanied them as they sought asylum. To be subject to nationality testing, an asylum applicant would have to first meet certain criteria, including claiming to be of Somali descent, and also being found not to be from Somalia, a finding determined after the asylum seeker had undergone preliminary language testing. When doubt was cast on the applicant's claims of national origin, testing was done through isotope analysis of hair and fingernail samples, and DNA analysis of samples collected

through a cheek swab, alongside language analysis as a means to—erroneously I argue here—determine nationality. These samples were said to
be voluntarily provided to the Asylum Screening Unit by asylum applicants (through signed consent forms) who were subjected to mtDNA (for
women) and Y chromosome (for men) testing, with the intention being
that the results would determine whether an asylum seeker claiming to
be from Somalia was in fact "genetically" Kenyan.[49] Here, an asylum applicant's claim of Somali origin was regarded as suspect, and ancestry was
conflated with nationality and citizenship, often with quite punitive ends
for those accused of "nationality-swapping." This pilot project ceased in
March 2011. In total, 198 DNA tests were carried out to determine familial
connections and 38 tests were conducted to determine country of origin.[50]
The UK Border Agency declined to continue testing asylum applicants
past the pilot project.

Itinerary 2: Surveillance at
the Airport Security Checkpoint

Safety is acted out in security theater, which consists of certain language,
forms, and customs, including the pictogram signage, overhead public address, and even the airline English stock phrases and instructions uttered
by those who labor in these spaces.[51] In many ways, the airport is designed
for spectatorship, where travelers, workers, and also those dropping them
off or picking them up at some point play the role of the audience. Discussing the theater metaphor at the airport, Peter Adey explains that in terms
of architecture, airports often encourage people watching and voyeurism,
where even the arrivals area is structured to draw attention to "the drama of
people meeting one another."[52] At the airport, the traveler is incited to speak
the truth through rites and rituals. With security theater we all have our
parts to play, whether workers, consumers, or travelers who are encouraged
to "Talk to TSA" by scanning with their smartphones QR (quick response)
codes found on TSA checkpoint signs to connect to online customer feedback forms. Travelers fill out customs forms, declare goods purchased or
being transported, answer questions concerning whether they packed their
bags themselves or left their luggage unattended at any time. Among other
practices, travelers are instructed to follow the directive not to joke about
bombs or explosives, or tell lies or other risky untruths.[53] These customs

and the directives in various airport screening zones—from the "no joking" signage and the instructions obliging travelers to purge themselves of liquids, snow globes, gels, and other prohibited items, to the communicating of color-coded threat advisories by way of overhead public address, and the virtual searches by way of whole-body imaging technology—all reveal the workings of pastoral power at the border.[54] This is a power that is individualizing, securitizing, and said to be beneficent. It is a power mediated by new technologies of bodily surveillance that enable post-9/11 mandates concerning security.

We can readily see the operation of pastoral power at airport screening zones, those corridors of indignity where some people labor and others learn about changing security imperatives and required performances.[55] There are choreographed "enhanced pat downs" for those who refuse or opt out of the TSA's advanced imaging technology (either a backscatter unit or a millimeter wave unit). The millimeter wave unit necessitates that travelers empty their pockets and put any items in a bin, then walk through the scanner, stand with their feet apart, and lift their arms over their heads, ideally with their fingertips touching. This unit makes use of radio-frequency energy that is projected onto the traveler's body and then reflected back from the body, producing a three-dimensional image that reveals concealed objects, if any. The backscatter units are full-body scanners that emit radiation in the process of producing an X-ray of the passenger's body, revealing any hidden objects.[56] Shoshana Magnet and Tara Rodgers have argued that the use of these body imaging technologies results in what they have insightfully called "virtual strip searches" that "serve up particular bodies for the viewing pleasure of TSA officers in ways that result in stratified mobilities for particular communities," including trans people, travelers with disabilities, and also those whose religious affiliation could be identified by jewelry worn on the body and other signifiers.[57] After passing through whole-body imaging technology, travelers who are singled out for further inspection are told, "I'm going to pat you down with the back of my hand" by the TSA agent performing the screening.[58] Perhaps it is thought that the back of the hand is less intimate, less invasive, or not an erotic form of touching. A touch of security that is clinical, not pleasurable. If this is the workings of pastoral power post-9/11, then the moment of salvation here should offer more, however, than merely having one's shoes, belts, and sometimes laptops returned after undergoing trace detection procedures—a technology used to determine the chemical signature of different types of explosives and incendiary devices left, if any, as residue on an individual's body, clothing, or possessions. That the plastic bins that hold our shoes, laptops, and others items as they pass through X-ray machines are now lined with advertisements for online shoe retailer Zappos.com, Instagram, and Sony Entertainment is very much in keeping with the theatrics involved in security at the airport.[59] Passenger screening is now complete, in many airports, with "thank you for participating in security" flashed on a television monitor or further signage encouraging travelers to fill out a TSA customer comment card and place it in a drop box.[60]

SOUTH PARK AND THE BLACK AND SASSY TSA AGENT

The animated television series *South Park* started its sixteenth season with the episode "Reverse Cowgirl." First airing in the United States in March 2012, this episode begins with Clyde's mother, Betsy Donovan, scolding him in front of his friends (the series' main characters Eric Cartman, Kyle Broflovski, Stan Marsh, and Kenny McCormick) for leaving the toilet seat up, an act to which Cartman says, "Dude, that sucks, Clyde. A mom shouldn't be able to put rules on toilet time like that. Toilet time is the last bastion of American freedom." Later in the episode, Clyde again leaves the toilet seat up, and his mother falls in, gets stuck, and dies from accidental flushing. At her funeral, a discussion ensues around the various ways that security, risk, and responsibility are gendered, with one of the mourners stating, "I'd like to say, on behalf of the departed, that it isn't a woman's responsibility to see that the seat is down. It's a man's responsibility to put it down. It's not that hard." In response to the death by toilet seat, a Toilet Safety Administration is created with the express duty of enforcing new government-mandated safety regulations: surprise toilet inspections, toilets fitted with safety harnesses to prevent users from accidentally falling in, checkpoints or screening zones set up at public and private restrooms complete with walk-through metal detectors, and bathroom security cameras concealed in black plastic domes installed and monitored at an off-site "discreet location." This *South Park* episode offers a satirical look at the TSA, a federal agency created in 2001 as an outcome of the Aviation and Transportation Security Act that took over operations from the Federal Aviation Administration. First an agency under the operation of the Department of Transportation and then moved to the Department of Homeland Security in 2003, the TSA now oversees security operations in mass transit systems including rail, aviation, seaports, pipelines, and other modes of transportation. The *South Park* episode is a critique of post-9/11 routines at the airport that are seen by many as an inconvenient but now necessary part of air travel. Some, however, think of these post-9/11 routines as a reactionary infringement on civil liberties. For example, in addressing a meeting of concerned citizens, Cartman asks, "Exactly how long are we going to sit around as our freedoms are stripped away one by one?" and leads a call to, as he puts it, "stand together and say we want the government out of our bathrooms."

This *South Park* episode mirrors the Don't Touch My Junk campaign and the National Opt-Out Day, November 24, 2010, that started when John Tyner, a software programmer from California, recorded video of his refusal to have his "junk" touched or patted down by a TSA agent at a screening zone at the San Diego International Airport on November 13, 2010. In August 2010, the TSA began a rollout of a new screening procedures policy, including the "enhanced pat down" that instructs TSA officers to use a slide-down approach with the palms of their hands when manually searching travelers.[61] When Tyner refused to pass through a full-body scanner, the attending TSA agent explained the pat down and "groin check" procedures and offered Tyner a private screening. Tyner responded, "We can do that out here but if you touch my junk I'm going to have you arrested." Tyner was eventually ejected from the airport, and when he posted a video recording of his ordeal, taken with his mobile phone, on YouTube, that video went viral, receiving over seventy thousand views the first day. Throughout Tyner's video, the stock phrases of security theater can be heard being played through the airport's overhead public address system: "Security is everyone's responsibility," sounding a collective responsibility for airport security. In the nearly thirty-minute video, Tyner asks the attending TSA officer about passenger opt-out rates, says that submitting to being "sexually molested" should not be a condition of flying, and volunteers instead to use the walk-through metal detector. On rights, Tyner had this to say during the recording: "arguably, the government took them away after 9/11." When asked if he thought he "looked like a terrorist" in an interview with a local newspaper, Tyner answered, "No. I'm 6-foot-1, white with short brown hair."[62] Being white with short brown hair, according to Tyner here, is not to look "like a terrorist." It is, then, echoing Ahmed, a "straightening device," and in so being it is meant to allow him an easy pass through the airport screening zone, a passing not weighted down by racial baggage.

South Park's "Reverse Cowgirl" lampoons all of the markers of what has come to be known as security theater: the signage ("Be Ready for Security" and "Your toilet safety is our number one priority"), long lines at public bathrooms, pat downs, metal detectors, and scripted questions ("Gots any metal in your pockets?"). In the episode there is a screening zone at the entrance of the restroom at an International House of Pancakes (IHOP), where patrons are told "Shoes off, belts off! Sharp objects go in the plastic tray." Known for its crass humor and raunchiness, *South Park* does not fail with this episode's depiction of the intersection of civil liberties, freedom, and toilets. Playing a pivotal part in this episode is Toilet Safety Administration officer R. Wiley. With her drop curls, gold bangles, doorknocker earrings, fuchsia nail polish, bright lipstick, and the standard-issue uniform of cobalt-blue shirt and black slacks, Officer Wiley conducts the screening of patrons inside the IHOP restroom, while Officer R. West looks on: "Do you mind if I touch your balls, sir?" she says, and wields a flashlight as she instructs the restroom's users, "I just need to check inside your asshole" (a line she repeats two other times throughout the episode), and "You're a big boy, aren't you sir?" as she wipes the restroom's patron. Both Officers Wiley and West are black and are depicted as doing the shitty work of bathroom attendant (figure 4.1). This scene plays on both the infantilization of the restroom user (and thereby airline passenger) and the erotic, through the body of the black woman as symbolic nursemaid and surrogate caregiver.

At another screening zone set up at Stan's house, Officers Wiley and West visually inspect Stan's father, Randy Marsh, with the use of a flashlight. After the inspection, the three Toilet Safety Administration agents stationed inside the bathroom stand around and continue their conversation, seemingly oblivious to Randy's presence as Agent Wiley, apparently in the middle of giving herself a manicure while on duty, files her nails. Later in the episode, Cartman (whom a news report names an "unknown terrorist") is able to get past a Toilet Safety Administration checkpoint with a gun and a baby. He drags a gagged and bound Agent Wiley by her hair into the purview of the agent monitoring the bathroom security cameras from a remote location, taunting the Toilet Safety Administration by leaving the toilet seat up in full view of the CCTV camera, and then disables the camera with spray paint. When asked by a news reporter about this "embarrassing" breach of security, Agent West, who viewers of the episode come to find out is the Toilet Safety Administration chief of operations, with gold door-

FIGURE 4.1. "Reverse Cowgirl," episode 1601, *South Park* (2012).

———

knocker earrings and long red nails, with her hand on her hip and rolling her neck, responds with an elongated "shit," as in "sheeeeeeeiiiiiiiit."

The lengthy catalog of controlling images that have plagued and overdetermined portrayals of black women are plentiful in this episode of *South Park*: first, the controlling image of the "bitch," a contemporary Sapphire and a representation that, as Patricia Hill Collins puts it, is "increasingly applied to poor and/or working-class Black women" and depicts them as "aggressive, loud, rude, and pushy."[63] Second is the "mammy" archetype—large-bodied, grateful, and devoted to her place of employment—except in this case she is not asexual; instead she engages in a somewhat predatory, but routine, groping of travelers. *South Park*'s "Reverse Cowgirl" also allows me to explore the ways that black women are characterized and also caricatured through popular culture, images, and ideas, particularly how their dual role in the domestic War on Terror as blue-collar service-sector workers and as working in service of the security of the state get popularly defined. This is a class of worker that makes airport security possible, where the power of the state to secure airports is racialized as black, however fleeting that power may be. The image of the black woman as the aggressive, sassy, and uninterested screening agent at U.S. airports is a not too uncommon composite and controlling image—or border patrolling image—in popular culture representations of commercial airplane travel and public safety.[64] She is now a common archetype that is emblematic of state power in popular representations of the airport. You can find this stock character in the "Bride of Ida" episode of *Malcolm in the Middle* that aired in 2006, when one of the show's main characters, Lois, is subject to a pat down when she sets off the metal detector at an airport, after voicing a complaint that "this airport's policy is that increased security should only inconvenience poor people."[65] Lois is met by Female Security Agent #2, a black TSA agent who, while putting on a pair of disposable latex gloves, says, "Ma'am, I need to touch your breasts" and "I'm required to probe with the back of my hand." Lois calls this probing a "a public feel-up." Here again, we see the eroticization of security, where it is the black woman's hands that probe the white traveler's body. In the movie *Soul Plane* (2004), she is Shaniece and Jamiqua, with the character Jamiqua, played by actor Mo'Nique, at one point stating to a traveler, "We Feds now, which means I can violate every last one of your civil rights. Now drop them draws," before donning latex gloves to grope and conduct a cavity check. She also appears in the Netflix series *Orange Is the New Black* (2014) as Cindy Hayes. Otherwise known as Black Cindy, in the episode "Comic Sans" it is revealed in a flashback scene that before her incarceration she was an unscrupulous TSA agent with a penchant for groping passengers and who often pilfered items from travelers' luggage.

Perhaps this archetype of the black woman as airport screening officer first entered popular culture with Shaneesha Turner in *Tracey Takes On . . .*, comedian Tracey Ullman's HBO sketch comedy show that aired 1996–1999. Shaneesha Turner first appeared in 1998, with Ullman, a white actor, performing in blackface as she played this character in the pre-TSA, pre-9/11 airport. Dressed in a blue uniform, gold doorknocker earrings, and long red nails, Shaneesha Turner would offer commentary on topics ranging from marriage, aging, lies, and her high blood pressure. Shaneesha Turner from *Tracey Takes On . . .*, *South Park*'s Officer Wiley, Shaniece and Jamiqua from *Soul Plane*, Ka-son on the sketch comedy series *Mad TV*, Black Cindy from *Orange Is the New Black*, Female Security Agent #2 in *Malcolm in the Middle*, and the TSA agent in a 2014 television ad for Old Navy jeans who exclaims, "Excuse me Miss, but I'm going to have to take a closer look," as she ogles a passenger while waving her handheld metal detector are all striking for the ways that they highlight what Collins has explained as two of the ongoing dimensions of African American women's oppression: labor exploitation as seen in their "longstanding ghettoization in service occupations," and controlling images of black women that are stereotyped representations of certain ideologies around black womanhood that originated in slavery and endure in the present day.[66]

While the black and sassy TSA agent might be a signifier of state power, that power is merely perceived. She comes to stand for something specific about working in the airport service sector: she might not be able to access the very thing that she is tasked with protecting—in the words of the TSA's mission, vision, and core values here—"freedom of movement."[67] In a 2004 survey of TSA screeners regarding job satisfaction, 73 percent disagreed that "disciplinary actions are applied fairly to employees" and 59 percent reported that they were considering leaving the TSA.[68] Of the over seventeen thousand screeners who responded to the survey, 59 percent disagreed that TSA employees are "protected from health and safety hazards on the job." With the repetitive lifting of passengers' heavy carry-on bags to perform luggage searches and the possibility of being hurt by sharp objects during these searches, on-the-job injuries for TSA screeners were among the highest of any federal employees in 2004, with a rate of 36 percent.[69]

THE ART OF SECURITY

As analyzed by Bennett, no-fly lists and passenger prescreening protocols have come up against critique from those that question "whether one should really care whether somebody on an airplane has connections with terrorism, so long as he/she is not going to harm that particular flight."[70] Bennett lays out four categories of responses to no-fly lists: "effectiveness, due process, discrimination, and security."[71] When it comes to discrimination and watch lists, ideas around the kinds of people who might commit terrorist acts and the behavioral patterns that could be indicative of terrorism are socially constructed. Inevitably, this leads to the profiling of many travelers based on race, ethnicity, religion, nationality, and other markers. Concerning the security problems with passenger prescreening and watch lists, people can attempt to board planes by using false identification or through impersonation, while computer and human errors can also occur, as Bennett writes.[72] Given this, such lists and prescreening protocols, coupled with the face-to-face passenger screening that takes place at airport security checkpoints, have come under much scrutiny. My discussion below explores the ways that artists represent security, transportation, and labor as a form of engagement with the protocols of the post-9/11 airport.

In *Baggage Allowance*, composer and media artist Pamela Z creatively and critically reveals some of the insecurities that come with contemporary air travel. *Baggage Allowance* is a text in three parts: a web portal, a live multimedia performance, and a gallery installation. When visitors first enter the web portal, a voice-over encourages them to "be nosy" and "thoroughly inspect every bag and open every trunk drawer" as "smart security takes time." The web portal is made up of five interactive parts, in some of which users are implored to become baggage inspectors, or at least to be an observing presence. For example, "Suitcase" is a video projection of Pamela Z curled in a fetal position, wrapped in a blanket, and enjoying a restless sleep inside a 24 × 16 × 9-inch vintage suitcase, tossing and at times looking directly at the viewer. The audio that accompanies "Suitcase" is of Pamela Z whispering about the weight of the worries of traveling and inspection: "So I just pack everything," "It would be so expensive to replace all these things," and "if the bag weighs too much they are going to charge me." *Baggage Allowance* is not only about the experiences of travel by train and plane, but also tells of memory, anxieties, and the psychic baggage that many people hold onto and drag around—the heavy stuff that weighs us down.

The live, multimedia performance begins with "Landing," where Pamela Z is dressed in dark clothing (though at one point during the performance she dresses herself in the entire contents of her luggage, putting on all of her clothes, in an effort to avoid paying a checked bag fee), carrying her roller bag, and descending the passenger stairway of a recently landed flight to the stage below. The stage is flanked by large projection screens that throughout the performance play images from the gallery installation: the view from the window of an airplane in flight, a moving baggage carousel as travelers collect their checked baggage, or a depiction of Pamela Z standing with her feet apart and with hands raised above her head as she assumes the position for a full-body scan. In the "Unknown Person" segment of the performance, Pamela Z sings the scripted questions of security theater: "Did you pack your own bags?" "Did any unknown person ask you to carry something?" "What is the purpose of your travel?" In one corner of the stage sits an antique electric fan on top of a stack of old suitcases. For most of the performance, Pamela Z stands by her MacBook Pro, equipped with a MIDI (Musical Instrument Digital Interface) controller called the BodySynth that allows her to control sounds, projected images, and other effects through her physical gestures, like a wave of her hand or a tapping of her feet, through the use of electrode sensors attached to her body that measure its electrical impulses. This gestural computing is what Herman S. Gray names as Pamela Z's "deeply embodied" approach to live performance, where, as he puts it, the "actual physical experience of the technology and its various uses are central to the total aural, sonic, and visual experience."[73] Through the use of this technology, Pamela Z layers and loops recordings of her own voice with, at times, recorded interviews of other people recounting their travel experiences.

Pamela Z's hour-long performance is filled with the sounds of travel: safety announcements by overhead public address, a plane engine's roar, and people telling their stories of airport security. In "Suitcase," when Pamela Z says, "I'm just hoping there will be enough to cover the bills while I'm away," "Maybe I should transfer some money from one of my credit cards," and "If the bag weighs too much they're going to charge me," she is voicing the cycle of debt. "Notice" sets to piano score the notice cards that are placed by the TSA in checked baggage to inform travelers that their bags were selected for physical inspection and searched for prohibited items, and that in the process locks may have been broken. The cards state that in the event that this is the case, the TSA "sincerely regrets having to do this." "Bag X-Ray" is part of the gallery installation for *Baggage Allowance*, and this piece allows users to play an active role in the installation as they are invited to place their bags on a conveyer belt, just as one would do with carry-on baggage at an airport's passenger screening zone. When a bag passes through the screening device, its contents are scanned and an X-ray image appears on a monitor, where it is revealed that a prohibited object is contained in the baggage: hypodermic needles, a gun, small animals, a beating heart, or an eggbeater.

Baggage Allowance is a play on travel and security theater, that through its depiction of attachment, possessions, and grief—such as a steam trunk that weeps—offers a window on the traveler's journey, including recorded interviews of what one packs and what is left behind. The live performance closes with "Heavy," during which an image of rough waters is projected on a large screen, and Pamela Z recounts the emergency landing of US Airways Flight 1549 on the Hudson River in January 2009. Flight 1549 experienced engine failure soon after takeoff due to its striking a flock of Canada geese. The landing in the Hudson River was successful and all 155 passengers and flight crew survived, in part because, as Pamela Z reminds her audience, the passengers followed the flight crew's directive to leave behind any baggage and personal belongings. She details the complex procedures by which the baggage from the wreckage of Flight 1549 was recovered from the Hudson River and returned to the passengers, stating that nearly thirty

FIGURE 4.2. Evan Roth, *TSA Communication* (2008). Courtesy of the artist.

thousand items were salvaged, telling her audience that each passenger, then, carried, on average, 193 items. Pamela Z also recounts her own inventory of the things she travels with and the things that she puts in storage: books, troubles, instruments, her kitchen sink, weapons-grade plutonium, and dark matter.

Conceptual artist Evan Roth's *Art in Airports* series offers a performance as inquiry into the airport's passenger screening zone. A piece called *TSA Communication*, part of this series, is an invitation for the "government to learn more about passengers than just the contents of their carry on bags." He first laser cuts messages into 13 × 10-inch sheets of stainless steel, which are then placed in carry-on luggage so that when the bags go through X-ray screening, the messages can be read by TSA workers and other airport security personnel. Messages such as "Mind your business" or "I am the frontline of defense, drawing on my imagination to creatively protect America from harm" are displayed on the baggage X-ray monitor, all the while concealing the contents of the carry-on luggage (figure 4.2). Also, *TSA Communication* consists of video secretly recorded by Roth as he takes his stenciled metal plates through X-ray baggage screenings at various airport security checkpoints and is questioned by security workers. Roth's TSA *Communication* caught the attention of the TSA and became part of the TSA's own communication when, in 2008, it was featured on the TSA's official blog, which warned travelers that "many folks who might think it's funny to 'talk back' to TSA won't be too happy when they find themselves spending extra time in the security line," if they were to make use of something like Roth's design.[74] The TSA's response to TSA *Communication*, as well as Roth's interactions with airport security workers, points to a dialogic relationship between art and airport security, where the art is not merely staged in airports but also affects TSA communications with the public.

Conclusion: *N'oublie pas*

One of this chapter's broad concerns has been how black women's experiences at airports can contribute to a different understanding of post-9/11 security practices, performances, and politics. In other words, I am suggesting here that many of the lessons of black feminisms can provide us a way to question the surveillance practices involved in the new configurations of travel at the airport and beyond. Black women, in their places of work, en route to and from their workplaces, sometimes at home and in places of leisure, are subjected to a scrutinizing surveillance. To talk back is a speech act that expresses "our movement from object to subject—the liberated voice," as bell hooks puts it.[75] DeShon Marman's assertion that he is just like everyone else is exactly such a speech act. Suaad Hagi Mohamud's use of DNA to challenge her abandonment in Kenya by airline authorities and the Canadian government, the "Discrim-FRO-nation" hair searches experienced by Laura Adiele, Timery Shante Nance, and Solange Knowles, and Malinda Knowles's removal from a flight under the accusation that she was not wearing underwear give us insight into some of the differential ways that black women negotiate the airport as a transportation place, meaning a place through which people pass in order to move from one location to another, and as a space where anxieties and ideologies surrounding race and security are legitimated and also refused.[76] Post-9/11, acts that could challenge institutionalized gendered racisms that often come into play at the airport are halted when they are interpreted as a questioning of security measures that are deemed necessary, and as such that very questioning and those who do the questioning come to be seen as a security threat or, as in the case of Malinda Knowles, deemed either in their hair or in their being as causing offense or as "unruly."

Launched on July 1, 2007, the digital art installation *Terminal Zero One* was exhibited in the presecurity area of Terminal 1 in Toronto's Lester B. Pearson International Airport. This digital art exhibition comprised five projects: *Dualterm, Arrivals and Departures,* ETA, *Touch and Go,* and *Passage Oublié.* This interactive experience invited travelers, workers, and visitors to the airport to use touch-sensitive screens and text messaging as a way to "engage in dialogue on issues of international security and human rights," as the curators put it in their statement on the exhibition. On my flights back to Austin from Toronto, I travel through Pearson Airport, so I want to focus here on my own experience with *Passage Oublié.* Created by Maroussia Lévesque, Jason Edward Lewis, Yannick Assogba, and Raed Moussa of Obx Laboratory for Experimental Media, *Passage Oublié* is an interactive artwork with a touch-screen kiosk that allows users, referred to as "Citizens of the World in transit," to send messages by text to a dedicated phone number or to the website www.passageoublie.org. These messages are then animated on the kiosk as flight trajectories on a map of eleven airports around the world involved in extraordinary renditions, either for rendition staging or for detainee dropoff for transfer to secret prisons for interrogation, including airports in Afghanistan, Egypt, Germany, Iraq, Jordan, and Guantánamo Bay in Cuba. *Passage Oublié*'s artists' statement informs me that "a rendition flight is a detainee-transfer practice where people, currently mostly Muslim men, are transported in rented commercial jets to interrogation sites around the world known as black sites" and that while there are legal forms of rendition, their focus with this interactive installation is illegal, extraordinary renditions. The artists' statement asks, "Are rendition flights an acceptable means of dealing with new terrorism threats? Let us know!" The statement informs me that "the survivors of Extraordinary Renditions tell of numerous human rights violations including torture" and asks that I critically interrogate my own implications in the practice of renditions, stating,

> You are here, at Pearson International Airport. As you are about to begin your journey, other people, elsewhere, are flying under different circumstances. Under the Extraordinary Rendition Program, these people are detained and transferred outside any legal system.

The detainees' journey often overlaps with that of regular passengers because the program uses rented jets for companies fronting government agencies. Have you been in an airport involved in rendition flights? You're about to find out.

This is what I mean by the possibilities of the airport as a site of learning, or as a critical pedagogical space where commercial air travel and emancipatory learning are both possible. *Passage Oublié* tells visitors to the installation that Pearson Airport is just a short flight away from Dulles International Airport in Washington, DC, which was used for rendition staging at that time. The installation explains that since the flight itineraries of commercial aircraft are publicly available, Planespotters.net began collating the flight schedules with information provided by released detainees to get a fuller picture of the extent of the flights to black sites. One submitted message suggested, "Rendition flights are avoiding advanced, industrialized countries' due process to extort information from people under circumstances that aren't justifiable," while another stated, "I'm an artist. I don't care about politics. Just basic humanity and morality." Other responses questioned the role of the Geneva Convention and the War on Terror: "I'm presuming that if they were covered by the Geneva convention some of the detainees are probably enemy combatants." My text message was simple: "N'oublie pas" (Don't forget). *Passage Oublié*'s touch screen made my experience with the record of rendition flights and the network of airports involved an intimate and tactile one. If I touched an airport icon on the screen, a pop-up would appear featuring a rendition report on that particular airport and messages sent by other users. The collection of these user-generated messages serves as a form of public dialogue on airport security, racial profiling, and renditions (figure 4.3). What this project makes clear is that art can be a way of critically and creatively questioning the policies, performances, and politics of post-9/11 air travel; particularly those opaque practices, like extraordinary rendition, that are made secret, left in the dark, or sent off to black sites.[77] Or, as its creators put it, "*Passage Oublié* is an undercover radical agent in a neutral setting. If renditions can camouflage themselves in airports, so can we."[78]

Some of the airport screening practices that I have examined in this chapter, such as searching black women's hair for potentially dangerous objects, are not on par with extraordinary rendition flights. However, as Lisa Parks points out in her analysis of looking and touching at the TSA se-

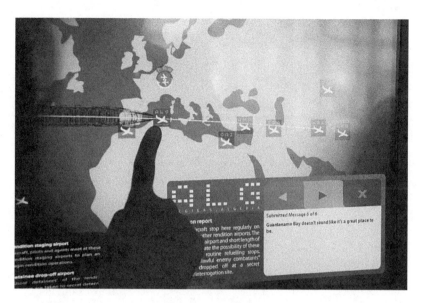

FIGURE 4.3. Maroussia Lévesque, Jason Edward Lewis, Yannick Assogba, and Raed Moussa, *Passage Oublié* (2007). Photo credit: Obx Labs.

curity checkpoint, these screening practices might be "symptomatic" of "a broader security regime in which looking authorizes touching and touching can become torture."[79] A project like *Passage Oublié*, where users can "look, touch, and contribute" to a critique of extraordinary rendition, as well as Solange Knowles's "little game" of "What did TSA find in Solange's Fro"?, Evan Roth's *TSA Communication*, and Pamela Z's *Baggage Allowance*, are ways of interrupting the promise of security that is said to come with backscatter machines, enhanced pat downs, no-fly lists, and the labeling of certain travelers as untrusted at the airport.

EPILOGUE

WHEN BLACKNESS ENTERS THE FRAME

In December 2009, Desi Cryer and Wanda Zamen, coworkers at Toppers
Camping Center in Waller, Texas, uploaded a video to YouTube titled "HP
Computers Are Racist." Cryer and Zamen tested out the new Hewlett
Packard MediaSmart computer, and they recorded what happened when
"Black Desi" and "White Wanda" used the computer's webcam. Cryer narrates the pair's video, at one point saying, "I think my blackness is interfer-
ing with the computer's ability to follow me," referring to the webcam's apparent inability to pan, tilt, zoom, follow, or detect any of Cryer's gestures.[1]
However, "as soon as white Wanda appears," the webcam's automated facial
tracking feature works, meaning only when "Black Desi gets in there, uh,
nope, no facial recognition anymore, buddy," Cryer says, also telling viewers, "The worst part is, I bought one for Christmas." Cryer ends the video
by saying, "I welcome responses to why the HP webcam does not pick up
Negroes." The video garnered close to three million views on YouTube.
Hewlett Packard later responded by first thanking Cryer and Zamen, and
then clarifying that it wasn't that their cameras "can't see black people," as
one CNN news report stated; it was that the technology "is built on standard
algorithms that measure the difference in intensity of contrast between the
eyes and the upper cheek and nose" and that "the camera might have difficulty 'seeing' contrast in conditions where there is insufficient foreground
lighting."[2] What Black Desi needed, according to HP, given their standard
algorithms, was better lighting. Or maybe a lantern.

When Black Desi asks that we watch what happens when his "blackness
enters the frame," he names what has been one of the driving concerns of
Dark Matters. That is, when blackness, black human life, and the conditions
imposed upon it enter discussions of surveillance, what does this then do

to those very discussions? Put another way, how is the frame necessarily reframed by centering the conditions of blackness when we theorize surveillance? That might look like situating the *Book of Negroes* as one of the earliest passports issued for crossing the Canada-U.S. border that identified race, gender, and other markers, where, as raised in chapter 2, doing so allowed for an exploration of what Hazel Carby calls, "narrative acts," where "the racialized subject is invented in the process of encounter, produced, in other words, as a subject dialogically constituted in and through its relationship to an other or others."[3] The making of the *Book of Negroes* was a historical moment where, particularly in the arbitration hearings held at Fraunces Tavern, black women, men, and children found creative ways to narrate their own freedom within a system that sought for them to remain unfree. These narrative acts constituted new forms of articulating postslavery freedom for black people within New York City at the time, and for those whose names would go on to be recorded as those of free people in the *Book of Negroes*. Similarly, as analyzed in chapter 3, by looking to the branding of enslaved people, where the brand worked not only to identify or verify but also as a mark of the mass marketing of the black subject as commodity during the transatlantic slave trade, I was able to draw connections between this early instantiation of biometric information technology and the ongoing biometric surveillance of the racial body.

The call to think about what happens when blackness enters the frame also gets at something else: subversion. Although Cryer and Zamen later released a statement saying that they did "not really think that a machine can be racist, or that HP is purposely creating software that excludes people of color" and that Black Desi's unsuccessful experience with it was "just a glitch,"[4] by uploading their video to YouTube, Cryer and Zamen were publicly sharing their critique of "standard algorithms" that function under a logic of prototypical whiteness. This is a logic that privileges users, in this case, in relation or proximity to blackness. Prototypical whiteness, as I explained in chapter 2, is the cultural logic that informs much of biometric information technology. It sees whiteness, or lightness, as privileged in enrollment, measurement, and recognition processes, and, as I argued in that chapter, prototypical whiteness is reliant upon dark matter for its own meaning. Dark matter being those bodies and body parts that trouble some biometric technology, like dark irises or cameras that "can't see black people" or that ask some Asian users, "Did someone blink?"[5] When particular surveillance technologies, in their development and design, leave out some subjects and communities for optimum usage, this leaves open the possibility of reproducing existing inequalities. This point is somewhat upheld in a 2010 U.S. National Research Council report on biometrics which argued that it is "incumbent upon those who conceive, design and deploy biometric systems to consider the cultural, social and legal contexts of these systems. Not attending to these considerations and failing to consider social impacts diminishes their efficacy and can bring serious unintended consequences," like the further marginalization, and in some cases the disenfranchisement, of people who because of industry-determined standard algorithms encounter difficulty in using this technology.[6] When dark matter troubles algorithms in this way, it amounts to a refusal of the idea of neutrality when it comes to certain technologies. But if algorithms can be troubled, this might not necessarily be a bad thing. In other words, could there be some potential in going about unknown or unremarkable, and perhaps unbothered, where CCTV, camera-enabled devices, facial recognition, and other computer vision technologies are in use?

The very thing that rendered Black Desi unseen in the "HP Computers Are Racist" video is what viewers of another YouTube video are instructed to employ in order to remain undetected by facial recognition technology. In her DIY (do-it-yourself) makeup tutorial on "how to hide from cameras," artist Jillian Mayer demonstrates how to use black lipstick, clear tape, scissors, white cream, some glitter, and black eyeliner to distort one's face in order to make it indiscernible to cameras and "look great."[7] Modeled in a format similar to popular makeup, hair, or other beauty tutorials on YouTube, Mayer tells her viewers that the most important thing "is to really break up your face." Mayer's tutorial is based on artist Adam Harvey's CV Dazzle project, which explores the role of camouflage in subverting face-recognition technology. Computer Vision (CV) Dazzle is a play on dazzle camouflage used during World War I, which saw warships painted with block patterns and geometric shapes in contrasting colors, so that rather than concealing a ship, dazzle camouflage was intended to make it difficult to visually assess its size and speed by way of optical illusion. So when Mayer instructs her viewers that when it comes to facial recognition, it "isn't about blending in" but rather "sticking out, yet remaining undetected" and that "black lipstick is a great way to cover lots of surface on your face quickly," she points out the productive possibilities that come from being unseen, where blackness, in this case applying black makeup, could be subversive in its capacity to distort and interfere when it comes to machine readability and standard algorithms. For this digital camouflage technique to be most effective, meaning for cv *Dazzle* to render the subject either unrecognized or a false match, it is often a matter of contrast. Adam Harvey's cv *Dazzle* Look Book features mainly white-looking women with hair styled in dissymmetrical ways that work to partially conceal their facial features and certain facial landmarks, like the space between the eyes. Harvey offers up "style tips for reclaiming privacy" and suggests that to decrease the possibilities of detection you should "apply makeup that contrasts with your skin tone in unusual tones and directions: light colors on dark skin, dark colors on light skin." Makeup could be used not only to prevent recognition but to obscure skin texture analysis as well. These tactics, however, do not explicitly challenge the proliferation of cctv and other computer vision technologies in public and private spaces, but rather leave it up to the individual to adapt.

One of the tasks of *Dark Matters* has been to situate the dark, blackness, and the archive of slavery and its afterlife as a way to trouble and expand understandings of surveillance. Of course, some things are still left in the dark: the open secret that is the operation of black sites for rendition, torture, detention, and disappearance of people suspected as terroristic threats, or Edward Snowden's revelations in the summer of 2013 of the National Security Agency's warrantless wiretapping, a program representing what he called "a dangerous normalization of governing in the dark."[8] In the beginning of this book, I named dark sousveillance as a form of critique that centers black epistemologies of contending with surveillance, and I later looked to freedom acts such as escaping from enslavement by using falsified documents and aliases, or the Totau as celebratory resistance performed right under the surveillant gazes of white audiences, and Solange's critique of tsa searches as "Discrim-fro-nation." Dark sousveillance is an analytical frame that takes disruptive staring and talking back as a form of argumentation and reading praxis when it comes to reading surveillance and the study of it, like my examples of ex-slave Sam, who was "remarkable in turning up the white of his eyes when spoke to" and Adrian Piper's *What It's Like, What It Is #3*. Routing the study of contemporary surveillance— whether that be biometric technologies or post-9/11 security practices at the airport—through the history of black enslavement and its attendant practices of captivity opens up the possibilities for fugitive acts of escape, resistance, and the productive disruptions that happen when blackness enters the frame.

NOTES

Introduction, and Other Dark Matters

1. Beauvoir, *The Force of Circumstance*, 606.
2. Bhabha, "Foreword," viii.
3. Beauvoir, *The Force of Circumstance*, 606.
4. Quoted in Geismar, *Fanon*, 185.
5. Cherki, *Frantz Fanon*, 162.
6. Fanon, "*Rencontre de la société et de la Psychiatrie.*" See Mirzoeff, *The Right to Look*; and Mirzoeff, "*We Are All Children of Algeria,*" for further discussion of Fanon's lectures in Tunisia. Mirzoeff notes that although Michel Foucault was in residence at the University of Tunis from 1966 to 1968, a mere six years after Fanon's residency, and Foucault taught a course called Madness and Civilization during his time at the University of Tunis, as yet no connection has been made in Foucault's published writings on the possibility of the influence of Fanon's thought on his own theorizing.
7. Fanon, *Rencontre de la société et de la Psychiatrie*, 10. In his biography of Fanon, *Frantz Fanon*, David Macey writes that much of Fanon's discussion here of the black condition in the United States is derived from literature, namely the works of Richard Wright and Chester Himes. On Himes, Macey writes that Fanon "misreads him badly" (326). "Quand un Noir tue un Noir, il ne se passé rien; quand un Noir tue un Blanc, toute la police est mobilisée" could be loosely translated from French to say: when a black person kills another black person, not much is remarked upon; but when a black person kills a white person, the entire police force is mobilized. See also singer-songwriter Frank Ocean's single "Crack Rock" from his album *Channel Orange* (2012) on the apparent inaudibility of black death and, similarly to Fanon's observation on black-on-black violence, police mobilization: "My brother get popped / And don't no one hear the sound."
8. Gendzier, *Frantz Fanon*, 99.
9. Mirzoeff, *The Right to Look*, 250. I would add here that Toni Cade Bambara (1970) also saw these possibilities that Mirzoeff alludes to, as she wrote that in Fanon's *A Dying Colonialism* he names how the anticolonial struggle necessitated a liberation from traditional gender roles, releasing people from "stultifying roleplaying, freeing them to fashion a new sense of self" (108). (Bambara) Cade, "On the Issue of Roles."

10. Wynter, "Towards the Sociogenic Principle," 3. Cited here is an earlier version of the chapter published in Gomez-Moriana and Duran-Cogan, *National Identities and Sociopolitical Changes in Latin America*.

11. Wynter, "Towards the Sociogenic Principle."

12. Fanon, *Black Skin, White Masks* (2008), 95.

13. Ibid., 92.

14. Hall, "Cultural Identity and Diaspora," 231.

15. Walcott, *Black Like Who?*, 132.

16. Ellison, *Invisible Man*, 9.

17. Collins, *Black Feminist Thought*, 18.

18. Winant, "The Dark Matter," 10.

19. Hammonds, "Black (W)holes and the Geometry of Black Female Sexuality," 139.

20. Baldwin, *The Evidence of Things Not Seen*, 44.

21. Bambara, "Preface" in Julie Dash, *Daughters of the Dust*, xii; bell hooks, *Black Looks*, 116.

22. Ferguson, *Aberrations in Black*, 77.

23. Ibid., 77.

24. Park, "The Conflict and Fusion of Cultures with Special Reference to the Negro," 129–130.

25. Ibid., 130. In *Aberrations in Black*, Ferguson discusses Park's address to the American Sociological Society through a reading of Baldwin's unpublished chapter. Ferguson notes that Baldwin was aware that this feminization was also about the queering of blackness, with the character Woodridge, a black queer professor who "represents the very nonconformity that Americanization programs were supposed to correct and canonical forms excluded," 59.

26. Ellison, *Invisible Man*, xv.

27. Gordon, *Ghostly Matters*, 143.

28. Ibid.

29. Hier and Greenberg, *The Surveillance Studies Reader*, 8–9.

30. Carson and Sabol, "Prisoners in 2011," 6. This report notes that "a larger percentage of whites (24%) were sentenced for property crimes than Hispanics (14%) or blacks (15%). The percentage of Hispanics (57%) and blacks (55%) in state prison held on violent offenses exceeded that for whites (49%). A higher percentage of whites (16%) were imprisoned for both rape and other sexual assaults than blacks (8%) and Hispanics (12%)" (9).

31. Influential works in the field, such as James Rule's *Private Lives and Public Surveillance* (1973), Gary T. Marx's *Undercover: Police Surveillance in America* (1988), Oscar Gandy's *The Panoptic Sort: The Political Economy of Personal Information* (1993), and William G. Staples's *Everyday Surveillance: Vigilance and Visibility in Postmodern Life* (2000), conceptualized the concerns of surveillance studies and theorized trends driving the expansion of surveillance from the mid-twentieth century on. David Lyon's *The Electronic Eye: The Rise of the Surveillance Society* (1994), *Surveillance Society: Monitoring Everyday Life* (2001), *Surveillance after September 11* (2003), *Surveillance Studies: An*

Overview (2007), and his numerous edited collections, articles, and chapters together are key to the formation of surveillance studies.

32. Lyon, "Technology vs. 'Terrorism,'" 673.

33. Lyon, *Surveillance Studies*, 25.

34. Ibid., 26–27.

35. Rule, *Private Lives and Public Surveillance*, 29.

36. Ibid., 38.

37. Marx, *Undercover*, 206.

38. Ibid., 217–219.

39. Ibid., 220.

40. Marx, "Surveillance and Society."

41. Staples, *Everyday Surveillance*, 48; Marx, *Undercover*, 214.

42. Gandy, *The Panoptic Sort*, 15.

43. Haggerty and Ericson, "Surveillant Assemblage," 611–613.

44. Fiske, "Surveilling the City," 81.

45. Goldberg, *The Threat of Race*, 67.

46. Fiske, "Surveilling the City," 85.

47. Ibid., 69.

48. Ibid., 71.

49. Lyon, *Surveillance after September 11*, 81.

50. Ibid., 83.

51. On April 22, 2013, Reddit general manager Erik Martin released an apology for the site's role in what he termed the "online witch hunts and dangerous speculation" that occurred during the aftermath of the Boston Marathon bombing where users of the site ("Redditors") incorrectly identified suspects using the /r/findbostonbombers subreddit page, a dedicated Google Doc, photographs uploaded to Flickr, and other crowdsourced information. See "Reflections on the Recent Boston Crisis," *Blog .Reddit*, April 22, 2013, accessed February 1, 2015, http://www.redditblog.com/2013/04/reflections-on-recent-boston-crisis.html.

52. Lyon, *The Electronic Eye*, 48.

53. Steven Poole and Anna Hart, "Beyond Selfies and Twerking . . . the Words That Really Mattered in 2013," *Guardian*, December 29, 2013, http://www.theguardian.com/lifeandstyle/2013/dec/29/selfies-twerking-words-really-mattered-2013.

54. Mann, Nolan, and Wellman, "Sousveillance," 333.

55. Mann, "Veillance and Reciprocal Transparency," 3.

56. Ibid., 6.

57. Ibid.

58. Ibid.

59. Wallace, *Constructing the Black Masculine*, 135; Butler, "Endangered/Endangering."

60. Butler, "Endangered/Endangering," 18.

61. Mann, Nolan, and Wellman, "Sousveillance," 333.

62. Douglass, *Narrative of the Life of Frederick Douglass*, 103.

63. "Run, nigger, run, de patrole's a commin' / Run, nigger, run, de patrole's a commin' / The nigger run, dat nigger flew / The nigger tore his shirt in two / Run, nig-

ger, run!" The interviewer who recorded ex-slave Aunt Ferebe Rogers noted that when asked about the song, "no amount of coaxing availed to make her sing the whole of the song, or to tell any more of the words." *Georgia Narratives*, vol. 4, part 3, in Work Projects Administration, *Born in Slavery: Slave Narratives from the Federal Writers' Project, 1936–1938*, 214. An extended version of this song made an appearance in the film *12 Years a Slave* (2013). Also see Sally E. Hadden, *Slave Patrols: Law and Violence in Virginia and the Carolinas* (Cambridge, MA: Harvard University Press, 2001).

64. Berry Smith, ex-slave, Scott County, *Mississippi Narratives*, vol. 9, in Work Projects Administration, *Born in Slavery*, 129.

65. Mabee, *Soujourner Truth*, 13.

66. Lyon, *Surveillance Studies*, 57.

67. The call for a "critical reinterpretation" of panopticism is made by David [Murakami] Wood in "Foucault and the Panopticon Revisited," an editorial in the journal *Surveillance and Society*, where in a discussion of the ways that panopticism is taken up by scholars and academics, Wood places it along with Majid Yar's (in the same issue) mapping of "appropriation and application; rejection; and qualified acceptance subject to empirically-dependent limitations" (236).

68. Ibid., 235.

69. Bentham, *The Works of Jeremy Bentham*, vol. 4, 41.

70. City of New York, *Minutes of the Common Council of the City of New York, 1675–1776*, vol. 4, 86.

71. Lyon, "Surveillance, Security and Social Sorting," 161–170.

72. Gilroy, "Scales and Eyes," 195.

73. Haggerty and Ericson, "Surveillant Assemblage," 613.

74. U.S. Bureau of Transportation Statistics, "Figure 1: World Wide Civil Aviation Hijackings, 1970–2000," *Transportation Statistics Annual Report*, 2001, accessed October 6, 2011, http://www.rita.dot.gov/bts/sites/rita.dot.gov.bts/files/publications/transportation_statistics_annual_report/2001/html/chapter_05_figure_01_114_table.html.

75. Asinof, *The Fox Is Crazy Too*, 16. Angela Davis was released from jail on February 23, 1972, on $102,500 bail.

76. U.S. Bureau of Transportation Statistics, "Figure 1: Worldwide Civil Aviation Hijacking."

77. "The Nixon Announcement," *New York Times*, September 12, 1970, 11.

78. Press briefing, May 16, 2002. In her testimony to the National Commission on Terrorist Attacks upon the United States (the 9/11 Commission), Rice stated that the intelligence community was aware of the possibility of a terrorist attack. See "Sociology and Psychology of Terrorism," CIA Report. In a section "Institutionalizing Imagination: The Case of Aircraft as Weapons" in the authorized edition of National Commission on Terrorist Attacks upon the United States, *The 9/11 Commission Report*, numerous scenarios, intelligence on possible suicide hijacking plots with aircraft originating overseas, and discussions of pre-9/11 protocol in place if such an event were to occur are discussed in detail.

1. Notes on Surveillance Studies

---

1. Jeremy Bentham to his father, Jeremiah Bentham, "On board a Turkish Caïk from Smyrna to Constantinople, E. of the Island of Metelin," letter 550, November 9, 1785, in Christie, *The Correspondence of Jeremy Bentham*, 387. The City of İzmir was formerly called Smyrna.

2. Bentham, *The Works of Jeremy Bentham*, vol. 1, 443–444.

3. Ibid., 444.

4. Ibid. This passage was first published in 1812 in Étienne (Stephen) Dumont's "Theorie des peines et des recompences." It was later translated into English by Richard Smith and published in 1825 as "Rationale of Punishment." Smith's English version was published in the 1843 Bowring edition of *The Works of Jeremy Bentham* as book 2 of *Principles of Penal Law*. However, it is not clear how faithful Dumont was to Bentham's original writings. The original manuscripts for *Principles of Penal Law* are held at the Bentham Project at the University College of London. According to Philip Schofield, director of the Bentham Project and general editor of the *Collected Works of Jeremy Bentham*, Hugo Bedau, who produced the transcripts, thought them to be written by Bentham in the 1770s, but "as so often is the case with Bentham's texts, it has a complex history." P. Schofield, personal communication, December 15, 2012.

5. Foucault, *Security, Territory, Population*, 125.

6. Bentham, *The Works of Jeremy Bentham*, vol. 4, 40.

7. Ibid.

8. Ibid., 39.

9. Foucault, *Discipline and Punish*, 200.

10. Ibid., 41.

11. Foucault, *Psychiatric Power*, 77.

12. Bentham, *The Works of Jeremy Bentham*, vol. 4, 41.

13. Foucault, *Discipline and Punish*, 49.

14. Ibid., 3.

15. See McKittrick, *Demonic Grounds*, chapter 4, in which she writes on the "surprise" that is Black Canada and Marie-Joseph Angélique.

16. Cooper, *The Hanging of Angélique*, 15.

17. Ibid., 18.

18. Ibid., 285.

19. McKittrick, *Demonic Grounds*, 117.

20. Foucault, *Discipline and Punish*, 6.

21. Ibid., 7.

22. Ibid., 10.

23. Bigo, "Security and Immigration," 81.

24. Bigo, "Globalized (In)Security," 35.

25. Stop and Frisk Data, New York Civil Liberties Union, accessed September 8, 2014, http://www.nyclu.org/content/stop-and-frisk-data.

26. Boyne, "Post-Panopticism," 299.

27. Ibid.

28. Ibid.

29. Gilliom and Monahan, *Supervision*, 49.

30. Ibid.

31. Lyon, *Surveillance Studies*, 57.

32. Haggerty, "Tear Down the Walls," 23.

33. Foucault, *Discipline and Punish*, 172.

34. Haggerty, "Tear Down the Walls," 33.

35. Ibid., 302.

36. Rhodes, "Panoptical Intimacies," 294, 287.

37. Ibid., 287.

38. Lyon, "The Search for Surveillance Theories," 5.

39. Ibid., 303.

40. Foucault, *Discipline and Punish*, 170.

41. Ibid., 177.

42. Ibid., 173.

43. Ibid., 178.

44. Ibid., 182.

45. Ibid., 189.

46. Wiegman, *American Anatomies*, 39.

47. Patterson, *Slavery and Social Death*.

48. Foucault, *Discipline and Punish*, 49.

49. Rediker, *The Slave Ship*, 45.

50. Gilmore, *Golden Gulag*, 28. The Centers for Disease Control quantify premature mortality rates by measuring individual deaths occurring prior to age seventy-five.

51. Best and Hartman, "Fugitive Justice," 13.

52. Foucault, Bülow, and Defert, "The Masked Assassination," 156.

53. Jackson, *Soledad Brother*, 4.

54. Phillips, "The Cargo Rap," 90.

55. Ibid., 165.

56. Ibid., 67.

57. Wacquant, *Punishing the Poor*, 148.

58. Phillips, "The Cargo Rap," 147.

59. Ibid., 154.

60. Ibid., 172.

61. Ibid.

62. Brand, *A Map to the Door of No Return*, 51–52.

63. Winant, *The New Politics of Race*, 82.

64. For recent and more detailed discussions of the *Brooks* (or *Brookes*) schematic diagram, see Cheryl Finley, *Committed to Memory: The Slave Ship Icon in the Black Atlantic Imagination* (PhD diss., Yale University, 2002); Rediker, *The Slave Ship*; Walvin, *Black Ivory*; Wood, *Blind Memory*.

65. "List of Voyages," Trans-Atlantic Slave Trade Database, accessed August 2, 2011, http://www.slavevoyages.org/tast/database/search.faces.

66. Clarkson, *The History of the Rise, Progress, and Accomplishment of the Abolition of the African Slave-Trade by the British Parliament*, vol. 2, 111.

67. Plymouth Committee of the Society for Effecting the Abolition of the Slave Trade, *Plan of an African Ship's lower Deck with Negroes stowed in the Proportion of only One to a Ton*.

68. *Stowage of the British Slave Ship "Brookes" under the Regulated Slave Trade Act of 1788*, Rare Book and Special Collections Division, Library of Congress, accessed September 9, 2014, http://memory.loc.gov/rbc/rbpe/rbpe28/rbpe282/28204300/001dr.jpg.

69. Clarkson, *The History of the Rise, Progress and Accomplishment of the Abolition of the African Slave-Trade by the British Parliament*, vol. 2, 115.

70. DuBois, "The Home of the Slave," 18.

71. Canot, *Memoirs of a Slave-Trader*, 57.

72. Ibid.

73. *Description of a Slave Ship*, printed by James Phillips. Also see Tinsley, "Queer Atlantic, Black Atlantic," for a queering of intimacy, bonding, and what she terms "erotic resistance" during the Middle Passage; Hartman on the violence of the archive of slavery in "Venus in Two Acts."

74. Slow-motion death is recounted by Harriet Ann Jacobs (Linda Brent) in *Incidents in the Life of a Slave Girl, Written by Herself*, where she describes slavery as a "living death," a life in which enslaved people are "slowly murdered" by abuse and vicious torment. Slavery is a condition where, Jacobs/Brent writes, "slaves, being surrounded by mysteries, deceptions, and dangers, early learn to be suspicious and watchful, and prematurely cautious and cunning" (234). Here Jacobs/Brent is describing the moment when her son Benjamin/Joseph reveals that he knew of her hiding place in the garret of her grandmother's home, but concealed this knowledge in order to protect her. Although the garret "was only nine feet long, and seven wide. The highest part was three feet high, and sloped down abruptly to the loose board floor," it was Jacobs/Brent's "loophole of retreat," a space of debilitating freedom. She writes of her ingenious escape: "Who can blame slaves for being cunning? They are constantly compelled to resort to it. It is the only weapon of the weak and oppressed against the strength of their tyrants." Jacobs hid there in a prison-like cell that was "the last place they thought of" for almost seven years and would write letters addressed from New York and Boston in order to fool those who wanted to see her captured. She eventually made her way to New York City. See also McKittrick, *Demonic Ground*.

75. Walvin, *Black Ivory*, 47.

76. Rediker, *The Slave Ship*, 9.

77. Clarkson, *The Substance of the Evidence of Sundry Persons*, 23.

78. James, *The Black Jacobins*, 9.

79. *Stowage of the British Slave Ship "Brookes."*

80. Spillers, "Mama's Baby, Papa's Maybe," 72.

81. *Description of a Slave Ship*, printed by James Phillips.

82. Ibid.

83. Ibid.

84. Clarkson, *The History of the Rise, Progress, and Accomplishment of the Abolition of the African Slave-Trade by the British Parliament*, vol. 2, 111.

85. Spillers, "Mama's Baby, Papa's Maybe," 72.

86. Haraway, *Simians, Cyborgs and Women*, 188.

87. Fanon, *Black Skin, White Masks* (1967), 112–116.

88. Haraway, *Simians, Cyborgs and Women*, 188.

89. "Remarks on the Slave Trade," *American Museum*, May 1789, 429–430.

90. Ibid.

91. Rediker, *The Slave Ship*, 311.

92. Tinsley, "Queer Atlantic, Black Atlantic," 199. The Middle Passage has been taken up, or remembered, in creative works, such as Amiri Baraka's play *Slave Ship* (1970); M. NourbeSe Philip's *Zong!* on the death and massacre of those forced overboard from the eighteenth-century slave ship *Zong*; Elizabeth Alexander's poem "Island Number Four" in *American Sublime*; Reginald Shepherd's collection of poetry *Some Are Drowning*; The O'Jays' album and single "Ship Ahoy" (1973); Caryl Phillips's novel *Crossing the River* (1994); and the 1991 television adaptation of George C. Wolfe's play *The Colored Museum*, featuring the sketch "Celebrity Slave Ship" where the Middle Passage is set onboard a commercial airplane. The *Brooks* appeared on the cover of Bob Marley's album *Survival* (1979). Given the *Brooks*'s repurposing with this text of survival rather than abolition, the image is now an "instant contextual filler," as Marcus Wood calls it, as the *Brooks* diagram has been reproduced, sampled, remixed, and reenacted into iconic status. In *Blind Memory*, Wood concludes that the *Description* is "best understood as a memorial to a disaster, not as a representation of what ever happened" (32). In July 2007, to mark the bicentenary of the abolition of the slave trade in 1807, Durham University Library Heritage Collections in the United Kingdom organized a reenactment where 274 school children acted as human cargo by lying flat on a printed-out replica of the hold of the *Brooks*. The students wore red T-shirts emblazoned with images of "cartoon figures," a term Hortense Spillers, in "Mama's Baby, Papa's Maybe," used to describe figures drawn to represent enslaved African cargo.

93. "Plantation Rules," 1844–1854, Tait Papers.

94. Ibid.

95. Hartman, *Scenes of Subjection*, 43.

96. Parenti, *The Soft Cage*.

97. *Georgia Narratives*, vol. 4, part 4, in Works Progress Administration, *Born in Slavery*, 322, at Manuscript and Prints and Photographs Divisions of the Library of Congress, Washington, DC, accessed May 22, 2014, http://memory.loc.gov/ammem /snhtml/snhome.html.

98. Plantation life as viewed by ex-slave Will Sheets, *Georgia Narratives*, vol. 4, part 3, in Works Progress Administration, *Born in Slavery*, 241. This transcription of Will Sheets's quote is not as it appears in the original, where the transcriptionist's choice of matching sound to written text in an exaggerated, stereotyped vernacular, I feel, reflects the racial logic of the time of the interview.

99. Anderson Furr, ex-slave, eighty-seven years of age, in *Georgia Narratives*, vol. 4, part 1, in Works Progress Administration, *Born in Slavery*, 349–350.

100. The descriptions here are taken from various advertisements found in Hodges and Brown, *Pretends to Be Free*. Advertisements quoted here, in order, are 230, 21, 326, 26, 308, 115, 401.

101. Ibid., 91–93, Advertisement 201, *Parker's New-York Gazette, or, The Weekly Post-Boy* #1008, April 29, 1762.

102. Fiske, "Surveilling the City," 81.

103. Advertisement in the *Richmond Whig*, January 6, 1836.

104. Advertisement in the *Alabama Beacon*, June 14, 1845.

105. Craft, *Running a Thousand Miles for Freedom*.

106. Ibid.

107. Similar to Ellen Craft, in her 1861 narrative, Harriet A. Jacobs recounts her use of a disguise of sailor's clothes as a means by which she evaded detection by giving off, through her dress, the impression of freedom. Jacobs, *Incidents in the Life of a Slave Girl*.

108. Goldberg, *The Racial State*, 189.

109. Ibid.

110. Ibid., 190.

111. Collins, *Fighting Words*, 20. Controlling images, post-Emancipation and during Reconstruction in the United States, were representational practices aimed at controlling black migration and mobilities from the Jim Crow South to the North. For example, the controlling image of the Zip Coon replaced that of the Sambo to mark black men as no longer conceived and stereotyped as docile, happy with, or naturally suited for enslavement (Sambo, mammy), but as dangerous (Zip Coon). See Collins, *Black Feminist Thought*.

112. Collins, *Fighting Words*, 20.

113. Ibid., 21.

114. hooks, *Black Looks*, 168.

115. Ibid., citing the biography of newspaper heiress Sallie Bingham, *Passion and Prejudice*, 270, in hooks's discussion of sight and invisibility.

116. Collins, *Black Feminist Thought*, 72.

117. Ibid.

118. Ibid.

119. Ibid.

120. Ibid., 72–73.

121. Turner, *Ceramic Uncles*, 73. Alongside the controlling image of the mammy is also the matriarch, the welfare mother, the black lady, and the Jezebel.

122. See bell hooks, "Homeplace: A Site of Resistance," in *Yearning: Race, Gender, and Cultural Politics* (Boston: South End Press, 1990), 41–49.

123. hooks, *Black Looks*, 168, 116.

124. Ibid., 116. For a discussion of James Baldwin and oppositional gazing, see Maurice O. Wallace, " 'I'm Not Entirely What I Look Like': Richard Wright, James Baldwin, and the Hegemony of Vision; or, Jimmy's FBEye Blues," in *Constructing the Black Masculine*. Wallace's examination of papers released by the FBI under the Freedom of Information Act regarding that agency's surveillance of writer James Baldwin reveal how the "fetishizing machinations of the racial gaze" were disrupted by Baldwin's "eye-

balling disposition" that "defies the hegemony of racial supervision on its own terms" (141). Wallace is referring here, in part, to the references made in the file to Baldwin as "huge-eyed [if] undersized" (137). Also see my discussion in chapter 2 of ex-slave Sam and his "reckless eyeballing" that, in fact, was not so reckless, but an act of subversion.

125. Wallace, *Constructing the Black Masculine*, 141.

126. Glaser, *Bo-Tsotsi*. Glaser places the entry of the term "tsotsi" in township vocabulary at around 1943–1944, and as referring "to a style of narrow-bottomed trousers that became popular among African youth in the early 1940s. In American gangland slang, the narrow-bottomed pants were called 'zoot suits.' It is possible that the word tsotsi comes directly from the word 'zoot-suit,' with a pronunciation shift" (50). The term later gained connotations that associated "tsotsi aesthetic" with criminal gang activity.

127. Robin Rhode in "Robin Rhode and Catharina Manchanda in Conversation" in Manchanda, *Catch Air*, 19.

128. Bentham, *The Works of Jeremy Bentham*, vol. 4, 39.

129. hooks, *Talking Back*, 9.

2. "Everybody's Got a Little Light under the Sun"

1. After the race is complete, some scenes are reenacted with participants in order for the film crew to capture better footage. A secondary film crew is sent out during the race, to lessen the chance that sighting a full film crew will give the trackers an advantage over the prey. *Mantracker* has filmed episodes outside of Canada, including California and Hawaii, and began its seventh season in May 2012, without Terry Grant as Mantracker.

2. Walcott, *Black Like Who?*, 14.

3. Ibid., 48.

4. Coined by sociologist Thomas Mathiesen, "The Viewer Society," the synopticon, in counterpoint to the Panopticon (where the few watch the many), allows for the many to watch the few, often by way of mass media in a viewer society, for example, reality television watching.

5. In this act, "negro cloth" includes duffel, kersey, osnaburg, blue linen, check linen, checked cotton, Scotch plaids, calico, and other coarse and unrefined cloths "and declares all garments of finer or other kind, to be liable to seizure by any constable as forfeited."

6. This quote is taken from the pair's application video, in which contestant Al St. Louis states incredulously, "Two black men being chased by a white man on a horse?" While it could be said that St. Louis and Thompson are framed in this episode through a narrative of uplift, it could also be argued that a certain element of minstrelsy or hamming it up for the camera is engaged by the two: losing a defective compass and leaving Mantracker to find it; paying homage to another reality television program that also makes use of surveillance footage of evasion and capture, *Cops*, by singing the lyrics to its theme song, reggae band Inner Circle's 1993 hit "Bad Boys." In deleted scenes avail-

able on DVD, contestant Al is filmed singing a rendition of the Negro spiritual "Nobody Knows the Trouble I've Seen" and alternately beatboxing "Go Down Moses."

7. Douglass, *Narrative of the Life of Frederick Douglass*, 33.

8. A "breeder" or foundation document is used to support one's identity claims in the application process for a more secure status document, such as a passport. In our contemporary moment, breeder documents, such as birth certificates and in some cases baptismal certificates, are said to be more easily forged and weak in terms of security. See Salter, *Rights of Passage*.

9. McKittrick, "'Their Blood Is There,'" 28.

10. McKittrick, "Math Whips."

11. Foucault, *Psychiatric Power*, 77.

12. Marriot, *On Black Men*, 9.

13. Sennett, *Flesh and Stone*, 80.

14. Now that the *Book of Negroes* is digitized and searchable online (http://www .blackloyalist.info/), it could be argued that this inventory bears some of the hallmarks of contemporary centralized traveler databases, complete with a "no-sail" list. For a detailed accounting of the inventory that is the *Book of Negroes*, see Hodges, *The Black Loyalist Directory*. Hodges's appendix includes tables, by colony and gender, of "All Negroes Who Claimed to Be Born Free," "All Negroes Who Claimed to Have Escaped," "All Negroes Who Were Free by Proclamation"—those who were indentured, enslaved, and emancipated.

15. For a longer discussion on the various watch lists, data collection practices, and programs in the regulation of airline travel and Canada-U.S. border crossings post-9/11, see Bennett, "What Happens When You Book an Airline Ticket?"

16. Carby, "Becoming Modern Racialized Subjects," 625.

17. Ibid., 627.

18. Gilroy, *The Black Atlantic*, 16.

19. In *Rights of Passage*, Mark B. Salter names the modern international passport system as a post–World War I formation that was codified by the League of Nations in 1920 with the expressed purpose of securing state borders and economic trade that is deemed legitimate, restricting the movements of refugees, and controlling the spread of disease through quarantine, all while facilitating travel between nations. Salter lays out the development of the modern passport from the doctrine of *ne exeat regno* (the right of the sovereign to determine who can leave the realm), to the emergence of safe conduct passes for merchants in thirteenth-century Europe, letters of marque issued to privateers that authorized the use of violence on the high seas in the name of the sovereign, and the post-Westphalian state system that saw the sovereign's monopoly on the legitimate means of violence. Radhika Mongia, in "Race, Nationality, Mobility," sees the passport system as having a "checkered, piecemeal, and counterintuitive development" (527), and considers the role of Indian emigration to Canada in the early twentieth century in this formation. I situate the *Book of Negroes* as part of this checkered development of the passport regime, notably because it emerged when the United States of America gained independence from Britain and it was written into

the terms of peace. Given that prior to the *Book of Negroes* what would eventually become the United States was still a British holding, no other document could have served the same function—a written record of the right to pass freely out of the United States that noted identifiers such as gender, race, place of birth, and, importantly, corporeal markers like scarring.

20. On November 7, 1775, John Murray, the fourth Lord Dunmore and governor of Virginia, issued a proclamation that promised freedom for male slaves who voluntarily fought with British forces. After the defeat of his forces in Virginia, Murray arrived in New York City in the summer of 1776 to occupy the city, establishing its military headquarters there. With Dunmore's Proclamation, and later Howe's 1778 Proclamation, then Clinton's Philipsburg Proclamation in 1779, this guarantee was extended to women and children, bringing about the "largest black escape in the history of North American slavery," with fugitives estimated at 25,000 to 55,000 in the "southern states alone" (Hodges, *The Black Loyalist Directory*, xiv). Sir Henry Clinton served as commander in chief of all British forces of North America from May 1778 until February 1782, when Sir Guy Carleton took up the post. See also Schama, *Rough Crossings*, 132–135.

21. *Pennsylvania Gazette*, July 17, 1776, quoted from Schama, *Rough Crossings*, 77.

22. Anderson, *Imagined Communities*, 35.

23. Foote, *Black and White Manhattan*, 190.

24. Hall, "Missing Dolly, Mourning Slavery," 70.

25. Allsopp and Allsopp, *Dictionary of Caribbean English Usage*, 110.

26. *Royal Gazette*, New York, June 14, 1783.

27. *Royal Gazette*, New York, July 21, 1783.

28. *New York Gazette*, October 27, 1783.

29. Walke, "Thomas Walke's Account of Capturing His Runaway Slaves in New York City."

30. Hartman, "Venus in Two Acts," 5.

31. Lyon, *Surveillance Society*, 51–53.

32. Iton, *In Search of the Black Fantastic*, 105. This term is also related to the performances that are often demanded and rendered necessary in dominant spaces (schooling, workplaces, the outdoors), so that minoritized peoples are not viewed as threatening to established norms.

33. Ibid.

34. The descriptions in the *Book of Negroes* of those who left New York also gesture to the intimate relations within the black and indigenous populations: "born free, her mother an Indian" or "better half Indian." Many thanks to Sharon Holland for pointing out this connection. For detailed discussions of the events of 1712 and 1741 in New York City and their effects on the regulation of the city life of black subjects, see Doolen, *Fugitive Empire*; Lepore, *New York Burning*; Harris, *In the Shadow of Slavery*; Burrows and Wallace, *A History of New York City to 1898*; Davis, *A Rumor of Revolt*. For seventeenth- and early eighteenth-century laws regulating free and enslaved blacks, see Hodges, *Root and Branch*.

35. City of New York, *Minutes of the Common Council of the City of New York, 1675–1776*, vol. 3, 30.

36. Ibid., vol. 4.

37. Ibid., vol. 4, 51.

38. Foucault, *Discipline and Punish*, 41.

39. *New York Weekly Journal*, vol. 113, January 5, 1735.

40. Ibid.

41. Hamilton, *Gentleman's Progress*, 88.

42. McKittrick, *Demonic Grounds*, 124.

43. City of New York, *Minutes of the Common Council of New York City 1784–1831*, vol. 1.

44. "Extract of a Letter from a Gentleman in Pennsylvania to His Friend in New York Dated March 24, 1784," *New York Journal and State Gazette*, April 15, 1784.

45. Fanon, *The Wretched of the Earth*, 19–20.

46. Harris, *In the Shadow of Slavery*, 41.

47. Lott, *Love and Theft*, 46; McAllister, *White People Do Not Know How to Behave*, 113; White, "Pinkster," 69.

48. McAllister, *White People Do Not Know How to Behave*, 112.

49. Thomas De Voe, *The Market Book*, cited in Lott, *Love & Theft*, 41–42.

50. "Where Slaves Danced: Catharine Market's Rise and Decline," *New York Times*, April 28, 1889.

51. Wynter, "Jonkonnu in Jamaica," 36.

52. Ibid., 37.

53. Ibid.

54. Ibid., 36. See also Wynter, "The Ceremony Found."

55. Wynter, "Jonkonnu in Jamaica," 36.

56. Wynter, "The Ceremony Found."

57. Carleton to Washington, May 12, 1783, in Carleton, Papers.

58. Hodges, *The Black Loyalist Directory*, xviii.

59. Eilbeck's death notice in the *American Beacon and Commercial Diary*, August 4, 1817, stated, "he never withheld from the labourer the reward of his industry, while hundreds can attest his forbearance towards those even who were the most unworthy of his indulgence." Here it is assumed that Eilbeck's "forbearance" was toward the laborer that was paid, and not enslaved.

60. Schama, *Rough Crossings*; Pybus, *Epic Journeys of Freedom*.

61. Lawrence Hill's *The Book of Negroes: A Novel*, has been adapted into a television miniseries that aired on Black Entertainment Television and the Canadian Broadcasting Corporation. The part of Samuel Fraunces is played by actor Cuba Gooding Jr., a casting decision that, I think, leaves Fraunces's blackness unambiguous.

62. Hartman, "Venus in Two Acts," 7.

63. Hill, *The Book of Negroes*, 294. For the novel's release in the United States, Australia, and New Zealand, it is titled *Somebody Knows My Name*, as the publisher reasoned that "Negroes" in the book's original title could cause offense with some audiences. The

Dutch edition of the book is titled *Het Negerboek*. A burning of the novel's cover was organized by a group of Afro-descended Dutch Surinamese to protest the book's title in Amsterdam in 2011. For more on this book burning, see Hill, *Dear Sir*.

64. Hill, *The Book of Negroes*, 306.

65. Ibid., 307.

3. B®anding Blackness

1. "An Instrument of Torture among Slaveholders," *Harper's Weekly* 6, no. 268 (February 15, 1862): 108.

2. "White and Colored Slaves," *Harper's Weekly* 8, no. 370 (January 30, 1864): 71.

3. Fanon, *Black Skin, White Masks* (2008), 89.

4. Gilroy, *Against Race*, 46.

5. "Branding Slaves," in *The Anti-slavery Almanac* (1840), Schomburg Center for Research in Black Culture, Manuscripts, Archives and Rare Books Division, Image ID: 413027, *North Carolina Standard*, July 18, 1838.

6. Wood, *Blind Memory*, 246.

7. Spillers, "Mama's Baby, Papa's Maybe," 67.

8. Atkins, "Voyage of John Atkins to Guinea," 269.

9. Omi and Winant, *Racial Formation in the United States*; Goldberg, *The Racial State*.

10. Goldberg, *The Racial State*, 110.

11. Ibid., 110–111.

12. Barbot, "John Barbot's Description of Guinea," 293.

13. Ibid., 294–295.

14. Feagin, *The White Racial Frame*, 2nd ed.

15. Ibid., 55.

16. Long, *The History of Jamaica*, 273.

17. Ibid., 382.

18. Ibid., 328. See also Mimi Sheller, "Quasheba, Mother, Queen," in *Citizenship from Below*.

19. Young, *Colonial Desire*, 181.

20. Barbot, "John Barbot's Description of Guinea," 290.

21. Platt, *The Martyrs, and the Fugitive*, 22.

22. Ibid.

23. Hall, "The After-Life of Frantz Fanon," 16.

24. Fanon, *Black Skin, White Masks* (2008), 91, 92.

25. McClintock, *Imperial Leather*, 33.

26. Ibid., 209.

27. Fanon, *Black Skin, White Masks* (2008), 93.

28. Ibid., 95.

29. Ibid., 94.

30. Ibid., 89.

31. Ibid., 114.

32. "Out of place" here, as explained further in chapter 2, gestures to the Caribbean vernacular usage of the term "out'a place," along with "facety," "farse," "bol'face," and "backchat"—all of which were and continue to be used to name subversive acts of looking and talking back.

33. Fanon, *Black Skin, White Masks* (2008), 94.

34. Clarkson, *The Substance of the Evidence of Sundry Persons*, 77.

35. Ibid., 77.

36. Hartman, *Lose Your Mother*, 79.

37. Postma, *The Dutch in the Atlantic Slave Trade*; Hartman, *Lose Your Mother*.

38. Postma, *The Dutch in the Atlantic Slave Trade*, 368.

39. Ibid., 52–53.

40. Williams, *Dessa Rose*, 229.

41. Morrison, *Beloved*, 73.

42. Ibid.

43. In his content analysis of fugitive slave notices that appeared in the *Royal Jamaica Gazette* during one week in June 1823, Clarkson, *The Argument That the Colonial Slaves Are Better Off*, writes that branding was not occasioned solely at the factories of the transatlantic slave trade, but took place in the colonies as a form of punishment and an identification practice by planters "that they may know them again" should the enslaved run away. Clarkson tells us that Creoles (those born in Jamaica) were branded, including "one individual branded with no less than ten capital letters."

44. Walvin, *Black Ivory*, 284, 250.

45. Hodges and Brown, *Pretends to Be Free*, 58, 69.

46. Ibid., 209.

47. Box 2, Folder 12 (December 8, 1761), 308, Thistlewood Papers, "Mark'd my New Negroes on the right Shoulder" (found adjacent is a diagram of Thistlewood's brand mark, TT, inside a triangle). Also see Hartman, "Venus in Two Acts," 1.

48. Box 3, Folder 14 (Wednesday, September 14, 1763), 227, Thistlewood Papers.

49. Box 4, Folder 21 (Friday, July 6, 1770), 110, Thistlewood Papers.

50. Box 4, Folder 21 (Sunday, July 1, 1770), 105, Thistlewood Papers.

51. Patterson, *Slavery and Social Death*, 59.

52. See Hartman, *Lose Your Mother*.

53. "White and Colored Slaves," 71.

54. See Fusco, "All Too Real."

55. For a discussion on the sale and collection of Black Americana, see Turner, *Ceramic Uncles and Celluloid Mammies*; Patterson, *Rituals of Blood*; and Spike Lee's film *Bamboozled* (2000).

56. See Orlando Patterson's discussion of the lynching as ceremony and sacrifice in the postbellum South in the chapter "Feast of Blood: 'Race,' Religion, and Human Sacrifice in the Postbellum South," in *Rituals of Blood*.

57. Fusco, "All Too Real."

58. Galloway, *Protocol*, 238.

59. Ibid.

60. Feagin, *The White Racial Frame* (2010), 172. Like Mendi + Keith Obadike's *Blackness for Sale*, conceptual artist damali ayo's *rent-a-negro* is an online critique of the objectification of black people. This satirical website worked as black antiracist counterframing, as visitors to the site could choose from a list of services, such as touching a black person's hair, that a professional black person would render for a set fee. See Catanese, "'How Do I Rent a Negro?'" for a more detailed discussion of ayo's *rent-a-negro*.

61. Gilroy, "Scales and Eyes," 190–196.

62. Gilroy, *Against Race*, 37.

63. Gilroy, "Scales and Eyes," 195.

64. Hall, "Introduction," 4.

65. Fanon, *Black Skin, White Masks* (2008), 90.

66. Gordon, "Is the Human a Teleological Suspension of Man?," 239.

67. Ibid.

68. Goldberg, *The Racial State*, 83.

69. Gordon, "Is the Human a Teleological Suspension of Man?," 239–240.

70. Gao and Ai, "Face Gender Classification on Consumer Images."

71. In June 2012, Facebook acquired Israeli-based face.com, in a deal said to be worth over $100 million. Face.com is promoted as the world's largest and most accurate face recognition platform, and created a smartphone app (KLIK) that allows users to take photographs that are then "auto-tagged," meaning the uploaded photographs are detected and then matched to friends' profiles ("a known set of users"); the subject's age ("age meter"), gender ("gender meter"), and mood can be guessed. Combined with GPS data, the app can also suggest the location of the subject. The company also created Celebrityfindr, a face recognition application that matches photos of celebrities with pictures posted on the social networking site Twitter. Lauren O'Neil, "Facebook Buys Facial-Recognition Platform Face.com," CBC News, June 19, 2012, accessed June 19, 2012, http://www.cbc.ca/newsblogs/yourcommunity/2012/06/facebook-buys-facial -recognition-platform-facecom.html.

72. Gao and Ai, "Face Gender Classification on Consumer Images," 175.

73. See Stephen Jay Gould's discussion of Samuel George Morton on *Crania Aegyptia* (1844) and *Crania Americana* (1839) in *The Mismeasure of Man*.

74. Gao and Ai, "Face Gender Classification on Consumer Images," 177.

75. Li, Zhou, and Geng, "Facial Pose Estimation," 173.

76. Ibid.

77. Once recorded on fiches or filing cards and accompanied by a photograph, this data could then be stored in filing cabinets, making indexing possible as a way of knowing the criminal body. With these files, or dossiers, came the creation of the database linking individual identity to bodily measurements. The fingerprint later replaced Bertillonage as the standard biometric for individualizing people and identifying suspects and repeat offenders.

78. Li, Zhou, and Geng, "Facial Pose Estimation," 178.

79. Nanavati, Thieme, and Nanavati, *Biometrics*, 36–37, emphasis mine.

80. Monahan, *Surveillance in the Time of Insecurity*, 114.

81. Pugliese, "*In Silico* Race and the Heteronomy of Biometric Proxies," 14.

82. Nanavati, Thieme, and Nanavati, *Biometrics*, 37. Also see Pugliese, "*In Silico* Race and the Heteronomy of Biometric Proxies," for further discussion of FTE rates and the notion that certain biometric technologies are "infrastructurally calibrated to whiteness" (5).

83. Dyer, *White*, 103.

84. Ibid.

85. Nanavati, Thieme, and Nanavati, *Biometrics*, 37.

86. The terms "dark matter" and "white prototypicality" are borrowed from Lewis R. Gordon's discussion of double consciousness in "Is the Human a Teleological Suspension of Man?"

87. Lao and Kawade, "Vision-Based Face Understanding Technologies," 346.

88. For example, Canada's Standing Committee on Citizenship and Immigration, *Building a Nation*, in advocating for biometrics, states, "We start with the use of photo identification, proposed as a security feature for the new card. The first thing to note is that human beings are not particularly acute at recognizing individuals from photograph identification, *particularly across cultural lines*. Moreover, glasses, hairstyles and (for men) facial hair may change, which may lead to questions even when the holder of the card is genuine" (emphasis mine). It is interesting to note here that biometric identifiers are suggested by the committee as a means to solve detection problems resulting from human beings' lack of ability to recognize individuals from photographs. I argue that what is suggested here is that digitized body data can be a technology to secure accurate and, presumably, fixed race and gender detection. Moreover, in this system it is apparently understood that only men have facial hair.

89. Balsamo, *Technologies of the Gendered Body*, 9–10.

90. Mayfield was held under the material witness statute of the USA Patriot Act for over two weeks and then released. Spanish authorities had earlier informed U.S. authorities that Mayfield's fingerprint was not a match with that found at the scene of the bombing on a knapsack used to contain detonating devices. See Cole, "Brandon Mayfield, Suspect."

91. Franklin, *The Real World of Technology*, 74.

92. Ibid., 74–75.

93. Gilroy, *Against Race*, 30.

94. Thacker, *The Global Genome*, 172.

95. See Lisa Nakamura's discussion of iPhone assembly and production at Foxconn's electronics manufacturing factories in "Economies of Digital Production in East Asia."

96. Böhlen (under the moniker "RealTechSupport"), "The Open Biometrics Initiative," 2.

97. Böhlen's Open Biometrics idea is that given the probabilistic nature of biometric data, a person should assemble an array of their own biometric data and—I'm borrowing from Foucault, *Archaeology of Knowledge*, here—"leave it to the bureaucrats and the police to see that our papers are in order" (17). For Böhlen, since it is now up to

the authorities to make determinations beyond a mathematical doubt, the biometric data that a person assembles can weaken statistical significance and can create "a new buffer zone for citizens in the age of big bio data." M. Böhlen, personal communication, September 6, 2014.

98. Böhlen, "The Open Biometrics Initiative," 2.

99. Ibid., 3.

100. Ibid.

101. A. O. Scott, "The Doodads Are Restless in Chicago," *New York Times*, July 16, 2004, accessed June 1, 2013, http://movies.nytimes.com/2004/07/16/movies/16ROBOT.html?_r=0.

102. Ibid.

103. To which the special advisor to the deputy director of operations of the NSA, Thomas Brian Reynolds (who we learn was born on September 11, 1940), played by actor Jon Voight, responds, "Liberal hysteria."

104. *Enemy of the State* pays homage to an earlier film on surveillance, *The Conversation* (1974), also starring Gene Hackman as wiretapping expert Harry Caul. Caul and Hackman's Brill in *Enemy of the State* share similar characteristics, indicating, perhaps, that the characters are one and the same.

105. Lyon, *Surveillance Studies*, 147.

106. Ibid.

107. Light, "Enemies of the State?," 44.

108. Balsamo, *Designing Culture*, 32.

109. Lyon, *Surveillance Studies*, 141.

110. Johanna Adorján, "Will Smith: George W Bush hat mich angelogen," *Frankfurter Allgemeine Zeitung*, September 8, 2004, accessed June 20, 2012, http://www.faz.net/aktuell/feuilleton/kino/will-smith-george-w-bush-hat-mich-angelogen-1178336.html. Translation mine. Thanks to Tamara K. Nopper for bringing it to my attention.

111. Jack Purcher, "An Avalanche of New Google Contact Lens Patents Come to Light," Patently Mobile, accessed April 14, 2014, http://www.patentlymobile.com/2014/04/an-avalanche-of-new-google-contact-lens-patents-come-to-light.html.

112. For a discussion of Cruise's films, see Lyon, *Surveillance Studies*, 146–148; and also Nakamura, *Digitizing Race*, 119–120.

113. Hanifa Harris, "Erasing Type: Hank Willis Thomas on What Advertisements Are Really Saying," *Time Lightbox*, April 19, 2011, accessed September 30, 2011, http://lightbox.time.com/2011/04/19/what-advertisements-dont-say/#1.

114. Federal Bureau of Investigation, "Expanded Homicide Data Table 2: Murder Victims by Age, Sex, and Race, 2013," Crime in the United States 2013, accessed February 13, 2015, http://www.fbi.gov/about-us/cjis/ucr/crime-in-the-u.s/2013/crime-in-the-u.s.-2013/offenses-known-to-law-enforcement/expanded-homicide/expanded_homicide_data_table_2_murder_victims_by_age_sex_and_race_2013.xls.

115. For the Centers for Disease Control and Prevention's *Years of Potential Life Lost Report (1999–2010)*, premature mortality or "premature death" is quantified by calculating the years of potential life lost when death occurs before the age of seventy-five.

116. Katie Zuppann, "Hank Willis Thomas, Unabridged," *Juxtapoz Art and Culture Magazine*, http://www.juxtapoz.com/Features/hank-willis-thomas-unabridged.

117. Teri Duerr, "Unbranded: An Interview with Hank Willis Thomas," *New York Art Beat*, March 5, 2009, accessed February 15, 2015, http://www.nyartbeat.com/nyablog /2009/03/unbranded-an-interview-with-hank-willis-thomas/.

118. It must also be noted that, although not discussed here, for many black fraternities and sororities in the United States and beyond, through scarification the brand is a mark of membership in a brotherhood or sisterhood.

119. "About Us," JPMorgan Chase, accessed September 13, 2014, http://www.jpmor ganchase.com/corporate/About-JPMC/about-us.htm.

120. John Friedman, "Chase's Historical Ledger: Chase Should Immediately Open Its Archives to Slavery Researchers," *The Nation*, September 24, 2000, http://www.the nation.com/article/chases-historical-ledger#.

121. Michael Vick was drafted first overall by the Atlanta Falcons in 2001, becoming the first black quarterback to be drafted first overall in an NFL draft. He played for the Falcons for six seasons. As of the end of the 2011 NFL regular season, Vick held the record for most rushing yards by a quarterback per season, per game, and over the span of his career.

122. It should be noted here that the black codes governing the lives of free Negroes during Reconstruction in the southern United States often included "cruel treatment to animals" as a punishable crime. In summarizing recurrent themes in Angela Y. Davis's theorizing on penal practices, Eduardo Mendieta names "social branding," where once a "black American has been in prison, he or she is permanently branded" and situates this as making it "more difficult for former black prisoners to regain entry into society than it is for their white counterparts." Davis and Mendieta, *Abolition Democracy*, 14. For more on social branding as a criminalizing process, see also Pager, "The Mark of a Criminal Record."

123. Wynter in Thomas, "Proud/Flesh Interviews."

124. Gilroy, *Against Race*, 41.

125. Fanon, *Black Skin, White Masks* (2008), 204.

4. "What Did TSA Find in Solange's Fro"?

1. Solange Knowles (@solangeknowles), Twitter post, November 14, 2012, https:// twitter.com/solangeknowles/status/268803217410895872.

2. "TSA Agents Demand to Search Woman's Afro," CBS DFW, September 21, 2011, http://dfw.cbslocal.com/2011/09/21/tsa-agents-demand-to-search-womans-afro/.

3. Solange Knowles (@solangeknowles), Twitter post, November 14, 2012, https:// twitter.com/solangeknowles/status/268803217410895872 12:50 pm and https://twitter .com/solangeknowles/status/268805914641960960 1:01 pm.

4. Goldberg, *The Threat of Race*, 9.

5. U.S. Customs Services, "Better Targeting of Airline Passengers for Personal Searches," 2.

6. *Bradley v. US Customs Service, et al.*, http://www.aclu.org/court/bradley_v_US Customs.html, copy on file with author. The class-action case, decided in September 2001, is *Yvette Bradley, Appellant v. the United States of America*, 299 F.3d 197 (3d Cir. 2001). See also "ACLU Sues U.S. Customs Service over Degrading Search in Case of 'Flying While Black,'" ACLU, May 12, 2000, https://www.aclu.org/racial-justice/aclu -sues-us-customs-service-over-degrading-search-case-flying-while-black.

7. *Bradley v. US Customs Service, et al.*

8. Ibid.

9. Ibid.

10. Ibid.

11. Ibid.

12. District Judge Nicholas H. Politan, Letter of Opinion and Order, *Bradley v. United States*, New Jersey District Court, 164 F. Supp. 2d 437 (September 10, 2001).

13. Salter, "Governmentalities of an Airport," 49–65.

14. Performance by the artist in August 2006 at SECT University of California at Irvine, Humanities Institute. See also Jay-Z's lyric "*Swoosh*, that's the sound of the border" in "Oceans," track five of the album *Magna Carta . . . Holy Grail* (2013).

15. While some of these passenger screening programs are governed solely by the state (for example, the Nexus Card managed by Canada Border Services Agency and U.S. Customs and Border Protection), traveler clearance programs, such as CLEAR's biometric CLEARcard used at CLEARlanes available at Orlando International Airport and San Francisco International Airport, for example, are managed by the private sector (www.clearme.com). However, in the case of the CLEAR program, the TSA section of the U.S. Department of Homeland Security dictates its parameters. Government-sponsored programs such as these mark the integration, or cooperation, of the private sector with the state to control and patrol borders. With this program, the traveler is issued a CLEARcard that contains the cardholder's biometric data (iris and fingerprint), once the traveler passes an assessment or is cleared. This assessment includes background screening, a "Security Threat Assessment" by TSA. This is not a one-time clearance, as the cardholder's status is continuously reviewed by TSA. If the cardholder's status changes and he or she is no longer deemed trusted, but a threat, membership in the program is deactivated. There is a $179 annual membership fee for the program. At present, CLEAR is available only to U.S. citizens and permanent residents.

16. Muller, "Travelers, Borders, Dangers," 127–143.

17. Bennett, "What Happens When You Book an Airline Ticket?," 133.

18. See French and Browne, "Surveillance as Social Regulation."

19. See Browne, "Digital Epidermalization."

20. Kelley, *Race Rebels*, 57.

21. Ibid., 63.

22. hooks, *Killing Rage*, 8.

23. Ibid., 8–11.

24. "TSA to Woman: We're Going to Have to Examine Your Hair," KING5, July 6, 2011, http://www.king5.com/news/local/TSA-to-woman-Were-going-to-have-to-examine -your-hair-125112189.html.

25. Joe Sharkey, "With Hair Pat-Downs, Complaints of Racial Bias," *New York Times*, August 15, 2011, accessed August 16, 2011, http://www.nytimes.com/2011/08/16/busi ness/natural-hair-pat-downs-warrant-a-rethinking.html.

26. Frances Martel, "Lady Accuses TSA of Racism for Extended Inspection of, Laughter at Her 'Poofy' Hair," Mediaite, July 9, 2011, http://www.mediaite.com/tv /lady-accuses-tsa-of-racism-for-extended-inspection-of-laughter-at-her-poofy-hair/.

27. For a detailed look of the spurious accounts published in print news media re-garding Jackson's death, see Foucault, Bülow, and Defert, "The Masked Assassination." One section in this chapter, "The Arsenal in Hair," recounts reports and rumors that Jackson used a wig, while other accounts claim Jackson's Afro was used to smuggle guns into the penitentiary (146).

28. Mercer, *Welcome to the Jungle*, 101. See also *Coffy* (1973), a blaxploitation film in which the lead character, Coffy, played by Pam Grier, hides weapons in her Afro.

29. Lisa Amin Gulezian, "Man Arrested for Not Pulling Up Pants on Plane," ABC7 News, June 16, 2011, http://abc7news.com/archive/8193594. In this same news report, San Francisco Police Department's Sgt. Michael Rodriguez notes that Marman was not threatening anyone directly.

30. Vic Lee, "Exclusive: Student Talks about Saggy Pants Arrest," ABC7 News KGO-TV San Francisco, June 18, 2011, accessed May 25, 2014, http://abc7news.com/archive /8197808/.

31. "Baggy Pants Get Man Booted from Plane," ABC News, video, accessed May 25, 2014, http://abcnews.go.com/US/video/baggy-pants-get-man-removed-from-plane -13866173.

32. Gulezian, "Man Arrested for Not Pulling Up Pants on Plane." In another story, Doyle is even more specific: "He's a big, tall, light-skinned black boy with dreadlocks. Gets on the plane with baggy pants. Right there you're stereotyped." R. J. Middleton, "Update: Police Address Baggy Pants Arrest," NBC Bay Area, June 17, 2011, http:// www.nbcbayarea.com/news/local/Mans-Baggy-Pants-Cause-Planes-Evacuation-Jail -Time-123994104.html.

33. Christina Caron, "JetBlue Sued: Underwear Altercation Humiliates Malinda Knowles," ABC News, July 26, 2011, http://abcnews.go.com/US/jetblue-sued-under wear-altercation-humiliates-malinda-knowles/story?id=14160167.

34. "Woman Kicked Off Flight over 'Panties,'" UPI, July 22, 2011, http://www.upi.com /Odd_News/2011/07/22/Woman-kicked-off-flight-over-panties/UPI-92381311365682/.

35. Allan Woods and John Goddard, "'No Excuse' for Woman's Plight," *Toronto Star*, August 13, 2009, A19.

36. Suaad Hagi Mohamud's appearance before the Government of Canada Stand-ing Committee of Foreign Affairs and International Development (CFAID), August 26, 2009. The OHIP card is the Ontario Health Insurance Plan identification card, which often includes a photograph. Canadian Tire Money is a popular currency or coupon, part of automotive, household, and sporting goods store Canadian Tire's loyalty pro-gram.

37. Minister Cannon's statement to the press on July 24, 2009. Accessed May 17, 2010, http://www.cbc.ca/news/world/suaad-hagi-mohamud-s-detention-in-kenya-1.785251.

38. Mohamud, CFAID Standing Committee, August 26, 2009.

39. Woodfield et al., "Exploring the Decision Making of Immigration Officers."

40. Lyon, *Identifying Citizens*, 13.

41. Fanon, *Black Skin, White Masks* (1967), 61.

42. Ibid., 60.

43. Ibid.

44. Lyon, "Under My Skin," 305.

45. Ahmed, *Queer Phenomenology*, 119.

46. Ibid., 121.

47. Ibid., 141.

48. "Skin Colour a Factor in Kenya Ordeal: Mohamud," CBC News, accessed August 21, 2009, http://www.cbc.ca/news/canada/skin-colour-a-factor-in-kenya-ordeal-mohamud-1.825003.

49. "Nationality-Swapping—Isotope Analysis and DNA Testing. UK Border Agency," accessed May 3, 2012, http://news.sciencemag.org/sites/default/files/nationality-swapping-DNA-testing.pdf.

50. Home Office, "20818 Human Provenance Pilot Project," Gov.UK, May 3, 2012, http://www.homeoffice.gov.uk/about-us/freedom-of-information/released-information1/foi-archive-immigration/20818-Human-Provenance-Pilot/.

51. See Gillian Fuller, "The Arrow—Directional Semiotics," where she argues that rather than universality, there is Eurocentric logic and literacy in airport pictograms and signage, where "the supposed international transparency of pictograms [is] clearly the imposition of a cultural/logical homogeneity in probably one of the most culturally heterogeneous spaces in the world" (235).

52. Adey, "May I Have Your Attention," 530.

53. See Salter, "Governmentalities of an Airport," for a discussion of "confessionary complex."

54. The Department of Homeland Security's Home Security Advisory System, a color-coded threat advisory scale, was in place from 2002 until April 2011, when it was replaced by the National Terrorism Advisory System. During its usage, the threat level was never lowered to "guarded" (blue) or "low" (green), but rather hovered at "elevated" (yellow). Only once was it raised to "severe" (red), in response to the August 2006 announcement by Scotland Yard that it had foiled a plot to detonate a liquid-based explosive on transatlantic flights from the U.K. to Canada and the United States.

55. Thanks to Rinaldo Walcott for the term "corridor of indignity."

56. Major U.S. airports began removing backscatter units in October 2012, while the European Union banned the use of these units in 2011 "in order not to risk jeopardizing citizens' health and safety." Michael Grabell, "X-Ray Body Scanners Removed from Major Airports," Salon.com, October 19, 2012, http://www.salon.com/2012/10/19/x_ray_body_scanners_removed_from_major_airports/.

57. Magnet and Rodgers, "Stripping for the State," 105.

58. Blogger Bob, "New TSA Pat-Down Procedures," The TSA Blog, November 11, 2010, http://blog.tsa.gov/2010/11/new-tsa-pat-down-procedures.html. As Bob Burns (Blogger Bob) of the TSA Blog Team said, "There's nothing punitive about it—it just

makes good security sense." That the backscatter unit is manufactured by Rapiscan (which some have termed "Rape-y-scan") is not without irony.

59. SecurityPoint Media contracts its SecureTray System of plastic bin advertising with companies such as Zappos paying the costs of bins, carts, and tables in the screening zones at participating airports. As Zappos put it, "By sponsoring the security bins, we absorb the cost that TSA would normally have to spend buying tables, bins, maintenance, etc. (not their primary function or responsibility). Since the airports that have the sponsored security bins don't have to put the money/time/energy into those efforts anymore, TSA can spend the money hiring/training more agents. And, due to the better training and additional resources, airports that have sponsors for their security bins have seen an average of a 16% improvement in wait time in getting through the lines." Aaron Magness, "Why Does Zappos Advertise in Airport Security Bins?," Zappos Blogs: tsa, January 11, 2011, http://blogs.zappos.com/taxonomy/term/18138.

60. The TSA regularly posts a roundup of noteworthy occurrences and items found by TSA agents at passenger screening zones, for example, "This Week in Review—Inert Detonator Discovered in Checked Bag": "Body Scanner Discoveries This Week—There were a total of 12 illegal and prohibited items discovered this week with the body scanners at HOU, SFO, LAX, MKE, SFO, SAN, ATL, OMA, SNA, MOB and PBI. Among the items were a punching weapon, strike anywhere matches, drugs, drug paraphernalia, and a gentleman at Houston (HOU) had a half full bottle of whiskey stuffed in his waistband. Finding these types of items in areas where explosives could also be hidden is a testament that the technology works. And while it isn't prohibited, a passenger wearing a chastity belt alarmed the body scanner at one of our checkpoints. I'm sure you can imagine where an undergarment such as this might be a problem at a security checkpoint. Especially if there is no key." The TSA Blog, June 8, 2012, http://blog.tsa .gov/2012/06/tsa-week-in-review-inert-detonator.html.

61. "New Logan Searches Blasted: TSA Tests Frisky Frisking Policy," Boston Herald, August 21, 2010, http://bostonherald.com/business/general/view/20100821new_logan _searches_blasted_tsa_tests_frisky_frisking_policy.

62. Robert J. Hawkins, "Oceanside Man Ejected from Airport for Refusing Security Check," U-T San Diego, November 14, 2010, http://www.utsandiego.com/news/2010 /nov/14/tsa-ejects-oceanside-man-airport-refusing-security/.

63. Collins, Black Sexual Politics, 123. Collins names the mammy image as a representational practice that, along with other controlling images (Jezebel, the black matriarch, the welfare queen), worked to justify black women's subordination. The "bitch" is, according to Collins, a "reworking of the image of the mule of chattel slavery. Whereas the mule was simply stubborn (passive aggressive) and needed prodding and supervision, the bitch is confrontational and actively aggressive" (123).

64. In a deleted scene from South Park's "Reverse Cowgirl" episode, it is revealed that both Officers West and Wiley share the same first name: "Roshaunda." For another instance of the stock character of the black woman as airport security guard, see the episode "Road to Rhode Island" of the Fox television series Family Guy. Airing on May 30, 2000, during that episode main character Stewie Griffin distracts the FAA officers conducting X-ray screening of his carry-on luggage, which contains an assault rifle

and other weaponry, by singing, "On the Good Ship Lollipop." After retrieving his bag from the conveyor belt, Stewie says, "Let's hope Osama bin Laden doesn't know show tunes." A character who appears to be Osama bin Laden then appears in the screening zone singing "I Hope I Get It" from the musical *A Chorus Line* while images of rifles and various weaponry smuggled in his carry-on baggage appear on the baggage X-ray monitor. This episode aired before the 9/11 hijackings and in later airings this scene was deleted. It is available in one of the DVD releases of season 2 of *Family Guy*.

65. "Bride of Ida," *Malcolm in the Middle*, first aired January 13, 2006.

66. Collins, *Black Feminist Thought*, 4.

67. "About TSA: Mission and Core Values," Transportation Security Administration, accessed June 20, 2014, http://www.tsa.gov/about-tsa/mission-vision-and-core-values.

68. TSA 2004 Organizational Assessment Survey, accessed through a FOIA request by the Project on Government Oversight, accessed June 20, 2014, http://pogo.org /m/hsp/hsp-tsa-screeners-2004.pdf (accessed through Wayback Machine Internet Archive).

69. Thomas Frank, "Airport Screeners' Injury Rate Declines but Still Exceeds Rates of Other Workers," *USA Today*, December 12, 2006, http://usatoday30.usatoday.com /news/washington/2006-12-12-tsa-injuries_x.htm.

70. Bennett, "Unsafe at Any Altitude," 66.

71. Ibid.

72. Ibid., 67.

73. Gray, *Cultural Moves*, 182.

74. Blogger Bob, "Message in a Carry-On," The TSA Blog, October 7, 2008, http:// blog.tsa.gov/2008/10/message-in-carry-on.html.

75. hooks, *Talking Back*, 9.

76. In March 2015, the ACLU announced that it had reached an agreement with the TSA, through an informal resolution process, that would see the retraining of TSA workers at both the Los Angeles International Airport and Minneapolis Saint Paul International Airport. This retraining is "to stress TSA's commitment to race neutrality in its security screening activities with special emphasis on hair patdowns of African-American female travelers." The agreement would also have the TSA "specifically track hair patdown complaints filed with MB (Multicultural Branch) from African-American females throughout the country to assess whether a discriminatory impact may be occurring at a specific TSA secured location." Letter to ACLU Staff Attorney Novella Coleman from Bryan W. Hudson, Policy Advisor with the Disability and Multicultural Division of the Office of Civil Rights and Liberties, Ombudsman and Traveler Engagement.

77. Other airport-specific art, photography, and fashion include Martha Rosler, *In the Place of the Public: Observations of a Frequent Flyer* (Berlin: Hatje Cantz, 1999); Vijay Iyer and Mike Ladd's jazz album *In What Language?* (New York: Pi Recordings, 2003); the music video for Kanye West's single "All Falls Down" (ft. Syleena Johnson) from his album *The College Dropout* (2004) in which West raps on a conveyor belt while going through baggage screening while an X-ray image of his skeleton is projected on a monitor; and the 4th Amendment Wear clothing line featuring T-shirts and underclothes with metallic ink-printed text of the Fourth Amendment to the U.S. Constitution.

78. Lévesque and Lewis, "What Else Do We Lose When We Make People Disappear?"

79. Parks, "Points of Departure," 192.

Epilogue: When Blackness Enters the Frame

1. Wzameno1, "HP Computers Are Racist," YouTube, December 10, 2009, https://www.youtube.com/watch?v=t4DT3tQqgRM.

2. Mallory Simon, "HP Looking into Claim Webcam Can't See Black People," CNN.com, December 23, 2009, http://www.cnn.com/2009/TECH/12/22/hp.webcams/.

3. Carby, "Becoming Modern Racialized Subjects," 625.

4. Brenna Ehrlich, "Creators of 'HP Computers Are Racist' Video Speak," Mashable, December 23, 2009, http://mashable.com/2009/12/23/hp-computers-are-racist/.

5. In 2009, Joz Wang used a Nikon Coolpix S630 camera to take pictures during a Los Angeles Angels baseball game. "Did someone blink?" appeared on the camera's LCD screen. For more, see Wang's blog post, "Racist Camera! No, I Did Not Blink . . . I'm Just Asian!," jozjozjoz, May 13, 2009, http://www.jozjozjoz.com/2009/05/13/racist-camera-no-i-did-not-blink-im-just-asian/. In 2009, ABC's television sitcom *Better Off Ted* took up the topic of race, automation, and machine intelligence with the episode "Racial Sensitivity." Set in the R&D lab of a large conglomerate, in this episode motion sensors are installed for overhead lighting, elevator buttons, water fountains, and automated doors to reduce costs. However, the new sensors cannot sense black employees' motions or "see black people." A senior manager states that company policy is "the opposite of racist because it's not targeting black people, it's just ignoring them. They insist that the worst people can call it is indifferent." Rather than replacing all of the new sensors, the company opts to install a "manual drinking fountain (for blacks)" next to the automated one, and provides every black employee with a "free white guy" who can then use his whiteness to make the sensors work for the black employee.

6. National Research Council, *Biometric Recognition*, 85.

7. Jill Mayer, "Makeup Tutorial HOW TO HIDE FROM CAMERAS," YouTube, May 30, 2013, http://youtu.be/kGGnnp43uNM.

8. James Risen, "Snowden Says He Took No Secret Files to Russia," *New York Times*, October 17, 2013, http://www.nytimes.com/2013/10/18/world/snowden-says-he-took-no-secret-files-to-russia.html?hp&_r=0.

BIBLIOGRAPHY

Archives and Government Documents

Book of Negroes or Headquarters Papers of the British Army in America 1783. UK National Archives PRO 30/55/100.

Carleton, Sir Guy, 1st Baron Dorchester. Papers, 1783. UK National Archives PRO 30/55.

Carson, Ann E., and William J. Sabol. "Prisoners in 2011." Washington, DC: U.S. Department of Justice, Office of Justice Programs, Bureau of Statistics, December 2012. Accessed February 2, 2013, http://www.bjs.gov/index.cfm?ty=pbdetail&iid=4559.

City of New York. *Minutes of the Common Council of the City of New York, 1675–1776*, volume 3 (February 1, 1712–November 8, 1729). New York: Dodd, Mead, 1905.

———. *Minutes of the Common Council of the City of New York, 1675–1776*, volume 4 (January 24, 1730–September 19, 1740). New York: Dodd, Mead, 1905.

Description of a Slave Ship. Printed by James Phillips, George Yard, Lombard Street, 1789. Object ID: 2026563. Beinecke Rare Book and Manuscript Library, Yale University.

Kent, Richard J., Jr. *Safe, Separated, and Soaring: A History of Federal Civil Aviation Policy 1961–1972*. Washington, DC: U.S. Department of Transportation, Federal Aviation Administration, 1980.

Library of Congress, Federal Research Division. "Sociology and Psychology of Terrorism: Who Becomes a Terrorist and Why?" CIA Report. 1999.

National Commission on Terrorist Attacks upon the United States. *The 9/11 Commission Report: The Final Report of the National Commission on Terrorist Attacks upon the United States*, authorized ed. New York: W. W. Norton, 2004.

National Research Council. *Biometric Recognition: Challenges and Opportunities*. Washington, DC: National Academies Press, 2010.

Politan, Nicholas H. District Judge Letter of Opinion and Order. *Bradley v. United States*, New Jersey District Court, 164 F. Supp. 2d 437, September 10, 2001.

Preston, Edmund. *Troubled Passage: The Federal Aviation Administration during the Nixon-Ford Term, 1973–1977*. Washington, DC: U.S. Department of Transportation, Federal Aviation Administration, 1987.

Provisional Articles to Treaty, 1782. George Washington Papers, 1741–1799, Series 4, General Correspondence, 1697–1799, United States and Great Britain. Washington, DC: Library of Congress.

Standing Committee on Citizenship and Immigration. *Building a Nation: The Regulations under the Immigration and Refugee Protection Act.* Canada, 2002. Accessed October 20, 2003, http://www.parl.gc.ca/InfoComDoc/37/1/CIMM/Studies/Reports/cimmrp04/13-chap5-e.html.

Tait, Charles William. Papers, 1844–1854. Box 2G451, Folder: Plantation Rules, undated. Dolph Briscoe Center for American History, University of Texas at Austin.

Thistlewood, Thomas. Papers. OBS MSS 176. James Marshall and Marie-Louise Osborn Collection, Beinecke Rare Book and Manuscript Library, Yale University.

Treaty of Paris, 1783. International Treaties and Related Records, 1778–1974. General Records of the United States Government, Record Group 11, National Archives, Washington, DC.

"TSA 2004 Organizational Assessment Survey." Accessed through a FOIA request by the Project on Government Oversight. http://pogo.org/m/hsp/hsp-tsa-screeners-2004.pdf (accessed through Wayback Machine Internet Archive).

"20818 Human Provenance Pilot Project." Gov.UK, May 3, 2012. https://www.gov.uk/government/publications/20818-human-provenance-pilot-project.

U.S. Customs Services. "Better Targeting of Airline Passengers for Personal Searches Could Produce Better Results." Washington, DC: Government Accountability Office, 2000. http://www.gao.gov/products/GGD-00-38.

Walke, Thomas. "Thomas Walke's Account of Capturing His Runaway Slaves in New York City." May 5, 1783. Record Group 360: Records of the Continental and Confederation and the Constitutional Convention, 1765–1821. Series: Papers of the Continental Congress, 1774–1789. File Unit: Letters Addressed to Congress, 1775–1784. National Archives Identifier: 2441090. National Archives Online Public Access. Accessed May 7, 2013, http://research.archives.gov/description/2441090.

Woodfield, Kandy, et al. 2007. "Exploring the Decision Making of Immigration Officers: A Research Study Examining Non-EEA Passenger Stops and Refusals at UK Ports." Home Office Online Report, January 2007. Copy on file with author.

Work Projects Administration. *Born in Slavery: Slave Narratives from the Federal Writers' Project, 1936–1938.* Washington, DC: Manuscript and Prints and Photographs Divisions of the Library of Congress, 1941.

Books and Articles
———

Adey, Peter. "'May I Have Your Attention': Airport Geographies of Spectatorship, Position, and (Im)mobility." *Environment and Planning D: Society and Space* 25, no. 3 (2007): 515–536.

Ahmed, Sara. *Queer Phenomenology: Orientations, Objects, Others.* Durham, NC: Duke University Press, 2006.

Alexander, Elizabeth. *American Sublime: Poems.* Minneapolis: Graywolf Press, 2005.

Allsopp, Richard, and Jeanette Allsopp. *Dictionary of Caribbean English Usage*. Cave Hill, Barbados: University of the West Indies Press, 2003.

Anderson, Benedict. *Imagined Communities: Reflections on the Origin and Spread of Nationalism*. London: Verso, 1991.

Asinof, Eliot. *The Fox Is Crazy Too: The True Story of Garrett Trapnell, Adventurer, Skyjacker, Bank Robber, Con Man, Lover*. New York: William Morrow, 1976.

Atkins, John. "Voyage of John Atkins to Guinea" (1735). In *Documents Illustrative of the History of the Slave Trade to America, Volume II: The Eighteenth Century*, edited by Elizabeth Donnan. Washington, DC: Carnegie Institution of Washington, 1931.

Baldwin, James. *The Evidence of Things Not Seen*. New York: Holt, Rinehart and Winston, 1985.

Balsamo, Anne. *Designing Culture: The Technological Imagination at Work*. Durham, NC: Duke University Press, 2011.

———. *Technologies of the Gendered Body: Reading Cyborg Women*. Durham, NC: Duke University Press, 1998.

Bambara, Toni Cade. Preface to *Daughters of the Dust: The Making of an African American Woman's Film*, by Julie Dash. New York: New Press, 1992.

(Bambara) Toni Cade. "On the Issue of Roles." In *The Black Woman: An Anthology*, edited by Toni Cade. New York: New American Library, 1970.

Barbot, John. "John Barbot's Description of Guinea" (1732). In *Documents Illustrative of the History of the Slave Trade to America, Volume I: 1441–1700*, edited by Elizabeth Donnan, 282–301. Washington, DC: Carnegie Institution of Washington, 1930.

Beauvoir, Simone de. *The Force of Circumstance*. Translated by Richard Howard. New York: G. P. Putnam's Sons, 1992.

Bennett, Colin J. "Unsafe at Any Altitude: The Comparative Politics of No-Fly Lists in the United States and Canada." In *Politics at the Airport*, edited by Mark B. Salter. Minneapolis: University of Minnesota Press, 2008.

———. "What Happens When You Book an Airline Ticket? The Collection and Processing of Passenger Data Post-9/11." In *Global Surveillance and Policing*, edited by Elia Zureik and Mark B. Salter. Portland: Willan, 2005.

Bentham, Jeremy. *The Works of Jeremy Bentham*, volume 1. Published under the Superintendence of his Executor, John Bowring. Edinburgh: William Tait, 1843.

———. *The Works of Jeremy Bentham*, volume 2. Published under the Superintendence of his Executor, John Bowring. Edinburgh: William Tait, 1843.

———. *The Works of Jeremy Bentham*, volume 4. Published under the Superintendence of his Executor, John Bowring. Edinburgh: William Tait, 1843.

Best, Stephen, and Saidiya Hartman. "Fugitive Justice: The Appeal of the Slave." *Representations* 92 (2005): 1–15.

Bhabha, Homi. "Foreword: Framing Fanon." In *The Wretched of the Earth*. New York: Grove Press, 2005.

Bigo, Didier. "Globalized (In)Security: The Field and the Ban-opticon." In *Traces 4: Translation, Biopolitics*, edited by Naoki Sakai and Jon Solomon. Hong Kong: Hong Kong University Press, 2006.

———. "Security and Immigration: Toward a Critique of the Governmentality of Unease." *Alternatives: Global, Local, Political* 27, no. 1 (2002): 63–92.

Bingham, Sallie. *Passion and Prejudice: A Family Memoir.* New York: Applause, 1991.

Böhlen, Marc. "The Open Biometrics Initiative." Real Tech Support, 2002. http://www.realtechsupport.org/pdf/OpenBiometrics.pdf.

Boyne, Roy. "Post-Panopticism." *Economy and Society* 29, no. 2 (2000): 285–307.

Brand, Dionne. *A Map to the Door of No Return: Notes to Belonging.* Toronto: Vintage Canada, 2002.

Browne, Simone. "Digital Epidermalization: Race, Identity and Biometrics." *Critical Sociology* 36, no. 1 (2010): 131–150.

Burrows, Edwin G., and Mike Wallace. *A History of New York City to 1898.* New York: Oxford University Press, 1999.

Butler, Judith. "Endangered/Endangering: Schematic Racism and White Paranoia." In *Reading Rodney King/Reading Urban Uprising,* edited by Robert Gooding-Williams, 15–22. New York: Routledge, 1993.

Canot, Theodore. *Memoirs of a Slave-Trader.* London: George Newnes, 1854.

Carby, Hazel V. "Becoming Modern Racialized Subjects: Detours through Our Past to Produce Ourselves Anew." *Cultural Studies* 23, no. 4 (2009): 624–657.

Catanese, Brandi. "'How Do I Rent a Negro?' Racialized Subjectivity and Digital Performance Art." *Theatre Journal* 57, no. 4 (2005): 699–714.

Césaire, Aimé. *Discourse on Colonialism.* Translated by Joan Pinkham. 1955. Reprint, New York: Monthly Review Press, 1972.

Cherki, Alice. *Frantz Fanon: A Portrait.* Ithaca, NY: Cornell University Press, 2006.

Christie, Ian R., ed. *The Correspondence of Jeremy Bentham: Volume 3, January 1781 to October 1788.* London: Athlone, 1971.

Clarkson, Thomas. *The Argument That the Colonial Slaves Are Better Off Than the British Peasantry.* Printed for the Whitby Anti-Slavery Society by R. Kirby, 1824. Internet Archive, accessed April 20, 2013, http://archive.org/details/oates71082042.

———. *The History of the Rise, Progress, and Accomplishment of the Abolition of the African Slave-Trade by the British Parliament,* volume 2. New York: Longman, Hurst, Rees, and Orme, 1808.

———. *The Substance of the Evidence of Sundry Persons: Collected in the Course of a Tour Made in the Autumn of the Year 1783.* London: Printed by James Phillips, George Yard, Lombard Street, 1789.

Cole, Ernest. *House of Bondage.* New York: Random House, 1967.

Cole, Simon. "Brandon Mayfield, Suspect." In *Suspect,* edited by John Knechtel, 170–185. Cambridge, MA: MIT Press, 2006.

Collins, Patricia Hill. *Black Feminist Thought: Knowledge, Consciousness and the Politics of Empowerment,* 2nd ed. London: Routledge, 2000.

———. *Black Sexual Politics: African Americans, Gender and the New Racism.* New York and London: Routledge, 2004.

———. *Fighting Words: Black Women and the Search for Justice.* Minneapolis: University of Minnesota Press, 1998.

Cooper, Afua. *The Hanging of Angelique: The Untold Story of Canadian Slavery and the Burning of Old Montréal.* Athens: University of Georgia Press, 2007.

Craft, William. *Running a Thousand Miles for Freedom; or, the Escape of William and Ellen Craft from Slavery.* London: William Tweedie, 1860. Electronic ed., Documenting the American South, http://docsouth.unc.edu/neh/craft/craft.html.

Davis, Angela Y., and Eduardo Mendieta. *Abolition Democracy: Beyond Empire, Prisons and Torture.* New York: Seven Stories Press, 2005.

Davis, Thomas J. *A Rumor of Revolt: The "Great Negro Plot" in Colonial New York.* New York: Free Press, 1985.

De Voe, Thomas F. *The Market Book.* New York: Burt Franklin, 1862.

Doolen, Andy. *Fugitive Empire: Locating Early American Imperialism.* Minneapolis: University of Minnesota Press, 2005.

Douglass, Frederick. *Narrative of the Life of Frederick Douglass, an American Slave, Written by Himself* (1845). Lanham, MD: Start, 2012.

DuBois, William E. B. "The Home of the Slave." In *Cabin, Quarter, Plantation: Architecture and Landscapes of North American Slavery,* edited by Clifton Ellis and Rebecca Ginsburg. New Haven, CT: Yale University Press, 2010.

Dyer, Richard. *White.* London: Routledge, 1997.

Ellison, Ralph. *Invisible Man.* New York: Vintage, 1989.

Fanon, Frantz. *Black Skin, White Masks.* Translated by Charles Lam Markmann. New York: Grove Press, 1967.

———. *Black Skin, White Masks.* Translated by Richard Philcox. New York: Grove Press, 2008.

———. *Rencontre de la société et de la Psychiatrie: Notes de cours, Tunis 1959–60.* Edited by Lilia Bensalem. Tunis: CRIDSSH-Université d'Oran, 1984.

———. *The Wretched of the Earth.* Translated by Constance Farrington. New York: Grove Press, 1963.

Feagin, Joe. *The White Racial Frame: Centuries of Racial Framing and Counter-Framing.* New York: Routledge, 2010.

———. *The White Racial Frame: Centuries of Racial Framing and Counter-Framing,* 2nd ed. New York: Routledge, 2013.

Ferguson, Roderick. *Aberrations in Black: Toward a Queer of Color Critique.* Minneapolis: University of Minnesota Press, 2004.

Fiske, John. "Surveilling the City: Whiteness, the Black Man and Democratic Totalitarianism." *Theory, Culture and Society* 15, no. 2 (1998): 67–88.

Foote, Thelma W. *Black and White Manhattan: The History of Racial Formation in Colonial New York City.* New York: Oxford University Press, 2004.

Foucault, Michel. *Archaeology of Knowledge and the Discourse on Language.* Translated by A. M. Sheridan Smith. New York: Pantheon, 1972.

———. *Discipline and Punish: The Birth of the Prison.* New York: Vintage, 1979.

———. *Psychiatric Power: Lectures at the Collège de France, 1973–1974.* New York: Picador, 2003.

———. *Security, Territory, Population: Lectures at the Collège de France, 1977–78.* New York: Palgrave Macmillan, 2007.

Foucault, Michel, Catherine Bülow, and Daniel Defert. "The Masked Assassination." In *Warfare in the American Homeland: Policing and Prison in a Penal Democracy*, edited by Joy James, 140–158. Durham, NC: Duke University Press, 2007.

Franklin, Ursula. *The Real World of Technology*. CBC Massey Lectures. Toronto: House of Anansi Press, 1999.

French, Martin A., and Simone A. Browne. "Surveillance as Social Regulation: Profiles and Profiling Technology." In *Criminalization, Representation, Regulation*, edited by Deborah Brock, Amanda Glasbeek, and Carmela Murdocca, 251–284. Toronto: University of Toronto Press, 2014.

Fuller, Gillian. "The Arrow—Directional Semiotics: Wayfinding in Transit." *Social Semiotics* 12, no. 3 (2002): 231–244.

Fusco, Coco. "All Too Real: The Tale of an On-Line Black Sale: Coco Fusco Interviews Keith Townsend Obadike." September 24, 2001. Accessed April 20, 2013, http://black netart.com/coco.html.

Galloway, Alexander. *Protocol: How Control Exists after Decentralization*. Cambridge, MA: MIT Press, 2004.

Gandy, Oscar H. *The Panoptic Sort: A Political Economy of Personal Information*. Boulder, CO: Westview, 1993.

Gao, Wei, and Haizhou Ai. "Face Gender Classification on Consumer Images in a Multiethnic Environment." In *Advances in Biometrics: Third International Conference on Biometrics*, edited by Massimo Tistarelli and Mark S. Nixon, 169–178. Berlin: Springer-Verlag Berlin Heidelberg, 2009.

Geismar, Peter. *Fanon*. New York: Dial, 1971.

Gendzier, Irene L. *Frantz Fanon: A Critical Study*. New York: Vintage, 1974.

Gilliom, John, and Torin Monahan. *Supervision: An Introduction to the Surveillance Society*. Chicago: University of Chicago Press, 2013.

Gilmore, Ruth Wilson. *Golden Gulag: Prisons, Surplus, Crisis, and Opposition in Globalizing California*. Berkeley: University of California Press, 2006.

Gilroy, Paul. *Against Race: Imagining Political Culture beyond the Color Line*. Cambridge, MA: Harvard University Press, 2001.

———. *The Black Atlantic: Modernity and Double Consciousness*. Cambridge, MA: Harvard University Press, 1993.

———. "Scales and Eyes: 'Race' Making Difference." In *Eight Technologies of Otherness*, edited by Sue Golding, 190–196. London: Routledge, 1997.

Glaser, Clive. *Bo-Tsotsi: The Youth Gangs of Soweto, 1935–1976*. Portsmouth, NH: Heinemann, 2000.

Goldberg, David T. *The Racial State*. Malden, MA: Blackwell, 2002.

———. *The Threat of Race: Reflections on Racial Neoliberalism*. Malden, MA: Wiley-Blackwell, 2009.

Gordon, Avery. *Ghostly Matters: Haunting and the Sociological Imagination*, 2nd ed. Minneapolis: University of Minnesota Press, 2008.

Gordon, Lewis. "Is the Human a Teleological Suspension of Man? Phenomenological Exploration of Sylvia Wynter's Fanonian and Biodicean Reflections." In *After Man,*

Towards the Human: Critical Essays on the Thought of Sylvia Wynter, edited by Anthony Bogues. Kingston, Jamaica: Ian Randle, 2006.

Gould, Stephen J. *The Mismeasure of Man.* New York: Norton, 1981.

Gray, Herman. *Cultural Moves: African Americans and the Politics of Representation.* Los Angeles: University of California Press, 2005.

Haggerty, Kevin D. "Tear Down the Walls: On Demolishing the Panopticon." In *Theorizing Surveillance: The Panopticon and Beyond*, edited by David Lyon, 23–45. Portland, OR: Willan, 2006.

Haggerty, Kevin D., and Richard V. Ericson. "The Surveillant Assemblage." *British Journal of Sociology* 51, no. 4 (2000): 605–622.

Hall, Rachel. "Missing Dolly, Mourning Slavery: The Slave Notice as Keepsake." *Camera Obscura: Feminism, Culture and Media Studies* 21, no. 1 (2006): 71–103.

Hall, Stuart. "The After-Life of Frantz Fanon: Why Fanon? Why Now? Why *Black Skin, White Masks*?" In *The Fact of Blackness: Frantz Fanon and Visual Representation*, edited by Alan Read, 12–37. London: Institute of Contemporary Arts, 1996.

———. "Cultural Identity and Diaspora." In *Identity: Community, Culture, Difference*, edited by Jonathan Rutherford, 222–237. London: Lawrence and Wishart, 1990.

———. "Introduction: Who Needs Identity?" In *Questions of Cultural Identity*, edited by Stuart Hall and Paul Du Gay, 1–17. London: Sage, 1996.

Hamilton, Alexander. *Gentleman's Progress: The Itinerarium of Dr. Alexander Hamilton 1744.* Published for the Institute of Early American History and Culture at Williamsburg, Virginia. Chapel Hill: University of North Carolina Press, 1948.

Hammonds, Evelyn. "Black (W)holes and the Geometry of Black Female Sexuality." *differences* 6, no. 2–3 (1994): 126–145.

Haraway, Donna. *Simians, Cyborgs and Women: The Reinvention of Nature.* New York: Routledge, 1990.

Harris, Leslie M. *In the Shadow of Slavery: African Americans in New York City, 1626–1863.* Chicago: University of Chicago Press, 2003.

Hartman, Saidiya. *Lose Your Mother: A Journey along the Atlantic Slave Route.* New York: Farrar, Straus and Giroux, 2007.

———. *Scenes of Subjection: Terror, Slavery and Self-Making in Nineteenth-Century America.* Oxford: Oxford University Press, 1997.

———. "Venus in Two Acts." *Small Axe* 26 (2008): 1–14.

Hier, Sean, and Joshua Greenberg. *The Surveillance Studies Reader.* Berkshire, UK: Open University Press, 2007.

Hill, Lawrence. *The Book of Negroes: A Novel.* Toronto: HarperCollins, 2007.

———. *Dear Sir, I Intend to Burn Your Book.* Edmonton: University of Alberta Press, 2013.

Hodges, Graham R. *The Black Loyalist Directory.* New York: Garland, 1996.

———. *Root and Branch: African Americans in New York and East Jersey, 1613–1863.* Chapel Hill: University of North Carolina Press, 1999.

Hodges, Graham R., and Alan E. Brown, eds. *Pretends to Be Free: Runaway Slave Advertisements from Colonial and Revolutionary New York and New Jersey.* New York: Garland, 1994.

hooks, bell. *Black Looks: Race and Representation*. Boston: South End Press, 1992.

———. *Killing Rage: Ending Racism*. New York: Henry Holt, 1995.

———. *Talking Back: Thinking Feminist, Thinking Black*. Boston: South End Press, 1989.

Iton, Richard. *In Search of the Black Fantastic: Politics and Popular Culture in the Post–Civil Rights Era*. New York: Oxford University Press, 2009.

Jackson, George. *Soledad Brother: The Prison Letters of George Jackson*. New York: Lawrence Hill, 1994.

Jacobs, Harriet A. *Incidents in the Life of a Slave Girl. Written by Herself*. Boston: Published for the author, 1861.

James, Cyril Lionel R. *The Black Jacobins: Toussaint L'Ouverture and the San Domingo Revolution*, 2nd ed. rev. New York: Vintage, 1989.

Kelley, Robin D. G. *Race Rebels: Culture, Politics, and the Black Working Class*. New York: Free Press, 1994.

King, Boston. "Memoirs of the Life of Boston King, a Black Preacher." *Methodist Magazine*, March–June 1798.

Lao, Shihong, and Masuto Kawade. "Vision-Based Face Understanding Technologies and Their Applications." In *Advances in Biometric Person Authentication*, edited by Stan Z. Li, Jianhuang Lai, Tieniu Tan, Guocan Feng, and Yunhong Wang, 339–348. Berlin: Springer, 2004.

Lepore, Jill. *New York Burning: Liberty, Slavery, and Conspiracy in Eighteenth-Century Manhattan*. New York: Vintage, 2005.

Lévesque, Maroussia, and Jason Edward Lewis. "What Else Do We Lose When We Make People Disappear? The Passage Oublié Project." *Wi: Journal of Mobile Media* 1, no. 1 (2008).

Li, Huaming, Mingquan Zhou, and Guohua Geng. "Facial Pose Estimation Based on the Mongolian Race's Feature Characteristic from a Monocular Image." In *Advances in Biometric Person Authentication*, edited by Stan Z. Li, Jianhuang Lai, Tieniu Tan, Guocan Feng, and Yunhong Wang, 172–178. Berlin: Springer, 2004.

Light, Andrew. "Enemies of the State? Electronic Surveillance and the Neutrality of Technology." In *Reel Argument: Film, Philosophy, and Social Criticism*. Boulder, CO: Westview Press, 2002.

Long, Edward. *The History of Jamaica or, General Survey of the Ancient and Modern State with Reflections on its situation, settlements inhabitants, Climate, Products, Commerce, Laws, and Government*. London: Printed for Lowndes, in Fleet Street, 1774.

Lott, Eric. *Love and Theft: Blackface Minstrelsy and the American Working Class*. New York: Oxford University Press, 1993.

Lyon, David. *The Electronic Eye: The Rise of Surveillance Society*. Minneapolis: University of Minnesota Press, 1994.

———. *Identifying Citizens: ID Cards as Surveillance*. London: Polity Press, 2010.

———. "The Search for Surveillance Theories." In *Theorizing Surveillance: The Panopticon and Beyond*, edited by David Lyon, 3–20. Portland, OR: Willan, 2006.

———. *Surveillance after September 11*. Cambridge, MA: Polity Press, 2003.

————. "Surveillance, Security and Social Sorting: Emerging Research Priorities." *International Criminal Justice Review* 17, no. 3 (2007): 161–170.

————. *Surveillance Society: Monitoring Everyday Life*. Buckingham: Open University Press, 2001.

————. *Surveillance Studies: An Overview*. Malden, MA: Polity Press, 2007.

————. "Technology vs. 'Terrorism': Circuits of City Surveillance since September 11th." *International Journal of Urban and Regional Research* 27, no. 3 (2003), 666–678.

————. "Under My Skin: From Identification Papers to Body Surveillance." In *Documenting Individual Identity: The Development of State Practices in the Modern World*, edited by Jane Caplan and John Torpey, 291–310. Princeton, NJ: Princeton University Press, 2001.

Mabee, Carleton. *Soujourner Truth: Slave, Prophet, Legend*. New York: New York University Press, 1995.

Macey, David. *Frantz Fanon: A Life*. London: Granta, 2000.

Magnet, Shoshana, and Tara Rodgers. "Stripping for the State." *Feminist Media Studies* 12, no. 1 (2012): 101–118.

Manchanda, Catharina. *Catch Air: Robin Rhode*. Wexler Center for the Arts. Columbus: Ohio State University, 2009.

Mann, Steve. "Veillance and Reciprocal Transparency: Surveillance versus Souveillance, AR Glass, Lifelogging and Wearable Computing." In *2013 IEEE International Symposium on Technology and Society (ISTAS)*, June 27–29, 2013, 1–12.

Mann, Steve, Jason Nolan, and Barry Wellman. "Sousveillance: Inventing and Using Wearable Computing Devices for Data Collection in Surveillance Environments." *Surveillance and Society* 1, no. 3 (2003): 331–355.

Marriot, David. *On Black Men*. New York: Columbia University Press, 2000.

Marx, Gary T. "Surveillance and Society." *Encyclopedia of Social Theory*, 2005. Accessed January 20, 2014, http://web.mit.edu/gtmarx/www/surandsoc.html.

————. *Undercover: Police Surveillance in America*. Berkeley: University of California Press, 1998.

Mathiesen, Thomas. "The Viewer Society: Michel Foucault's Panopticon Revisited." *Theoretical Criminology* 1, no. 2 (1997): 215–234.

McAllister, Marvin. *White People Do Not Know How to Behave at Entertainments Designed for Ladies and Gentlemen of Colour: William Brown's African and American Theatre*. Chapel Hill: University of North Carolina Press, 2003.

McClintock, Ann. *Imperial Leather: Race, Gender and Sexuality in the Colonial Contest*. New York: Routledge, 1995.

McKittrick, Katherine. *Demonic Grounds: Black Women and the Cartographies of Struggle*. Minneapolis: University of Minnesota Press, 2006.

————. "Math Whips." Paper delivered at the Archive and Everyday Life Conference, McMaster University, Hamilton, Ontario, May 8, 2010.

————. "'Their Blood Is There, and They Can't Throw It Out': Honoring Black Canadian Geographies." *TOPIA: Canadian Journal of Cultural Studies* no. 7 (spring 2002): 27–37.

Mercer, Kobena. *Welcome to the Jungle: New Positions in Black Cultural Studies*. New York: Routledge, 1994.

Mirzoeff, Nicholas. *The Right to Look: A Counterhistory of Visuality*. Durham, NC: Duke University Press, 2011.

———. *"We Are All Children of Algeria": Visuality and Countervisuality, 1954–2011*. Durham, NC: Duke University Press, 2011. http://scalar.usc.edu/nehvectors/mirzoeff /index.

Monahan, Torin. *Surveillance in the Time of Insecurity*. New Brunswick, NJ: Rutgers University Press, 2010.

Mongia, Radhika V. "Race, Nationality, Mobility: A History of the Passport." *Public Culture* 11, no. 3 (1999): 527–556.

Morrison, Toni. *Beloved*. New York: Vintage, 2007.

Muller, Benjamin J. "Travelers, Borders, Dangers: Locating the Political at the Biometric Border." In *Politics at the Airport*, edited by Mark B. Salter, 127–143. Minneapolis: University of Minnesota Press, 2008.

(Murakami) Wood, David. "Foucault and the Panopticon Revisited. *Surveillance and Society* 1, no. 3 (2003): 234–239.

Nakamura, Lisa. *Digitizing Race: Visual Cultures of the Internet*. Minneapolis: University of Minnesota Press, 2008.

———. "Economies of Digital Production in East Asia: iPhone Girls and the Transnational Circuits of Cool." *Media Fields: Critical Explorations in Media and Space*, no. 7 (2011): 1–12.

Nanavati, Samir, Michael Thieme, and Raj Nanavati. *Biometrics: Identity Verification in a Networked World*. New York: Wiley, 2002.

Omi, Michael, and Howard Winant. *Racial Formation in the United States: From the 1960s to the 1990s*, 2nd ed. New York: Routledge, 1994.

Pager, Devah. "The Mark of a Criminal Record." *American Journal of Sociology* 108, no. 5 (2003): 937–975.

Parenti, Christian. *The Soft Cage: Surveillance in America from Slave Passes to the War on Terror*. New York: Basic Books, 2003.

Park, Robert E. "The Conflict and Fusion of Cultures with Special Reference to the Negro." *Journal of Negro History* 4, no. 2 (1919): 111–133.

Parks, Lisa. "Points of Departure: The Culture of US Airport Screening." *Journal of Visual Culture* 6, no. 2 (2007): 183–200.

Patterson, Orlando. *Rituals of Blood: Consequences of Slavery in Two American Centuries*. New York: Civitas, 1998.

———. *Slavery and Social Death: A Comparative Study*. Cambridge, MA: Harvard University Press, 1985.

Philip, M. NourbeSe. *Zong!* Middletown, CT: Wesleyan University Press, 2011.

Phillips, Caryl. *Crossing the River*. London: Bloomsbury, 1993.

———. "The Cargo Rap." In *Higher Ground: A Novel in Three Parts*. London: Viking, 1989.

Platt, Smith H. *The Martyrs, and the Fugitive; Or a Narrative of the Captivity, Sufferings, and Death of an African Family, and the Slavery and Escape of Their Son*. New York: Daniel Fanshaw, 1859.

Plymouth Committee of the Society for Effecting the Abolition of the Slave Trade. *Plan of an African Ship's lower Deck with Negroes stowed in the Proportion of only One to a Ton.* Plymouth, England, 1789.

Postma, Johannes. *The Dutch in the Atlantic Slave Trade, 1600–1815.* Cambridge: Cambridge University Press, 1990.

Pugliese, Joseph. "*In Silico* Race and the Heteronomy of Biometric Proxies: Biometrics in the Context of Civilian Life, Border Security and Counter-Terrorism Laws." *Australian Feminist Law Journal* 23 (2005): 1–32.

Pybus, Cassandra. *Epic Journeys of Freedom: Runaway Slaves of the American Revolution and Their Global Quest for Liberty.* Boston: Beacon, 2006.

Rediker, Marcus. *The Slave Ship: A Human History.* New York: Viking, 2007.

Rhodes, Lorna A. "Panoptical Intimacies." *Public Culture* 10, no. 2 (1998): 285–311.

Rule, James P. *Private Lives and Public Surveillance.* London: Allen Lane, 1973.

Salter, Mark. "Governmentalities of an Airport: Heterotopias and Confession." *International Political Sociology* 1, no. 1 (2007): 49–66.

———. *Rights of Passage: The Passport in International Relations.* Boulder, CO: Lynne Rienner, 2003.

Schama, Simon. *Rough Crossings: The Slaves, the British, and the American Revolution.* New York: HarperCollins, 2007.

Sennett, Richard. *Flesh and Stone: The Body and the City in Western Civilization.* New York: Norton, 1994.

Sheller, Mimi. *Citizenship from Below: Erotic Agency and Caribbean Freedom.* Durham, NC: Duke University Press, 2012.

Shepherd, Reginald. *Some Are Drowning.* Pittsburgh: University of Pittsburgh Press, 1994.

Spillers, Hortense. 1987. "Mama's Baby, Papa's Maybe: An American Grammar Book." *Diacritics* 17, no. 2 (1987): 64–81.

Staples, William E. *Everyday Surveillance: Vigilance and Visibility in Postmodern Life,* 2nd ed. Lanham, MD: Rowman and Littlefield, 2014.

Thacker, Eugene. *The Global Genome: Biotechnology, Politics and Culture.* Boston: MIT Press, 2005.

Thomas, Greg. "Proud Flesh Inter/Views: Sylvia Wynter." *Proudflesh: A New Afrikan Journal of Culture, Politics and Consciousness,* no. 4 (2006). http://www.africaknowledge project.org/index.php/proudflesh/article/view/202.

Thomas, Hank Willis. *Pitch Blackness.* New York: Aperture, 2008.

Tinsley, Omise'eke Natasha. "Queer Atlantic, Black Atlantic: Queer Imaginings of the Middle Passage." *GLQ* 14, no. 2–3 (2008): 191–215.

Turner, Patricia A. *Ceramic Uncles and Celluloid Mammies: Black Images and Their Influence on Culture.* Charlottesville: University of Virginia Press, 1994.

Wacquant, Loïc. *Punishing the Poor: The Neoliberal Government of Social Insecurity.* Durham, NC: Duke University Press, 2009.

Walcott, Rinaldo. *Black Like Who? Writing Black Canada,* 2nd rev. ed. Toronto: Insomniac Press, 2003.

Wallace, Maurice O. *Constructing the Black Masculine: Identity and Ideality in African American Men's Literature and Culture, 1775–1995*. Durham, NC: Duke University Press, 2002.

Walvin, James. *Black Ivory: Slavery in the British Empire*. Hoboken, NJ: Wiley-Blackwell, 2001.

White, Shane. "Pinkster: Afro-Dutch Syncretization in New York City and the Hudson Valley." *Journal of American Folklore* 102, no. 403 (1989): 68–75.

Wiegman, Robyn. *American Anatomies: Theorizing Race and Gender*. Durham, NC: Duke University Press, 1995.

Williams, Sherley Ann. *Dessa Rose*. New York: HarperCollins, 1999.

Winant, Howard. "The Dark Matter." *Racial and Ethnic Studies* 35, no. 4 (2012): 600–607.

———. *The New Politics of Race: Globalism, Difference, Justice*. Minneapolis: University of Minnesota Press, 2004.

Wood, Marcus. *Blind Memory: Visual Representations of Slavery in England and North America, 1780–1865*. New York: Routledge, 2000.

Wynter, Sylvia. "The Ceremony Found: Black Knowledges/Struggles, the Color Line, and the Third Emancipatory Breaching of the Law of Cognitive Closure." Keynote lecture delivered at the Eighth International Conference of the Collegium for African-American Research, Bremen, Germany, March 28, 2009.

———. "Jonkonnu in Jamaica: Towards the Interpretation of Folk Dance as a Cultural Process." *Jamaica Journal* 4, no. 2 (1970): 34–48.

———. "Towards the Sociogenic Principle: Fanon, the Puzzle of Conscious Experience of 'Identity' and What It's Like to Be 'Black.'" In *National Identities and Sociopolitical Changes in Latin America*, edited by Antonio Gomez-Moriana and Mercedes Duran-Cogan, 30–66. New York: Routledge, 2001.

Young, Robert. *Colonial Desire: Hybridity in Theory, Culture, and Race*. London: Routledge, 1995.

INDEX

Abdulmutallab, Umar, 137
Aberrations in Black (Ferguson), 10
abolitionists, 21, 91–93, 99. *See also* slavery
Absolut No Return (Thomas), 125
Absolut Power (Thomas), 125
Absolut Vodka, 124–25
Abu-Jamal, Mumia, 3
ACLU (American Civil Liberties Union),
    133–34, 188n76
Adey, Peter, 145
Adiele, Laura, 138, 156
African Americans. *See* blacks
After Earth (film), 122
Ahmed, Sara, 143
airline English, 137–38, 145
airports: black women and, 135–36, 140–45,
    147–52; no-joking protocol and, 145–46;
    passenger screening zones and, 69, 136–46;
    security theater and, 27–29, 39, 131–36,
    145–59, 184n15; trusted traveler programs
    and, 39, 135–36, 152–56. See also *South Park*
    (TV show); TSA (Transportation Security
    Administration)
Alexander, Elizabeth, 172n92
Algeria, 2, 5
Ali, Muhammad, 44
alienation, 6, 105
"All Falls Down" (West), 188n76
American Beacon and Commercial Diary,
    177n59
American Express, 124
American Museum, 50
American Revolution, 7, 25, 66–69, 71, 87
American Sociological Society, 11, 166n25
Angélique, Marie-Joseph, 36–38

Ann (ship), 85
anthropometry, 111–12, *112*. *See also* biometric
    technology; facial recognition
antiblack racism and, 5, 9–11, 21, 61, 95, 105,
    110, 143. *See also* blacks; race; racism
Anti-hijacking or Air Transportation Security
    Act (1974), 28
antisurveillance, 21–22, 163–64
Arar, Maher, 135–36
Archaeology of Knowledge (Foucault), 181n97
Archer, Dinah, 86
Art in Airports (Roth), 134, *155*, 155–56
Asians, 111–13, 162
Assogba, Yannick, 157–59
Atkins, John, 93
auctionism, 104–8
Aviation and Transportation Security Act,
    147

"Babylon System" (Marley), 50
backchat, 72, 99, 179n32
backscatter units, 146, 159, 186n56
Bad Boys (film), 122
"Bad Boys" (Inner Circle), 174n6
Baggage Allowance (Pamela Z), 8, 134, 152–56,
    159
"Bag X-Ray" (Pamela Z), 154
Baines, John, 86
Baker, Josephine, 3
Baldwin, James, 2, 10, 166n25, 173n124
Balsamo, Anne, 114, 121
Bambara, Toni Cade, 6, 10, 165n9
Banks, Nathaniel P., 91
banopticon, 38–39

performances: black expressive practices and, 80–83; commodity racism and, 97–98; freedom practices and, 21, 54–55, 64–69, 74–77, 84–88, 91–93, 137, 156–59, 162; gestural computing and, 152–56; pedagogy and, 134–45, 157–59; punishment and, 35–37, 51–52, 68, 97–102, 118; security theater and, 2, 27, 51–52, 131–36, 145–59

Persuasive Games, 136–37

Phenix (ship), 100

Philadelphia Enquirer, 89

Philipsburg Proclamation, 71, 176n20

Phillips, Caryl, 8, 43–45, 67, 172n92

phrenology, 95, 112

Pinkster, 81

Piper, Adrian, 8, 33, 57–62, 164

Planespotters.net, 158

Plan of an African Ship's lower Deck with Negroes stowed in the Proportion of only One to a Ton (Plymouth Committee), 47

plantations, 12, 21–26, 32, 42–45, 50–55, 82, 90–91, 95–102

Platt, Smith H., 96–97

Plymouth Committee of the Society for Effecting the Abolition of the Slave Trade, 47

policing, 13, 39, 122

Politan, Nicholas H., 134

popular biometric consciousness, 27, 121

postpanopticism, 32, 38–42, 168n167

premature death, 43–44, 50, 97, 124, 182n115

Priceless #1 (Thomas), 123–25, 125

Principles of Penal Law (Bentham), 169n4

print (technology), 11, 25, 51–55, 66–76, 83–88, 175n8

prisons, 40, 43. *See also* panopticon

Private Lives and Public Surveillance (Rule), 14

prototypical whiteness, 26–27, 92, 110, 113–18, 122, 162, 181n86

Public Enemy, 66

Pugliese, Joseph, 113

race: biometric information and, 25–27, 39, 70–74, 89–102, 108–20, 140–45; black mobility and, 11, 21, 24–25, 62–83, 91, 136–59, 161; epidermalization and, 5–7, 16–17; gender's intersections with, 10–11, 26–29, 57–58, 94, 110–11, 128–29, 131–36, 156–59;

racial baggage and, 28–29, 131–36, 148–49; sorting and, 14–18, 26, 55–57, 77–83, 93–102, 109–18; white racial frame and, 95, 180n60

racial epidermal schema, 49

racializing surveillance, 8, 16–18, 21, 32, 42, 50–58, 68, 78, 82, 91–92, 97–102, 114, 128, 161–64

"Racial Sensitivity" (*Better Off Ted*), 189n5

racism: antiblack racism and, 5, 9–11, 21, 61, 95, 105, 110, 143; black antiracist counterframing and, 108, 180n60; commodity racism and, 97–98; facial recognition technology and, 109–12, 112, 161–64, 180n71, 181n88, 189n5; gender and, 131–36, 156–59; policing strategies and, 13; racial baggage and, 28–29, 131–36, 148–49; scientific racism and, 95–97, 111–14; sexuality and, 10–11, 50, 96–97, 101, 146–51, 171n73; surveillance's resistance and, 6–7, 9–10, 12–13, 21, 23, 31–32, 36–38, 173n124; TSA and, 131–56. *See also* airports; blacks; controlling images; epidermalization; gaze, the

Ramsey, Cato, 74, 87

Ranger (ship), 85

reality television, 38, 63–69, 174n1, 174n6

RealTechSupport, 116–18, 181n97

Reddit, 18, 167n51

redditveillance, 18

Rediker, Marcus, 42, 48, 50

Regulation Act, 48

Reveley, Willey, 33

"Reverse Cowgirl" (*South Park*), 147–52, 187n64

Rhizome, 108

Rhode, Robin, 33, 58–59

Rhodes, Lorna, 40–41

Rice, Condoleezza, 28, 168n78

Richie, Lionel, 61

Rights of Passage (Salter), 175n19

Roberts, Charles, 53–54

Robeson, Paul, 44

Rodgers, Tara, 146

Rodriguez, Dylan, 10

Rogers, Aunt Ferebe, 167n63

Roth, Evan, 134, 155, 159

Royal Gazette, 54, 72, 85, 101

Rule, James, 14

"Run, Nigger, Run" (song), 22, 167n63
runaway notices, 11, 21–23, 26, 50–57, 71–73, 82, 91–93, 100, 179n43

Salter, Mark B., 135, 175n19
San Antonio International Airport, 138
Sartre, Jean-Paul, 2
Scarred Chest (Thomas), 126
Scott, A. O., 119
Seattle-Tacoma Airport, 138
Secondary Security Screening Selection, 69
security theater, 2, 27, 51–52, 131–36, 145–59
Sennett, Richard, 68
sexuality: erotic resistance and, 50, 171n73; race and, 10–11, 96, 101, 149
Shakur, Assata, 2
Sheets, Will, 172n98
sick leave, 6
Sierrra Leone, 86
signifying, 57
sky marshals, 28
slavery: abolitionism and, 91–93, 99; Bentham and, 31–32; branding and, 42, 89–102, 118–19, 128, 162, 179n43; escape from, 5, 11, 21–22, 25–26, 36–37, 52–55, 61–76, 83–102, 171n74; freedom practices and, 21, 54–55, 64–69, 74–77, 84–88, 91–93, 137, 156–59, 162; gender and, 25, 102–3; Middle Passage and, 42, 45–50, 172n92; mobility and, 11, 22, 24–25, 68–76, 83–88; plantation rules and, 51–52; racializing surveillance and, 16–17, 26; as slow-motion death, 48, 171n74; surveillance and, 7–8, 11–13, 22, 24–26, 31–32, 42, 45–57, 66–69, 76–83. *See also* blackness; *Book of Negroes*; Coobah; Door of No Return; mobility; Thistlewood, Thomas
Slavery and Social Death (Patterson), 102
Slave Ship (Baraka), 172n92
Smith, Berry, 22, 169n4
Smith, Tommie, 45
Smith, Will, 27, 111, 119–23, 123
SNCC (Student Nonviolent Coordinating Committee), 3
Snowden, Edward, 164
Society for the Propagation of the Gospel, 100, 118
sociogeny, 7

Soledad Prison, 43
solitary confinement, 40, 43
sorting, 14, 16–18, 26, 38–42, 48–49, 55–57, 77–83, 93–102, 109–18
sousveillance, 18–19, 19, 20–21, 54, 66–68, 164. *See also* dark sousveillance
South Africa, 58–59
South Park (TV show), 134, 147–52, 187n64
Spillers, Hortense, 49, 89, 93
Staples, William, 15–16
St. Louis, Al, 64–69, 88, 174n6
stop-and-frisk tactics, 11, 39
Stowage of the British Slave Ship "Brookes" under the Regulated Slave Trade Act of 1788, 47
straightening devices, 144–45, 148
"Suitcase" (Pamela Z), 153–54
surveillance: academic disciplines and, 12–24; control and, 33–42, 57–58, 63–69, 116–19; definitions of, 5–6, 13, 16–18, 20; documents and, 11, 25, 51–55, 66–76, 83–88, 100–102, 175n8; neutrality thesis and, 121–29; policing strategies and, 13, 39; racism and racialization and, 5–10, 12–13, 16, 21, 24, 37–38, 42, 50–57, 66–83, 91–102, 128–29, 161–64; resistance methods and, 6–7, 12, 22, 23, 24, 28–29, 33, 52–55, 57–62, 64–69, 77–83, 88, 131–36; security theater and, 2, 27, 39, 51–52, 63–64, 131–36, 145–59; slavery and, 7–13, 21–26, 31–32, 42, 45–57, 66–69, 76–83; sousveillance and, 18–19, 19, 22–23; technologies of, 8–9, 14–18, 22–25, 27, 29, 32–38, 52–55, 66–83, 89–93, 108–19; War on Terror and, 12–14, 17–18, 27–28, 115, 134–37, 146–52, 157–59, 186n54
Surveillance Studies (Lyon), 24
The Surveillance Studies Reader (Hier and Greenberg), 12–13
surveillant assemblages, 16, 26
Survival (Marley), 172n92
Swoosh, 125–26
Sylvania (plantation), 51–52
synopticon, 38–39

Tait, Charles William, 51–52
talking back, 33, 36, 60–62, 72, 99, 156, 179n32
Taulbert, Violet, 85

Taylor, Charley, 103
technologies. *See* biometric technology; branding; DNA analysis; fingerprinting; lantern laws; print (technology); surveillance; *specific technologies*
Terminal Zero One (exhibit), 134, 157–59
Thacker, Eugene, 116
ThE StRaNgEst ThINg, 103
Thibault, Claude, 36
Thistlewood, Thomas, 26, 101–2
Thomas, Hank Willis, 8, 27, 92–93, 123–29, *125*
Thompson, Garfield, 64–69
Timberland, 124
Tinsley, Omise'eke Natasha, 50
torture, 78–79, 89–93, 102, 111–13, 162. *See also* branding; slavery
Totau. *See* dance
Tracey Takes On . . . , (TV show), 151–52
Trapnell, Garrett Brock, 27
travel (airline): border agents' discretionary power and, 28, 136, 143; "dangerous" markers and, 38, 138, 158; trusted traveler program and, 39, 128, 135–36, 152–56
Treaty of Paris, 71, 74, 83
trusted traveler program, 39, 128, 135–36, 152–56
Truth, Sojourner, 22
TSA (Transportation Security Administration), 27–28, 69, 131–36, 145–59, 164, 184n15, 187n60, 188n76
TSA Communication (Roth), *155*, 155–56, 159
Tubman, Harriet, 44
Tunisia, 2, 5, 165n6
Turner, Patricia A., 58
Twitter, 13, 132, 180n71
Tyner, John, 148
Types of Mankind (Nott and Gliddon), 111

UAVs, 8, 119, 128
uberveillance, 18. *See also* surveillance
Ullman, Tracey, 151–52
Underground Railroad, 22, 37, 63–66
United Kingdom, 142, 144–45
United Negro Improvement Association, 10
United States: air transportation and, 27–28, 131–36, 145–50, 184n15, 187n60, 188n76; citizenship metrics and, 114–15; Customs department of, 133–36, 184n15; international migration and, 25, 66–69; prison system of, 40–44, 67–68; surveillance by, 1–2, 55–57; War on Terror and, 12–18, 27–28, 115, 134–37, 146–52, 157–59. *See also* mobility; race; slavery
univeillance, 19–20
U.S. Immigration and Naturalization Service, 136
U.S. Secure Flight program, 68–69

veillance, 18, *19*, 21
Veillance Plane, 18, 20–21
Vick, Michael, 27, 126, 183n121
video surveillance, 6, 13, 17–18, 20, 38, 119, 149, 163
Virginia Gazette, 84
visibility, 11–15, 21, 24–25, 29, 66–68, 76–83, 91, 109–14, 122–23, 161–64
visual surplus, 76–77, 79

Wacquant, Loïc, 44
Walcott, Rinaldo, 8, 65
Walker, Jonathan, 92
Wallace, Maurice O., 20, 58, 173n124
Wallace, Michele, 9
War on Terror, 12–14, 17–18, 134–37, 146–52, 157–59, 186n54
Washington, George, 83
Washington Post-Times Herald, 1
Washington State Department of Corrections, 40
webcams, 109, 161. *See also* video surveillance
West, Kanye, 188n76
What It's Like, What It Is #3 (Piper), 8, 33, 60–62, *62*, 164
Wheatley, Phillis, 44
whiteness: biometric surveillance and, 110–11; gaze of, 7, 49–50, 79–83, 91–108, 120–22; prototypicality of, 26–27, 92, 110, 113–18, 122, 162, 181n86; as straightening device, 144–45; surveillance technology and, 79–83, 161–64; unmarked nature of, 17, 110–11, 113, 116–19, 121–22, 162–63; white racial frame and, 95, 180n60. *See also* epidermalization; race; surveillance